# eBay®

# TOP 100

## Simplified®

## Tips & Tricks

by Julia Wilkinson

From
**maranGraphics**®

&

**WILEY**
Wiley Publishing, Inc.

**Visual**

**eBay®: Top 100 Simplified® Tips & Tricks**

Published by
Wiley Publishing, Inc.
111 River Street
Hoboken, NJ 07030-5774

Published simultaneously in Canada
Copyright © 2004 by Wiley Publishing, Inc.,
Indianapolis, Indiana
Certain designs, text, and illustrations Copyright
© 1992-2004 maranGraphics, Inc., used with
maranGraphics' permission.

maranGraphics, Inc.
5755 Coopers Avenue
Mississauga, Ontario, Canada
L4Z 1R9

Library of Congress Control Number: 2004102357
ISBN: 0-7645-5595-2
Manufactured in the United States of America
10 9 8 7 6 5 4 3 2 1

1K/SU/QT/QU/IN

## Trademark Acknowledgments

## Important Numbers

For U.S. corporate orders, please call maranGraphics at
800-469-6616 or fax 905-890-9434.

For general information on our other products and
services or to obtain technical support please contact
our Customer Care Department within the U.S. at
800-762-2974, outside the U.S. at 317-572-3993 or
fax 317-572-4002.

## Permissions

Wiley Publishing, Inc.

| **U.S. Corporate Sales** | **U.S. Trade Sales** |
|---|---|
| Contact maranGraphics at (800) 469-6616 or fax (905) 890-9434. | Contact Wiley at (800) 762-2974 or fax (317) 572-4002. |

# CREDITS

**Project Editor:**
Maureen Spears

**Acquisitions Editor:**
Jody Lefevere

**Product Development Manager:**
Lindsay Sandman

**Copy Editor:**
Marylouise Wiack

**Technical Editor:**
Ina Steiner

**Editorial Manager:**
Robyn Siesky

**Permissions Editor:**
Carmen Krikorian

**Editorial Assistant:**
Adrienne Porter

**Manufacturing:**
Allan Conley
Linda Cook
Paul Gilchrist
Jennifer Guynn

**Special Help:**
Sherry Kinkoph

**Cover Design:**
Anthony Bunyan

**Book Design:**
maranGraphics, Inc.

**Production Coordinator:**
Nancee Reeves

**Layout:**
Beth Brooks
LeAndra Hosier
Kristin McMullan
Kathie S. Schnorr

**Screen Artist:**
Jill A. Proll

**Illustrators:**
Ronda David-Burroughs
David E. Gregory

**Proofreader:**
Sandra Profant

**Quality Control:**
Susan Moritz
Angel Perez
Brian H. Walls

**Indexer:**
Sherry Massey

**Vice President and Executive Group Publisher:**
Richard Swadley

**Vice President and Publisher:**
Barry Pruett

**Composition Director:**
Debbie Stailey

## ABOUT THE AUTHOR

Julia Wilkinson is fortunate to have nice mail carriers, who put up with her many incoming and outgoing eBay packages. She is a writer with 15 years experience in online communities and Web content production. She worked for America Online (formerly Quantum Computer Services) from 1988–1997, and was Director of Community for womenCONNECT.com from 1997–1999.

Julia is the author of *My Life at AOL*, Best *Bang for Your Book* and several ebooks about the online auction business, including *What Sells on eBay for What*. Her writing has appeared in various publications, including *Reader's Digest*, *The Washington Post*, *Virginia*, and *AuctionBytes Update*. Julia publishes her own monthly newsletter, Yard Salers and eBayers. Julia holds a B.A. from the University of Virginia and lives in Virginia with her husband, children, their pet parakeets, Super and FluffPuff, and their fish, Scales.

## AUTHOR'S ACKNOWLEDGMENTS

Thanks to my husband, Nick Gallagher, for his support during this book; and to my kids, Lindsay and Kyle, for understanding why I didn't cook as much. I'd also like to thank the folks at Wiley: To Project Editor Maureen Spears, for all her help and expertise; to Acquisitions Editor, Jody Lefevere, for her faith in me; and to Copy Editor Marylouise Wiack for her thoroughness. A big thanks to Ina Steiner, for her Technical Editing and great suggestions, and to David Steiner for his industry knowledge. Also, thanks to Sherry Kinkoph, for helping out in a pinch. Finally, thanks to the gang on the eBay Clothing, Shoes and Accessories board for their cheerful helpfulness.

*For Nick, Lindsay and Kyle.*

maranGraphics is a family-run business
located near Toronto, Canada.

At **maranGraphics**, we believe in producing great computer books—one book at a time.

Each maranGraphics book uses the award-winning communication process that we have been developing over the last 28 years. Using this process, we organize screen shots and text in a way that makes it easy for you to learn new concepts and tasks.

We spend hours deciding the best way to perform each task, so you don't have to! Our clear, easy-to-follow screen shots and instructions walk you through each task from beginning to end.

We want to thank you for purchasing what we feel are the best computer books money can buy. We hope you enjoy using this book as much as we enjoyed creating it!

Sincerely,

**The Maran Family**

Please visit us on the Web at:
# www.maran.com

# HOW TO USE THIS BOOK

**eBay®: Top 100 Simplified® Tips & Tricks**
includes the 100 most interesting and useful tasks you can perform with eBay. This book reveals cool secrets, and timesaving tricks guaranteed to make your eBay experience more productive.

## Who is this book for?

Are you a visual learner who already knows the basics of eBay, but would like to take your eBay experience to the next level? Then this is the book for you.

## Conventions In This Book

### ❶ Steps

This book walks you through each task using a step-by-step approach. Lines and "lassos" connect the screen shots to the step-by-step instructions to show you exactly how to perform each task.

### ❷ Tips

Fun and practical tips answer questions you have always wondered about. Plus, learn to do things with eBay that you never thought were possible!

### ❸ Task Numbers

The task numbers, ranging from 1 to 100, indicate which self-contained lesson you are currently working on.

### ❹ Difficulty Levels

For quick reference, symbols mark the difficulty level of each task.

Demonstrates a new spin on a common task

Introduces a new skill or a new task

Combines multiple skills requiring in-depth knowledge

Requires extensive skill and may involve other technologies

# TABLE OF CONTENTS

 **Smart Searching on eBay**

Task #1   Expand Your Search Depth .................................................4

  #2   Perform an Advanced Search ......................................6

  #3   Research Completed Items for Market Prices ............8

  #4   View What Others Have Bought ...............................10

  #5   Supplement Your Searches with Browse ....................12

  #6   Using Categories to Refine Searches .......................14

  #7   Find Hot Items .........................................................16

  #8   Search While You Sleep ...........................................18

  #9   Find eBay's Hidden Gems .......................................20

 #10   Create Photo Albums of Search Results ..................22

 #11   Find It Fast with eBay's Site Map .............................24

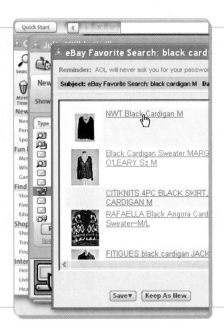

**Using Smart Shopping on eBay**

Task #12   Watch an Item You Want to Buy ..............................28

  #13   Ask a Seller a Question ...........................................30

  #14   Save Time with Feedback Tools ..............................32

  #15   Buy Regionally to Save Shipping .............................34

  #16   Find Unique Items in Other Countries .......................36

  #17   Get Bid Alerts with the eBay Toolbar .....................38

  #18   Shop for Last-Minute Bargains ................................40

  #19   Using Gallery View to Quickly Shop .......................42

  #20   Buy Multiple Items to Save on Shipping ...................44

  #21   Factor In Hidden Costs ............................................46

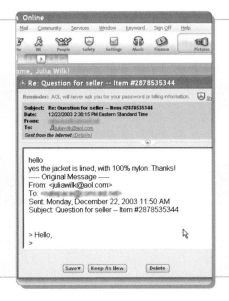

## Improve Your Bidding & Buying Strategies

Task #22 Using Proxy Bidding to Your Advantage .............................................50

#23 Snipe with Last-Second Bidding ................................................52

#24 Snipe While You Sleep ................................................54

#25 Out-Snipe Snipers with Advanced Techniques .............................56

#26 Make Odd Numbers Work for You ................................................58

#27 Check Prices of Common Items ................................................59

#28 Get a Low Price with Dutch Auctions ................................................60

#29 Buy a Car with eBay Motors ................................................62

#30 Find Real Estate Bargains ................................................64

#31 Support a Good Cause ................................................66

#32 Join the Elite Fray of Live Auction Bidding ................................................68

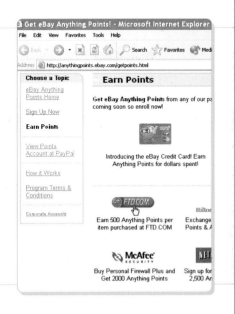

## Paying For Items Painlessly

Task #33 Find the Right Payment Options ................................................72

#34 Set Up a PayPal Account ................................................74

#35 Add PayPal Funds ................................................76

#36 Withdraw Funds from PayPal ................................................78

#37 Save Time with Auction Payments ................................................80

#38 Get Discounts with Anything Points ................................................82

#39 Using Escrow to Buy Your Item ................................................84

#40 Troubleshoot After-Sale Problems ................................................86

#41 Resolve Payment Disputes with SquareTrade .............................88

#42 Using Feedback to Build Goodwill ................................................90

# TABLE OF CONTENTS

 **Smart Selling on eBay**

Task #43 Avoid Problems with Trademark Protection ...............................94

#44 Check That eBay Allows Your Item ..............................................96

#45 Set an Auction Length ................................................................97

#46 Determine When to Use Buy It Now ............................................98

#47 Create a Fixed-Price Listing ......................................................99

#48 Sell in Bulk with Dutch Auctions ...............................................100

#49 Protect Your Item with a Reserve ..............................................101

#50 Save Money on Listing Fees ......................................................102

#51 Give Your Listing a Background Color ......................................103

#52 Jazz Up Your Listing with Listing Designer Graphics ..................104

#53 Save Time with Pre-filled Information ........................................106

#54 Make a Second-Chance Offer ..................................................108

**Using Effective Seller Tools**

Task #55 Using Photoshop Elements to Edit a Picture ..........................112

#56 Copyright Your Auction Photographs ......................................114

#57 Track Listing Visits with a Free Counter ....................................116

#58 Start an Auction with the Scheduler ........................................117

#59 Create Auction Listings with Turbo Lister ..................................118

#60 Research Auctions with Deep Analysis ....................................122

#61 Determine the Best Auction Days ............................................124

#62 View eBay Seller Newsletters ..................................................125

**Boost Your Sales with Advanced Selling Techniques**

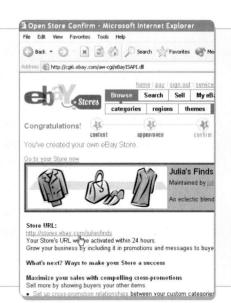

Task #63  Benefit from PowerSellers ................................................128

#64  Save Money with Image-Hosting................................................130

#65  Add Multiple Images in Slideshow Format .............................132

#66  Using Statistics to Measure Sales ..........................................134

#67  Get Organized with Selling Manager .....................................136

#68  Improve Your Listings with eBay's HTML Editor ...........................138

#69  Market Your Goods with an eBay Store ...................................140

#70  Create Your Own Store with Vendio ......................................142

#71  Cross-Promote Your eBay Store Items ...................................144

#72  Manage Cross-Promoted Item Categories ..............................146

# Maximize Your Item's Exposure

Task #73  Emphasize Listings with Your About Me Page ......................150

#74  Give Shoppers a Preview with Gallery ...................................152

#75  Place Your Item on eBay's Home Page ...................................154

#76  Using Bold and Highlighting to Emphasize Auctions .................156

#77  Maximize Visibility with Featured Auctions ...........................158

#78  Call Attention to Your Other Auctions ...................................160

#79  Showcase Thumbnails of Related Auction Items .......................162

#80  Appeal to Buyers with SquareTrade's Seal of Approval ............164

#81  Attract Traffic to Your Auction ..............................................166

#82  Boost All Auctions with a Strategic Item .................................168

## Smart Shipping for Sellers

Task #83 Create Good Terms of Sale ...................................................172

#84 Retrieve Shipping Information .......................................................174

#85 Place a Shipping Calculator in Your Listing ...........................176

#86 Save Time and Money with Flat Rates ...............................178

#87 Print Your Own Stamps ...............................................................180

#88 Protect Yourself with Delivery Confirmation and Insurance ......182

#89 Using U-Pic to Insure Packages ...............................................184

#90 Using eBay to Purchase Packing Supplies ...........................186

#91 Order Free Supplies ...................................................................188

#92 Send Large, Valuable, or Fragile Items ...............................190

## Tap into the eBay Community Gold Mine

Task #93 Find a Home in the Discussion Boards ...............................194

#94 Browse the Discussion Boards ...............................................196

#95 Get Answers with Live Chat ...................................................198

#96 Get Answers with Message Boards .......................................200

#97 Using eBay University to Take Classes ...............................202

#98 Network with eBay Groups ...................................................204

#99 Find Outside Auction Communities .......................................206

#100 Stay Informed with Industry Newsletters ...........................208

# CHAPTER 1

# Smart Searching on eBay

With millions of items for sale on eBay, and more every day, finding what you want can be very time-consuming. Good search skills can help you find bargains and save time.

Although you can sort through listings using the eBay Browse feature, the huge number of items in many categories can make browsing overwhelming. Because of this, many people prefer to use searches rather than to browse on eBay.

However, you can use tips and tricks to make your searches more effective. The eBay search pages feature different parameters that narrow down your hunt for a specific type of item. You can even combine browsing and searching as a search strategy.

In addition to eBay's search features, you can use third-party tools, such as timeBLASTER, to save time and more easily narrow down the items you seek from the millions of listings on eBay.

You can benefit from eBay's search features as both a buyer and a seller. As a buyer, you can use search tricks, such as searching for listings with typos and transpositions, to find items that other buyers may overlook. As a seller, you can use parameters, such as Completed Items only, to research items that are similar to those you sell. Because eBay shoppers expect good deals, it is critical for you to have a good idea of what kind of sales price you can expect for your items. That way, you know what you can afford to spend on inventory and still make a reasonable profit.

# TOP 100

**#1**   Expand Your Search Depth . . . . . . . . 4

**#2**   Perform an Advanced Search . . . . . . . . . 6

**#3**   Research Completed Items for Market Prices . . . . . . . . . . . . . . . . . . . . 8

**#4**   View What Others Have Bought . . . . . . . . . . . 10

**#5**   Supplement Your Searches with Browse . . . . . . . . 12

**#6**   Using Categories to Refine Searches . . . . . . . . . . 14

**#7**   Find Hot Items . . . . . . . . . . . . . . . . . . . . . . . . 16

**#8**   Search While You Sleep . . . . . . . . . . . . . . . . . 18

**#9**   Find eBay's Hidden Gems . . . . . . . . . . . . . . . 20

**#10**   Create Photo Albums of Search Results . . . . . . . . . . . . . . . . . . . . . 22

**#11**   Find It Fast with eBay's Site Map . . . 24

# Expand your
# SEARCH DEPTH

You can increase the number of hits you receive on a search by searching items by both title and description. The Search title and description option on the eBay Basic Search tab allows you to retrieve items that contain keywords in both the item description and the item title.

If you search using titles only, you may miss a large percentage of the available items. For example, if you search for blue Wedgewood — a popular type of collectible china — with the title and description option activated, you may receive 50 items. A

similar search without this option activated may result in 19 items, which would result in your missing more than half of the items you seek.

You may miss items when you use the titles-only search because sellers do not always include the keywords you expect in their titles. This occurs when sellers do not have enough space to fully describe their item in the title, do not choose the most appropriate words, or have several ways to describe the item.

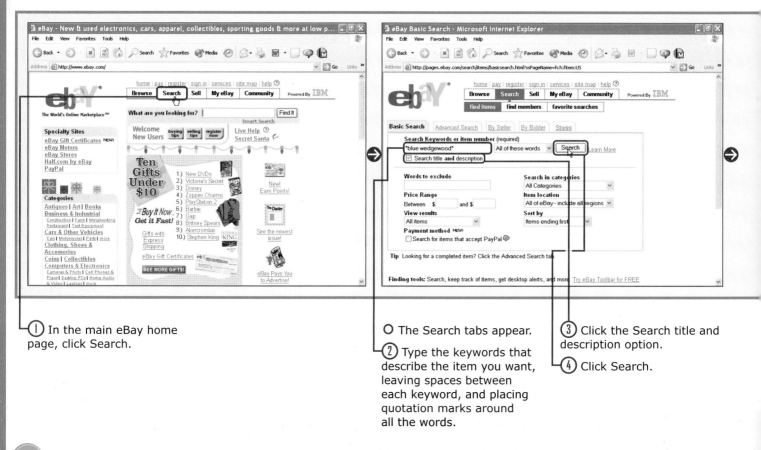

① In the main eBay home page, click Search.

○ The Search tabs appear.

② Type the keywords that describe the item you want, leaving spaces between each keyword, and placing quotation marks around all the words.

③ Click the Search title and description option.

④ Click Search.

## Buyer Beware! ☀

Carefully read the descriptions of items on which you intend to bid. Although your keywords may appear in an item description, you may not want the item. For example, if you type **"blue Wedgewood"** to look for that type of china, a search may yield an item with blue Wedgewood in its description, but the description may refer to an ottoman of blue Wedgewood color.

## Did You Know? ☀

You can also access the Basic Search tab by clicking the Smart Search link on the eBay home page, below and to the left of the Find It button. Or, you can simply type your search words into the text box located just to the right of the What are you looking for? prompt.

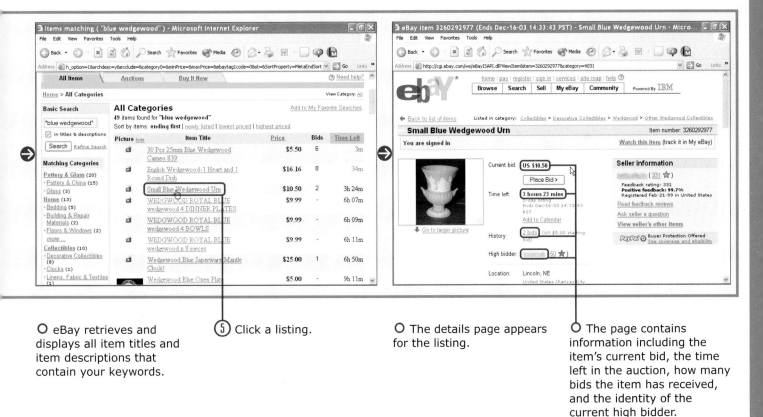

O eBay retrieves and displays all item titles and item descriptions that contain your keywords.

⑤ Click a listing.

O The details page appears for the listing.

O The page contains information including the item's current bid, the time left in the auction, how many bids the item has received, and the identity of the current high bidder.

# Perform an
# ADVANCED SEARCH

You can perform a more powerful search on eBay by using the Advanced Search tab instead of the Basic Search tab. The Advanced Search tab contains all the features of eBay's basic search, as well as additional parameters that can narrow down your search.

Although using all of these options together may severely limit your search, you may want to combine some of them to optimize your search. For this reason, it is important to understand how each option can benefit you.

The Words to exclude option allows you to eliminate certain keywords from the search. For example, if you know you want metal and not wooden toy trains, you can enter **wooden** in this option box.

The Buy It Now Items only option displays items for immediate purchase and is especially useful if you see a bargain. For more on this feature, see tasks #9 and #46.

The Gift Items only option yields listings that the sellers designate as gifts. In some cases, the seller may even offer gift wrapping and shipping to the gift recipient.

The Advanced Search feature also facilitates international searching. For more information on international searching, see task #15.

---

① In the eBay home page, click Search.

O The Search tabs appear.

② Click the Advanced Search tab.

③ Type the word or phrase for the item you want to find.

④ Click the desired Expand search Item type options.

O You can click the Buy It Now Items only option to show items for immediate purchase.

O You can click the Gift Items only option to see items that make good gifts.

## More Options! ☼

When you click the
Completed Items only option, you
receive hits for auctions that have
ended. This is useful when you want to
research how past items have sold. For
more information on this option, see task #3.

## More Options! ☼

In the Sort by list, on both the Basic and Advanced
Search tabs, you can select different sort options.
The Items ending first option lists auctions about
to end first. The Newly listed items first option
displays auctions that have just gone live first,
followed by those about to end. The Lowest
prices first option shows items from the
cheapest to the most expensive. The
Highest prices first option shows items
from the most expensive to the cheapest.

DIFFICULTY LEVEL

─⑤ Type the words you want
to exclude.

─○ You may need to scroll
your screen.

─○ You can click here and
select how to sort your list.

─⑥ Click Search.

○ The search results
appear.

○ This example lists all Buy
It Now, non-wooden Thomas
Tank engine gift items, with
auctions that end first at the
top of the list.

# Research Completed Items for
# MARKET PRICES

You can use the Completed Items only option in the Advanced Search tab to research the final selling prices for different types of items for the last two weeks. As a buyer, this information gives you an idea of what to expect as a final bid. As a seller, this information allows you to estimate what market prices you can expect for your own, similar items. Knowing an item's recent market price helps you avoid buying inventory at a price that is too high to yield a profit.

To see what has sold for the most and least money, you can use the Sort by menu to select either the Highest prices first or Lowest prices first option. Viewing the highest prices shows you the items that can make you the most money; viewing the lowest prices shows you what items to avoid selling.

Please note that items that do not meet their reserve, or asking prices, are not good reflections of a particular item's market value, nor should you use them for research purposes.

① In the Advanced Search tab, type a keyword or phrase.

*Note: See task #2 for more information on accessing the Advanced Search tab.*

② Click the Completed Items only option.

③ Click here, and then click Highest prices first.

○ You may have to scroll to see this option.

④ Click Search.

## Savvy eBaying! ※

For a thorough search, try different word combinations for items. For example, consider using the words antique glass as well as Depression glass, as different sellers may select different names or descriptions for their items.

**DIFFICULTY LEVEL**

## Buyer Beware! ※

Various factors can influence the final sales price of an item, including condition, age, color, and season.

## Buyer Beware! ※

Look at a variety of hits in the search returns, because the highest and lowest prices may not reflect the average sales price of a certain type of item. The Bids column on the results page shows the number of bids the item received and indicates the level of interest in it. Lower numbers in this column usually indicate lower interest.

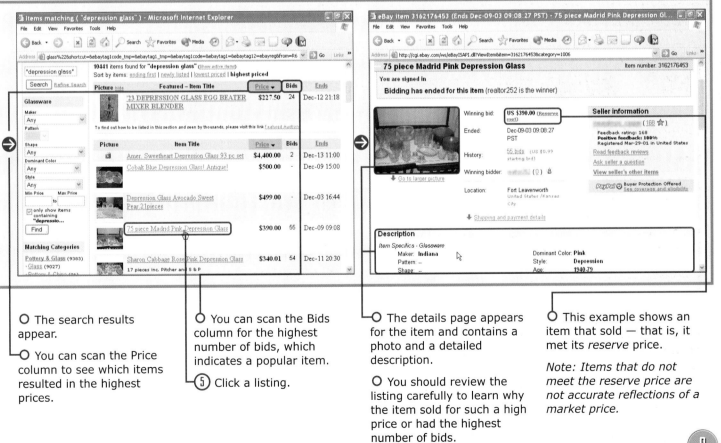

O The search results appear.

O You can scan the Price column to see which items resulted in the highest prices.

O You can scan the Bids column for the highest number of bids, which indicates a popular item.

⑤ Click a listing.

O The details page appears for the item and contains a photo and a detailed description.

O You should review the listing carefully to learn why the item sold for such a high price or had the highest number of bids.

O This example shows an item that sold — that is, it met its *reserve* price.

*Note: Items that do not meet the reserve price are not accurate reflections of a market price.*

# View what
# OTHERS HAVE
# BOUGHT

You can use the By Bidder tab in the eBay search page to view what other users bid on and buy. The By Bidder feature allows you to benefit from other people's shopping skills because they may find a great item you would otherwise miss. If you often bid against certain users in key categories, take note of their user IDs and use them in a By Bidder search.

On the By Bidder tab, you can type the bidder's eBay ID, and a list of the items that person is bidding on appears with information about those auctions,

including an item number, a start and end date and time, price, title, current high bidder, and seller.

You can choose not to include completed items if you only want to see the items on which a user is currently bidding. You can also select the No, only if high bidder option to eliminate auctions the user lost. Finally, you can select how many results you want per page: 5, 10, 25, 50, 75, 100, 200, or All items on one page.

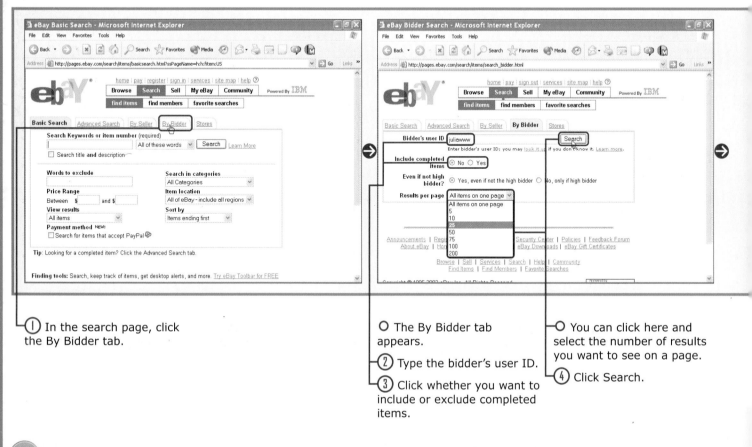

① In the search page, click the By Bidder tab.

○ The By Bidder tab appears.

② Type the bidder's user ID.

③ Click whether you want to include or exclude completed items.

─○ You can click here and select the number of results you want to see on a page.

④ Click Search.

# Savvy Selling! ☀

The By Bidder tab is a good tool to learn what your customers want. For example, if you sell bubble wrap and you see your repeat customers bidding on tape and envelopes, consider adding those items to your inventory.

# Did You Know? ☀

Have you received e-mails from an eBay member who does not specify his or her user ID? If you have completed previous transactions with this member, you can look up the corresponding user ID. In the By Bidder tab, click the look it up link, and then type the e-mail address in the Request user ID option box. eBay prompts you through a security screen, at which point you can click Search to retrieve the user's ID.

# #4

## DIFFICULTY LEVEL

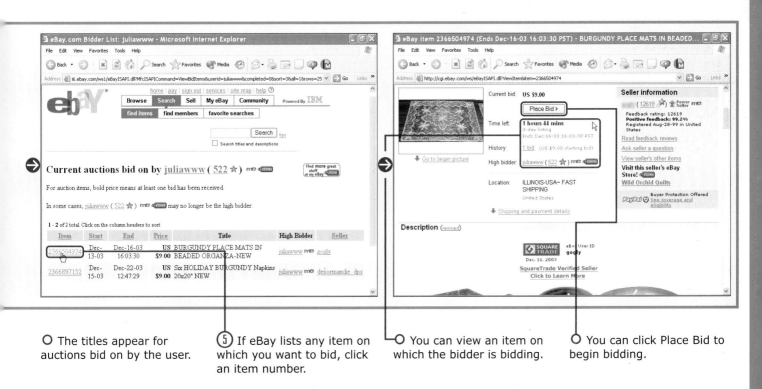

○ The titles appear for auctions bid on by the user.

⑤ If eBay lists any item on which you want to bid, click an item number.

○ You can view an item on which the bidder is bidding.

○ You can click Place Bid to begin bidding.

# Supplement your searches with
# BROWSE

You can increase your chances of finding items if you supplement your searches by browsing in the appropriate eBay category. This is because some sellers use titles or descriptions that you may not find when you perform a search for them.

Some eBay treasure-hunters actively use this search method to find listings where a seller has an item whose true value they do not realize. For example, one eBay browser bought an old manuscript written by a famous author; the seller did not know that the writer of the manuscript was famous. The buyer found this manuscript by looking for clues to its origin in the seller's description.

Because eBay offers a steadily growing number of category choices, you must check similar categories to obtain a thorough search. For example, under the Jewelry and Watches category, some items make sense in both the subcategories of Loose Beads and Loose Gemstones. Although some sellers list items in a second category, not all sellers do. Sellers sometimes have items that can belong in more than two categories.

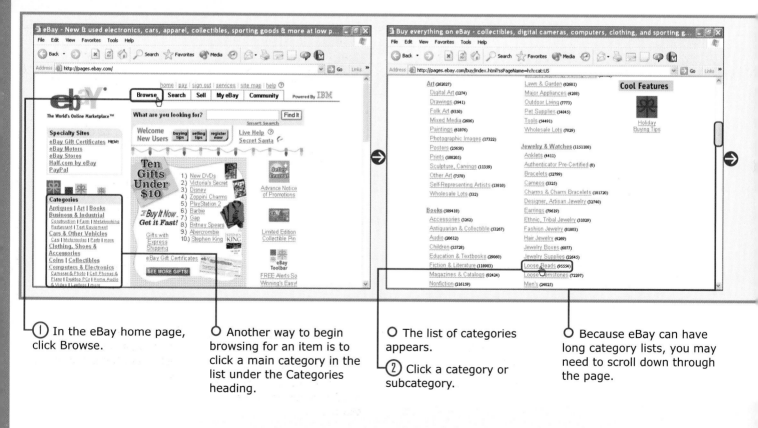

○① In the eBay home page, click Browse.

○ Another way to begin browsing for an item is to click a main category in the list under the Categories heading.

○ The list of categories appears.

○② Click a category or subcategory.

○ Because eBay can have long category lists, you may need to scroll down through the page.

## More Options! ❊

To get a quick overview of eBay's categories, click the see all eBay categories link, located beneath the Everything Else link on the eBay home page. The see all eBay categories link allows you to see all the first- and second-level eBay categories on one page, which can quickly help familiarize you with the various category options as they currently stand.

DIFFICULTY LEVEL

## Everything Else

Gifts | Health & Beauty | more
*see all eBay categories*

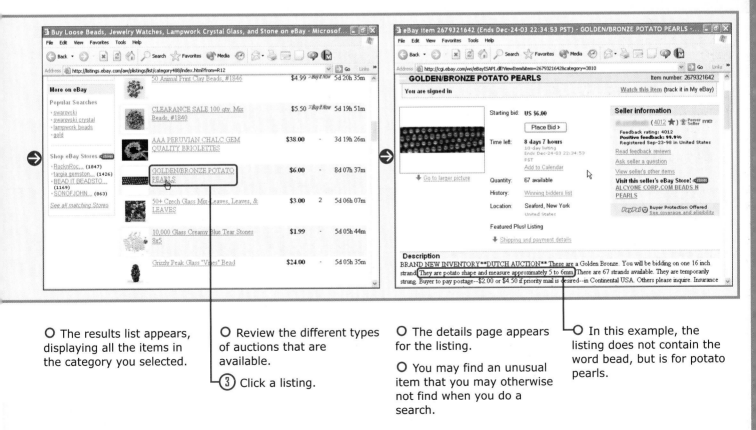

O The results list appears, displaying all the items in the category you selected.

O Review the different types of auctions that are available.

③ Click a listing.

O The details page appears for the listing.

O You may find an unusual item that you may otherwise not find when you do a search.

O In this example, the listing does not contain the word bead, but is for potato pearls.

# Using categories to
# REFINE SEARCHES

You can combine browsing and searching to narrow down your search. This technique allows you to take advantage of eBay's large category hierarchy by moving through the many category layers — sometimes referred to as *drilling down* — to access the items you want. Because eBay's categories can consist of many layers, you may need to drill down into several subcategories before you find the item you want.

Combining the Search and Browse features is especially useful when you want to browse for a specific item but do not know in which category that item belongs. You may also find this technique

useful if the item can potentially fall into several different categories. For more information on browsing, see task #5.

You can combine the Browse and Search features by using the Matching Categories list, which appears on the left side of the page after you do a search. eBay often lists more than one category here, and presents you with a list of matching categories.

When you perform a search and then enter a matching category, eBay's search continues to filter out items according to your search words.

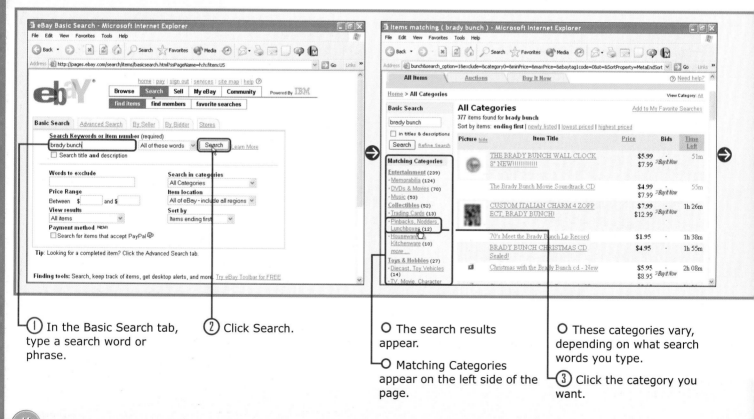

① In the Basic Search tab, type a search word or phrase.

② Click Search.

○ The search results appear.

○ Matching Categories appear on the left side of the page.

○ These categories vary, depending on what search words you type.

③ Click the category you want.

## More Options! ※

You can also perform a
search within any given category.
In the eBay home page, click
Browse. Once you drill down into a
category with actual auction listings on the
right, you can type search words into the Basic
Search box on the upper left, and then click the
Only in this category option ( ☐ changes to ☑ )
directly beneath it.

DIFFICULTY LEVEL

## Did You Know? ※

You can find search results grouped by
category for eBay's top keyword searches
at keyword.ebay.com. From there, you
can browse a list of keywords that eBay
buyers and sellers use most often. If
you click a keyword, you receive a list
of categories containing the keyword
along with a Gallery containing photos
of items related to that keyword.

O The search results
appear.

O eBay narrows down the
Matching Categories to
smaller categories.

④ Click another category
under Matching Categories.

O eBay displays the search
results, further narrowing
down the items.

# Find
# HOT ITEMS

You can read the Hot Items by Category document, located in Seller Central, to determine which items sold well recently. eBay staff creates a list of items they deem hot sellers in each category. eBay defines *hot items* as recent items with bidding growth significantly outpacing new listings growth, or where the bid-to-item ratios are higher than other products in the same parent category.

As a seller, you can read the Hot Items by Category list to get ideas for things you can sell that can make you the most money. You can place the hot

items information to work and experiment with new types of products to see what sells.

Because the hot items list changes regularly, it is a good idea to check it frequently to get the best idea of what sells well in a particular category.

As an alternative to the steps in this task, you can also use a pay service that does the tedious work of searching for hot items for you. One service is andale's What's Hot. To use andale's service, go to www.andale.com.

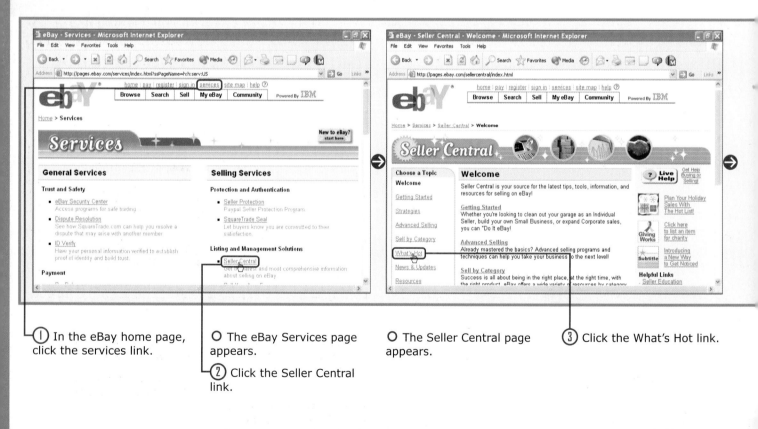

① In the eBay home page, click the services link.

○ The eBay Services page appears.

② Click the Seller Central link.

○ The Seller Central page appears.

③ Click the What's Hot link.

# Did You Know? ☀

You can see previous lists of Hot Items in the Hot Items Folder in the eBay Community area. In any eBay page, click Community, and then click the Discussion Boards link. Next, click the Hot Items link. Click a specific category folder, and you can see the lists of Hot Items for that category.

DIFFICULTY LEVEL

The hot products in the Computers & Electronics category for the week of 09/25/03:

**Desktop PCs**
700MHz to 1GHz
400-650MHz
**Gadgets & Other Electronics**
Air Purifiers
Home Automation
Other Gadgets
**Home Audio & Video**
Wholesale Lots
Home Audio
**Office Products**
Calendars, Planners
Copiers & Supplies
Laminating Machines, Supplies
Presentation A/V
**Portable Audio & Video**
MP3 Players
Voice Recorders

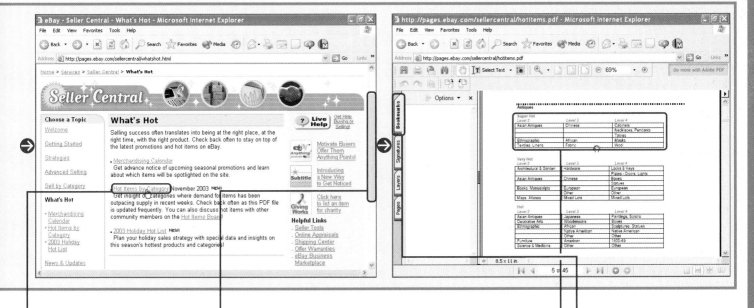

○ The What's Hot page appears.

④ Click the Hot Items by Category link.

○ You may need to scroll down to access this link.

○ The Hot Categories Report, which is in Adobe Acrobat's pdf format, appears.

*Note: If you do not already have the Adobe Acrobat Reader, eBay may prompt you to download it.*

⑤ Click the Bookmarks tab to view the report.

○ You can see the Hot Products by category.

# Search
# WHILE YOU SLEEP

You can use eBay's My Favorite Search feature to have the system regularly scan for a certain type of item. This is a convenient and timesaving way to locate a particular item without having to perform multiple manual searches. This technique is especially useful when you are not in a hurry, and can take your time to find an item over days, weeks, or even months.

You can give the search a name. For example, if your search is for a medium-sized, black cardigan, you can name the search black cardigan M. You can

also designate for how long you want eBay to e-mail you the daily results of the search — with options ranging from 7 days to 12 months.

You can opt whether eBay e-mails your search results using the Email me daily whenever there are new items option. You can also check the saved search anytime in the My Favorite Searches area located in My eBay's Favorites tab.

---

① In the Basic Search tab, type a search word or phrase.

② Click Search.

○ The search results appear.

③ Click the Add to My Favorite Searches link.

## Did You Know? ☀

When you find the item you want, you can delete its Favorite Search to make room for new searches. Click My eBay in the eBay home page, or any other eBay page, and then click the Favorites tab. Click the option next to the name of the search, and then click Delete. eBay lets you save up to 100 searches.

## More Options! ☀

If you especially like items from a specific seller or store, and you want to quickly and easily view new items, you can save them as favorites. In the My eBay page, click the Favorites tab, and then click My Favorite Sellers/ Stores. Click Add new Seller/Store, and type the seller's user ID or the store name. Then click Save Favorite.

○ The Add to My Favorite Searches page appears.

④ Type a name for your search.

⑤ Click the Email me daily whenever there are new items option.

⑥ Click here, and select a time frame for the search.

⑦ Click Submit.

○ eBay e-mails your Favorite Search results to you.

*Note: You must sign on to your e-mail service to check the Favorite Searches e-mail.*

# Find eBay's
# HIDDEN GEMS

You can find great items that other eBay users may miss by searching for alternate spellings and typo variations of words. Because many searchers overlook alternate spellings, fewer people view and bid on these listings, allowing you to find wonderful bargains.

For example, if you look for Lilly Pulitzer brand clothing, which tends to sell very well on eBay, you may want to search under the spelling Lily Pulitzer, as this is a common misspelling of the brand name. Another common error sellers make is transposing

two letters. You can almost always find items with this mistake. For example, try DNKY instead of DKNY, or Evlis instead of Elvis.

As an example, a recent search on DNKY brought up 24 listings, only three of which had bids. These listings without bids give you an opportunity to find bargains. Compare that to the correct spelling, DKNY, where, out of the first 50 items, 30 have bids.

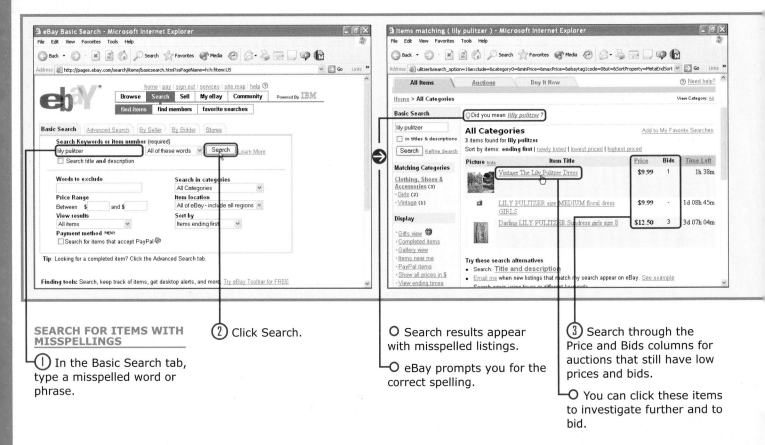

**SEARCH FOR ITEMS WITH MISSPELLINGS**

① In the Basic Search tab, type a misspelled word or phrase.

② Click Search.

○ Search results appear with misspelled listings.

○ eBay prompts you for the correct spelling.

③ Search through the Price and Bids columns for auctions that still have low prices and bids.

○ You can click these items to investigate further and to bid.

## eBay Savvy! ※

A misspelled item with a Buy
It Now option is great because
you can buy it immediately at a low
price and prevent other typo-hunters
from finding it. For more information on the
Buy It Now option, see tasks #2 and #46.

## eBay Savvy! ※

Try searching for both newly listed and Buy It Now
items to increase your chances of finding a bargain,
because the good deals go quickly. When you
browse, look for the new today items.

## Did You Know? ※

When you deliberately search for items with
incorrect spellings, you can ignore the eBay
search engine's prompt near the top of the
page that suggests the correct spelling.

DIFFICULTY LEVEL

---

**SEARCH FOR ITEMS WITH TRANSPOSITIONS**

① In the Basic Search tab, type a word or acronym with transposed letters.

② Click Search.

O The search results appear.

③ Search through the Price and Bids columns for auctions that still have low prices and bids.

O You can click these items to investigate further and to bid.

# Create photo albums of
# SEARCH RESULTS

Have you ever scrolled through numerous eBay listings of similar items, clicking into each one to find the specific one that you want? You can reduce the time you spend finding items by using a tool called timeBLASTER, which was invented by an avid stamp collector who spent long hours on eBay. With timeBLASTER, you can reduce searches that take 20 hours a week to an hour a week. timeBLASTER is great for sellers, too. One sports trading card dealer uses a standing timeBLASTER search to monitor market prices.

timeBLASTER automatically searches eBay, downloads the item descriptions and photos, and creates photo albums of the results by neatly lining up rows of photos and item information. Instead of scrolling through many pages of listings and clicking each auction to see photos, you can view the search results in a compact, easy-to-view format. You can also easily bid on or watch an item directly from the Photo Album page.

Before you can use timeBLASTER, you must first download and install the timeBLASTER software from the Web site, www.timeblaster.com/tbeindex.shtml.

① In the timeBLASTER main page, click Create New Search.

◯ A Search Description window appears.

② Type a name for your search.

③ Type the items for which you are searching.

④ Click Save.

⑤ In the Save dialog box that appears, click Save.

⑥ Click Create Photo Album Now.

## Did You Know? ☀

The timeBLASTER software for eBay is only available for Windows PCs. You can view a free animated demonstration of how the software works on the timeBLASTER Web site. The example in the demonstration is of a search for Roseville vases, a popular collector's item. timeBLASTER offers a 30-day free trial. A one-year subscription to the service costs $39.95, and timeBLASTER pays you $4 for every friend you refer who buys a one-year subscription.

**#10**

**DIFFICULTY LEVEL**

## Did You Know? ☀

You can run searches automatically by clicking Turn Scheduled Searches On from the main timeBLASTER page. Running a scheduled search allows you to do searches at night or any time that is most convenient for you so you can do other things while the search runs.

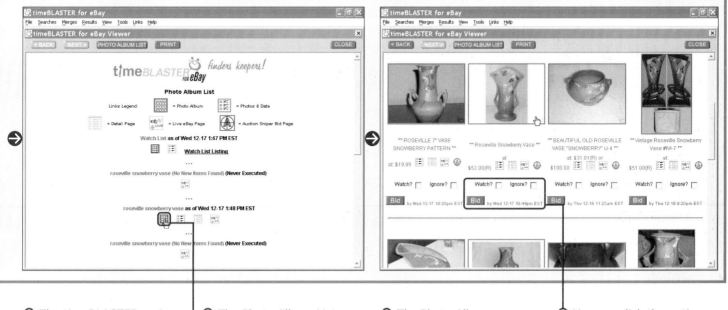

O The timeBLASTER main page reappears, showing the status of the newly created search.

⑦ Click View Photo Albums.

O The Photo Album List appears.

⑧ Click a photo album icon of an album you want to view.

O The Photo Album appears, allowing you to view photos and titles of multiple items on one page.

O You can click the options to watch, bid on, or ignore an item.

# Find it fast with eBay's
# SITE MAP

One of the easiest ways to find a particular section of the eBay site is to use the site map. Because eBay can be many layers deep in some areas, the site map acts as a valuable tool, displaying the broad array of features, services, and information available on the eBay site, and enabling you to navigate to a particular link. The site map can save you time and frustration in trying to find a specific part of eBay, because it compactly organizes all of the eBay links on one page.

You can access the eBay site map from any eBay page by using the link that appears at the top right of every page.

The site map is organized as a series of links under headings that describe every area on eBay, such as Browse, Sell, Search, Services, and Community. New features and areas are easy to find, because they are marked with a bright yellow NEW! icon.

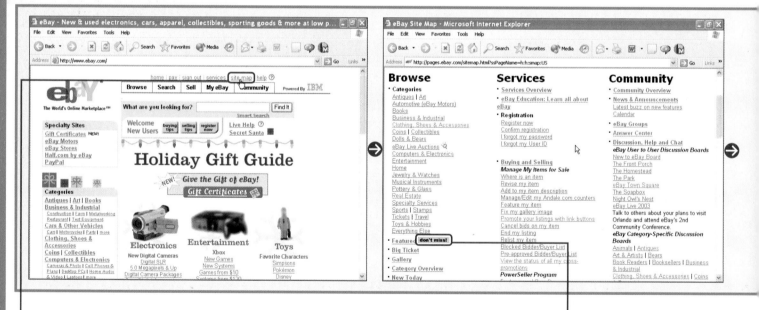

① In the eBay home page, click the site map link.

○ The eBay site map page appears.

○ Links to all eBay areas appear in the lists on this page.

○ Special items feature a don't miss! icon.

## More Options! ※

If you cannot find what you need on eBay's site map, you can search eBay's Help section. Click the help link, located just to the right of the site map link on any eBay page. You search the help database by typing your search words in the box at the top of the help window, and then clicking Search Help. You can also browse a complete alphabetical list of help topics by clicking the A-Z index tab in the eBay Help Center window.

## Did You Know? ※

If you still cannot find what you need using the site map or the eBay Help Center, you can use the Contact Us link, under eBay Help at the left of the Help Center search page.

**#11**

DIFFICULTY LEVEL

○ You can scroll down to see the entire site map.

② Click the link that interests you.

○ This example uses the Category overview with numbers link.

○ The Category Overview with Category Numbers page appears, allowing you to find an eBay area that you may not otherwise notice.

○ You can use the numbers in the Sell Your Item Form to specify the category in which to list your item.

○ You can click a main Category link to view the subcategories with numbers below it.

# CHAPTER 2

# Using Smart Shopping on eBay

With all the competition for shopping on eBay, it helps to use some tricks to buy the items you want at the right time and for the right price.

You can use eBay's tools, such as the Watch an Item option, to mark an item you may not be sure you want to buy, but do not think you can find later in the sea of eBay items. You can also use tools like the eBay Toolbar Alert to set up an alarm on your computer so you know when your auctions are about to end.

To ensure you have all the important details you need about an item, you can use the Ask seller a question link.

Checking a seller's feedback rating is critical to your success as a buyer.

You can save time finding negative or neutral feedback with tools like Gutcheck.

To find good deals, you can look for auctions that are about to end and have few to no bids, and you can use the Buy It Now feature when the price is right. You can also shop for items in other countries, for which you may have less competition.

Other things you can do to save money include buying items within your own geographical area, and buying several things from the same seller to save on shipping. Remembering hidden costs, such as shipping, handling, and insurance, helps you spend your money wisely.

# TOP 100

**#12**    Watch an Item You Want to Buy . . . . 28

**#13**    Ask a Seller a Question . . . . . . . . . . . . . 30

**#14**    Save Time with Feedback Tools . . . . . . . . . 32

**#15**    Buy Regionally to Save Shipping . . . . . . . . . 34

**#16**    Find Unique Items in Other Countries . . . . . . . . 36

**#17**    Get Bid Alerts with the eBay Toolbar . . . . . . . . 38

**#18**    Shop for Last-Minute Bargains . . . . . . . . . . . 40

**#19**    Using Gallery View to Quickly Shop . . . . . . 42

**#20**    Buy Multiple Items to Save on Shipping . . . 44

**#21**    Factor In Hidden Costs . . . . . . . . . 46

# WATCH AN ITEM
## you want to buy

You can track items that interest you by using the Watch this item feature. When you browse through many pages of listings, you may find it confusing to go back to an earlier page and find an item that interests you. The Watch this item feature makes it very easy to keep track of all the items you may want to buy, because you can mark an item on which you may want to bid, and then continue to browse for similar items before you decide to bid on one of them.

You can view a complete list of all the items you are watching in My eBay under the Items I'm Watching heading. The list shows you the item numbers, titles, current prices, number of bids, time left in the auction, and the seller's user ID. You can even bid on the item directly from the Items I'm Watching list.

Once the auctions end for the items you are watching, you can delete them to make room for more items.

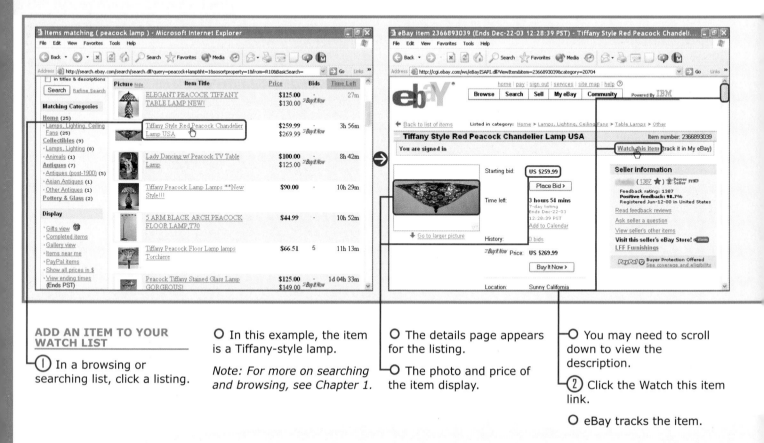

**ADD AN ITEM TO YOUR WATCH LIST**

① In a browsing or searching list, click a listing.

○ In this example, the item is a Tiffany-style lamp.

*Note: For more on searching and browsing, see Chapter 1.*

○ The details page appears for the listing.

○ The photo and price of the item display.

○ You may need to scroll down to view the description.

② Click the Watch this item link.

○ eBay tracks the item.

# More Options! ☀

For a quick, easy way to review items you want, you can use the My Recently Viewed Items or My Recent Searches features, which eBay displays at the bottom of search results and listings. Both features list the last three items you viewed or your last three searches.

**# 12**

**DIFFICULTY LEVEL**

# Did You Know? ☀

You can watch up to 30 items. As a reminder, eBay e-mails you a daily list of auctions that you are watching that end within 36 hours. If you do not want to receive this e-mail list, you can go to My eBay, click the Preferences tab, click Change my notification preferences, and then deselect the Item Watch Reminder option ( ☐ changes to ☑ ).

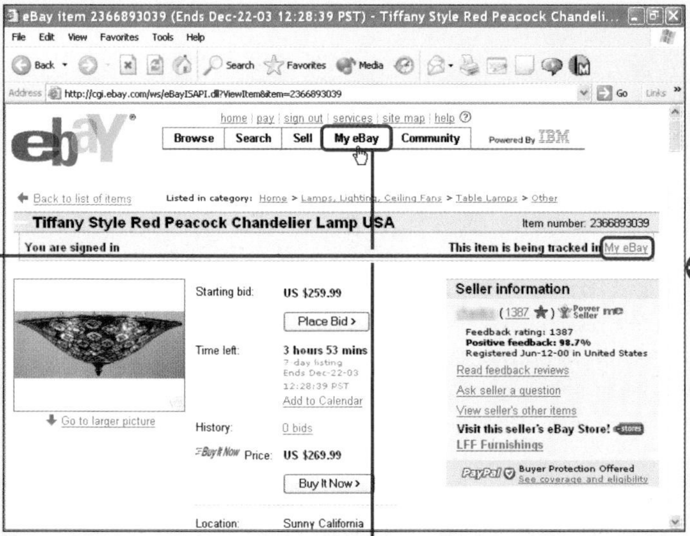

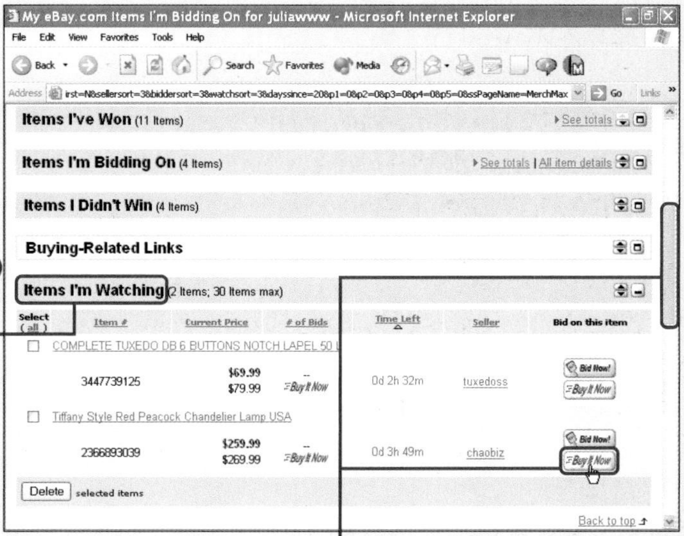

**VIEW AN ITEM ON YOUR WATCH LIST**

① Click the My eBay link.

○ You can also access the My eBay page from any eBay page by clicking My eBay.

○ The My eBay page appears.

○ You can view the item under the Items I'm Watching heading.

○ You may need to scroll down the page.

○ You can bid on the item directly by clicking the Buy It Now button.

# ASK A SELLER
## a question

You can get more information about an item before you buy it using the Ask seller a question link. Because of privacy concerns, eBay does not publish a user's e-mail address, name, address, or phone number. Therefore, this link is the only way you can communicate directly with a seller, unless an auction is over and you win an item, at which point eBay sends your e-mail address directly to the seller.

If the seller does not include key details in the auction's description, such as the measurements of an item of clothing, an item's age, or the shipping cost to your location, this option allows you to do further research. Getting detailed and complete information on an item helps you to avoid buying something you do not want.

eBay sends your question to the seller's e-mail address. The seller can then e-mail you back with the answers to your question. You can specify if you want to receive a blind carbon copy, or Bcc, of the e-mail for your records.

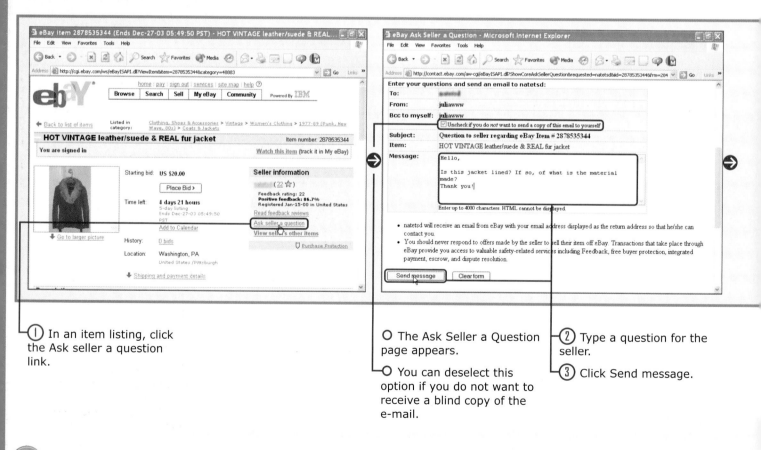

① In an item listing, click the Ask seller a question link.

○ The Ask Seller a Question page appears.

○ You can deselect this option if you do not want to receive a blind copy of the e-mail.

② Type a question for the seller.

③ Click Send message.

## Did You Know? ※

You can request an eBay member's contact information during an active transaction. Also, in a successful closed transaction, winning bidders and sellers can request each other's contact information. To request contact information, click Search, and then click Find Members. Type the user ID of the member and the item number in the option boxes, and then click Submit. eBay tells you that it has processed your request and e-mails you the contact information.

## Caution! ※

It is against eBay's rules to ask a seller to sell you an item outside the eBay system. Also, transactions outside the eBay Web site do not offer the same protections that eBay offers, such as buyer protection, dispute resolution, mediation, and feedback.

—O eBay confirms that your e-mail has been sent to the seller.

—O If you selected the Bcc to myself option on the Ask Seller a Question screen, eBay tells you that you will receive it shortly.

④ Launch your e-mail application, and check your e-mail.

⑤ Open the e-mail from the seller.

—O The item number appears in the subject.

—O The seller's response helps you make a more informed decision about whether to purchase the item.

# Save time with
# FEEDBACK TOOLS

Before you bid on an item, it is critical to perform a thorough check of a seller's feedback rating to determine a seller's integrity. Located next to the seller's eBay ID, a seller's *feedback rating* tells you how many transactions a seller has completed, as well as what percentage of these transactions resulted in positive comments from buyers. eBay also allows you to read a seller's feedback comments.

To save time scrolling through hundreds of feedback comments, you can download the free Gutcheck tool at www.teamredline.com/gutcheck/fdefault.asp and

view just the negative and neutral comments together on one page. With Gutcheck, you can also easily see information about the auction that a comment references.

Preferably, the seller's percentage of positive feedback comments should be very high — 100 percent, or close to it. Keep in mind that even the best sellers have a few neutral or negative comments, especially if they complete numerous transactions. That is why it is important to read what those comments say.

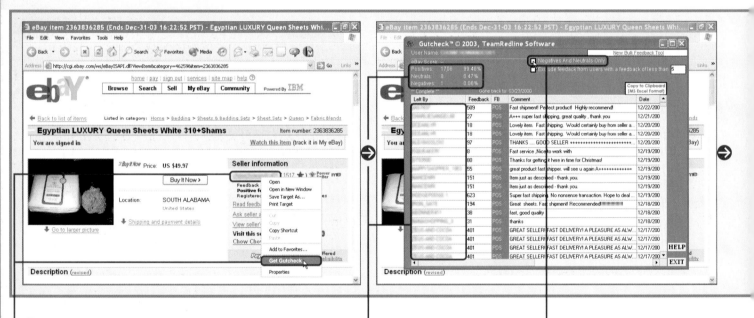

① In an item listing, right-click the seller's feedback rating number or eBay ID.

② Click Get Gutcheck.

*Note: The steps in this section assume that you have Gutcheck installed.*

○ The Gutcheck software opens.

○ You can see how many, and the percentage of, positive, negative, and neutral comments the seller has.

○ A condensed list of the comments appears below the eBay score.

○ This example shows a seller with a good Positives feedback rating of greater than 99 percent.

③ Click the Negatives and Neutrals Only option.

## More Options! ※

You can export your Gutcheck feedback data to other applications, such as Microsoft Excel. From the first Gutcheck Feedback page, click the Copy to Clipboard option above the Date column. Gutcheck informs you that the data is copied to the clipboard. Open Excel, and click Paste or press Ctrl+V.

## More Options! ※

With Gutcheck's GiveSomeBack Bulk Feedback Tool, you can simultaneously leave multiple positive feedback comments for specific or all pending transactions. You can also use a feedback comment from a stored list to avoid retyping commonly used feedback comments. You can download the Bulk Feedback Tool at www.teamredline.com/gsb. The Bulk Feedback Tool works only for positive feedback because most eBay buyers typically give negative feedback comments sparingly.

DIFFICULTY LEVEL

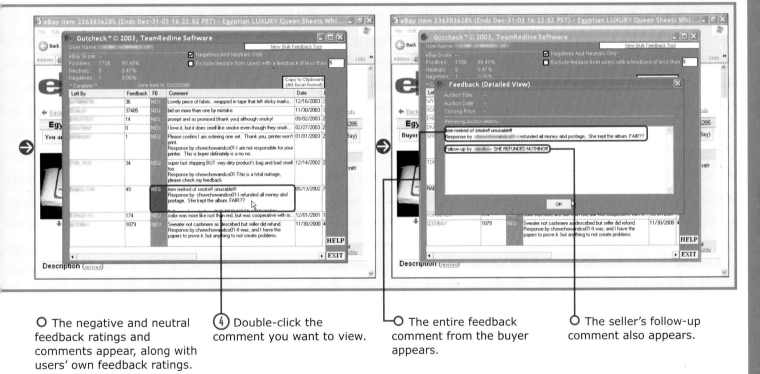

○ The negative and neutral feedback ratings and comments appear, along with users' own feedback ratings.

④ Double-click the comment you want to view.

○ The entire feedback comment from the buyer appears.

○ The seller's follow-up comment also appears.

# Buy regionally to
# SAVE SHIPPING

You can save a lot of money on the shipping of heavy items if you find an item you want on eBay that is located near where you live. You can use eBay's Item location menu on the Basic Search tab to select the closest city to where you live and then perform a search. If you win the item, you can reduce the cost of shipping, or you can simply drive to the seller's location and pick up the item.

For example, if you want a bicycle and you live near the Washington, D.C., area, you can select that city in the Item location menu and perform a search. If

you can drive to other nearby locations to pick up an item, you can also perform additional searches for other cities near you.

You should check the item's description to find out if the seller permits you to pick it up in person. If this information is not in the description, you can use the Ask seller a question link. For more information on the Ask seller a question feature, see task #13.

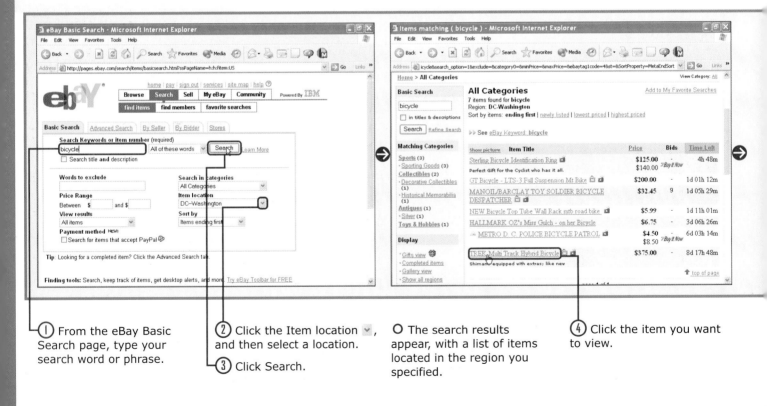

① From the eBay Basic Search page, type your search word or phrase.

② Click the Item location ▾, and then select a location.

③ Click Search.

● The search results appear, with a list of items located in the region you specified.

④ Click the item you want to view.

# Buyer Beware! ⁑

Although buying a heavy item regionally on eBay often makes sense, if an item is expensive or fragile and shipping is a fraction of its cost, sometimes you are better off searching the whole country or the world on eBay and paying for the shipping. You can use a special shipping service, such as Craters and Freighters. For more information on shipping large, valuable, or fragile items, see task #92.

**# 15**

DIFFICULTY LEVEL

# More Options! ⁑

If you live near more than one city, you can perform more than one regional search in case the item you want is located in another city near you. For example, if you live in northern Virginia, you can search in Baltimore, Md., as well as in Washington, D.C.

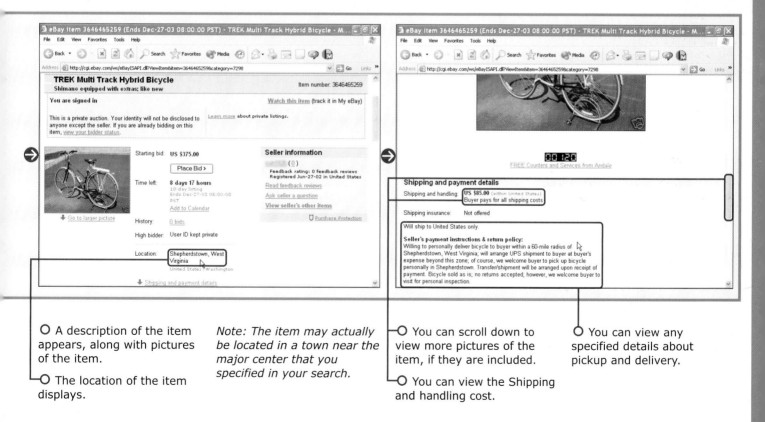

○ A description of the item appears, along with pictures of the item.

○ The location of the item displays.

*Note: The item may actually be located in a town near the major center that you specified in your search.*

○ You can scroll down to view more pictures of the item, if they are included.

○ You can view the Shipping and handling cost.

○ You can view any specified details about pickup and delivery.

# Find unique items in
# OTHER COUNTRIES

You can shop for items from around the world by using the Location/International options in the eBay Advanced Search page. This is a great way to find unique items that are hard to locate in your own country.

For example, you can search for authentic Celtic jewelry by using the Items located in option under the Location/International heading to find items in Ireland.

If the seller does not state in the auction description that they ship to your country, you can use the Ask seller a question link to find out if they do. For more

information on the Ask seller a question feature, see task #13.

You can also use the Items available to option to search for items that sellers ship to your country, although this usually brings up a mixture of both local and international items.

Another way to find unique items is to select the Any country from the Items available to option. However, you may discover that sellers do not ship their items to your country, so you need to check the item description for shipping details.

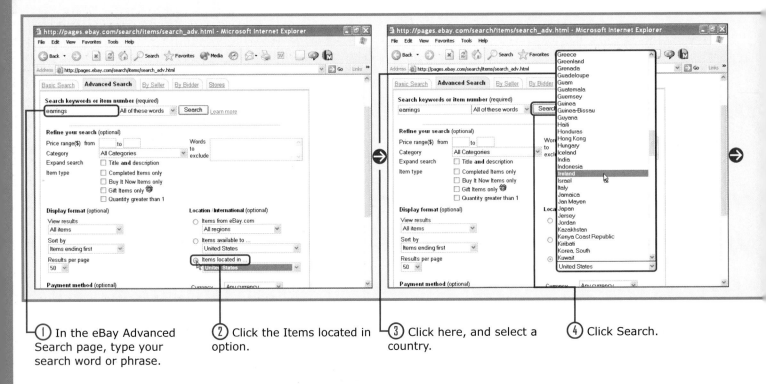

① In the eBay Advanced Search page, type your search word or phrase.

② Click the Items located in option.

③ Click here, and select a country.

④ Click Search.

## More Options! ※

Another way to search for
items in different countries is
to go directly to the international
eBay site of that country, using that
country's domain name. For example, to
look for items in Germany, you can go to
www.ebay.de. For a list of eBay's worldwide
sites with links to each, scroll to the lower left
of the eBay home page and look under Global
Sites. However, remember that these sites appear
in each respective country's native language.

## Buyer Beware! ※

When you buy internationally on eBay, you must pay
with whatever currency the seller specifies. You can
view a currency converter at www.pages.ebay.com/
services/buyandsell/currencyconverter.html. For more
about international buying, go to www.pages.ebay.com/
internationaltrading/findingitems.html.

**#16**

DIFFICULTY LEVEL

○ The search results appear
for the list of items located in
the country you specified.

⑤ Click the item you want
to view.

○ The details page appears
for the listing.

⑥ View the Shipping and
payment details section to
determine if the seller ships
to your country.

○ You may need to scroll
down to see the Shipping
and payment details.

# GET BID ALERTS
## with the eBay Toolbar

You can use the eBay Toolbar to receive a notice on your desktop reminding you to bid on an auction on which you have already bid and that is about to end. Called a *Bid Alert*, these notices are especially helpful when you bid on numerous items and want to expend less time keeping track of when their auctions end.

Although the eBay Toolbar is free, you must download the toolbar from www.pages.ebay.com/ ebay_toolbar/ and install it before you can perform

the steps in this task. Once installed, you can specify how many minutes before the auction ends that you want to receive your Bid Alert.

You do not have to be online or have your browser window open to see the Bid Alert. The alert appears on your desktop and links you to the item's auction page on eBay.

eBay automatically removes ended auctions from your Bid List in the Bid Alert menu. However, if you win the auction, the item appears in the Items I've Won menu, which you access via the Items Won button.

**SET BID ALERT PREFERENCES**

① Click here, and then click eBay Toolbar Preferences.

○ The eBay Toolbar Preferences window appears.

② Click here, and select when you want eBay to send you a Bid Alert.

○ You can click here and select an option to dismiss the notification.

○ You can click here to receive Audio notification.

③ Scroll down, and click Save Changes.

○ Your new eBay Toolbar settings take effect.

## More Options! ※

You can check the items on
which you have bids at any time
by using the Bid Alert menu. In the
eBay Toolbar, click the Bid Alert icon
(🔍). You can select an item from the
menu to view the item's auction. eBay
refreshes your Bid List when you bid on a
new item. You refresh your bid list manually
by clicking 🔍 and then clicking Refresh Bid List.

## #17

DIFFICULTY LEVEL

## Did You Know? ※

You can receive watch alerts for your Watch List
items. For information on how to watch an item,
see task #12. When an auction you are watching
is about to end, eBay sends an audio notification,
and an alert appears in the lower right corner
of your desktop.

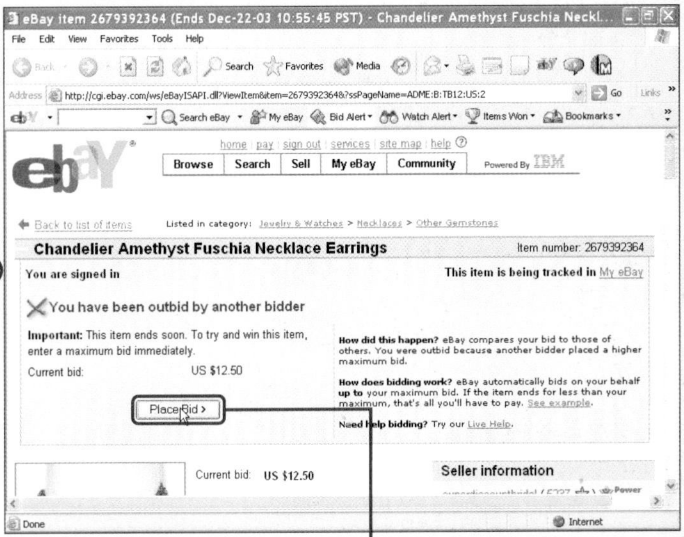

**USING A BID ALERT**

O At the time you specified
before the end of the auction,
the Bid Alert appears on the
lower right corner of your
desktop.

O If you have the default
Audio notification selected
in your eBay Toolbar
preferences, you hear
a noise.

① Click the Bid Alert.

O Your browser opens, and
the item's auction page
appears.

O eBay allows you to bid on
the item before the auction
ends.

# Shop for
# LAST-MINUTE
# BARGAINS

You can take advantage of great deals by bidding on soon-to-end auctions with few or no bids. You can find a nice, low-price item that many eBay buyers overlook because of a poor title or misspelled name. For more on running a search for such items, see task #9.

When you browse categories, you can sort the various auctions by their ending time to find appealing items with few or no bids. eBay displays auctions that close in the next five hours as going, going, gone. You can also sort listings by ending today, which shows you auctions with a closing date of today.

You can also apply these parameters with search results by simply checking the auctions that are ending first.

Although you can find some great bargains with the going, going, gone feature, items may have no bids for a good reason. For example, the item may have a flaw or be outdated. Always read the auction description carefully to make sure you do not bid on something you do not want.

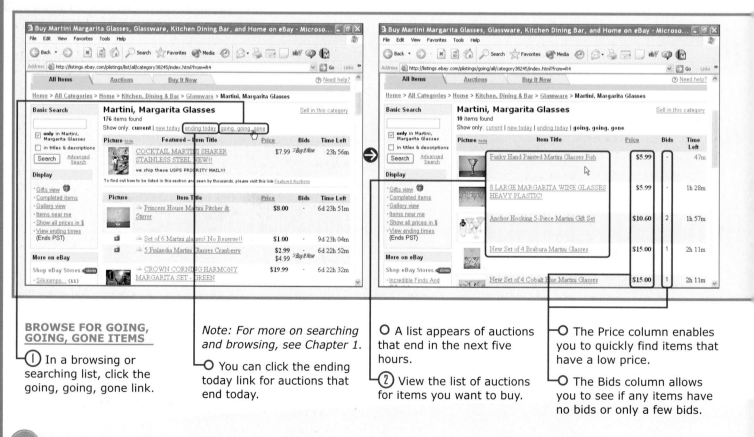

**BROWSE FOR GOING, GOING, GONE ITEMS**

① In a browsing or searching list, click the going, going, gone link.

*Note: For more on searching and browsing, see Chapter 1.*

○ You can click the ending today link for auctions that end today.

○ A list appears of auctions that end in the next five hours.

② View the list of auctions for items you want to buy.

○ The Price column enables you to quickly find items that have a low price.

○ The Bids column allows you to see if any items have no bids or only a few bids.

# #18

## More Options! ☀

You can also sort items while browsing using the new today link, on the top of a browsing list, which shows listings that just started today. Sorting by new today is useful when you want to find good items that have just gone live, decreasing the possibility that other eBay buyers may view the same bargain.

## eBay Savvy! ☀

You can also check for items whose auctions are about to end and that have a Buy It Now icon ( =Buy It Now ). When =Buy It Now appears next to an item that you want, you can buy it right away and not worry about losing the item to another bidder. For more information on using the Buy It Now feature, see tasks #2, #9, #19, and #46.

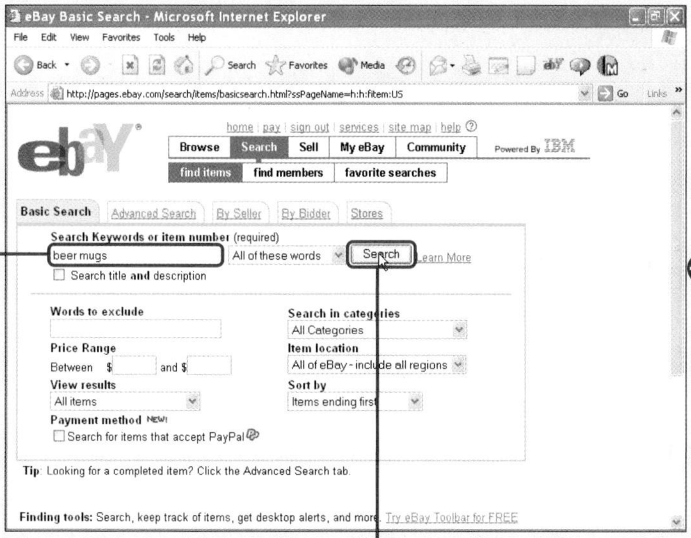

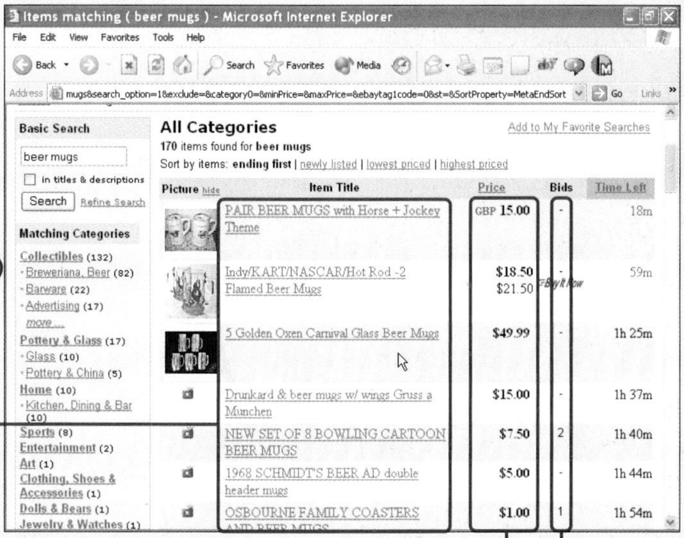

---

**SEARCH FOR ENDING FIRST ITEMS**

① In the eBay Basic Search tab, type your search word or phrase.

② Click Search.

○ A list of auctions appears, sorted by the auctions ending first.

*Note: This is the default sort setting for the search.*

③ View the list of auctions for items you want to buy.

○ The Price column enables you to quickly find items that have a low price.

○ The Bids column allows you to see if any items have no bids or only a few bids.

# USING GALLERY VIEW
## to quickly shop

Have you ever been in a situation where you need to find a gift quickly for that special someone? You can combine two options on eBay, the Gallery view and the Buy It Now features, to expedite your shopping.

The Gallery view option allows you to view the items in an eBay search or browse results list as neatly aligned rows of photos, and you can efficiently scan the pictures to see if there are any items you want.

When you combine the Gallery view option with the Buy It Now feature, you not only find what you want

more quickly, but you can also purchase it right away.

To find Buy It Now items, you can use the Buy It Now option on the Advanced Search page, or the Buy It Now tab above a category name next to the All Items and Auctions tabs. The Buy It Now tab appears whether you are browsing or searching. For information about finding bargains with Buy It Now, see tasks #2, #9, #19, and #46.

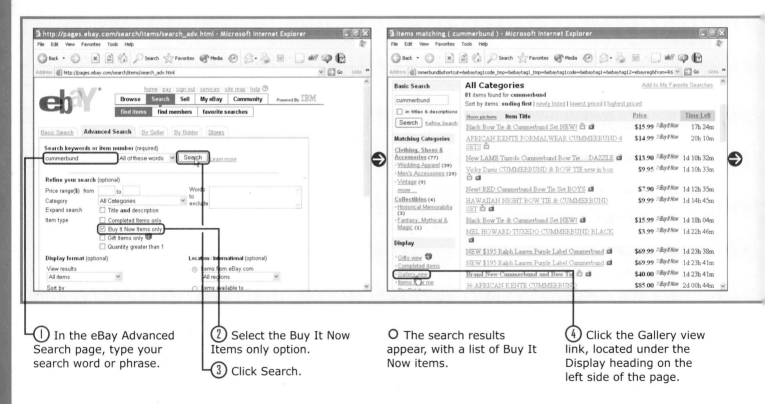

① In the eBay Advanced Search page, type your search word or phrase.

② Select the Buy It Now Items only option.

③ Click Search.

○ The search results appear, with a list of Buy It Now items.

④ Click the Gallery view link, located under the Display heading on the left side of the page.

# More Options! ※

Another way to quickly
view photos of items is to
use the timeBLASTER tool, which
downloads photos of eBay items for
offline viewing in a Photo Album format.
For more information, see task #10.

## Did You Know? ※

Items can either have a Buy It Now price
in addition to a starting bid price, or they
can have only a Buy It Now price, with
no option to bid — this is known as a
*fixed-price listing*.

## Did You Know? ※

The Buy It Now option disappears after a buyer places
a bid unless the auction has a reserve price, in which
case the Buy It Now option remains until someone
bids at or above the reserve price.

# #19

DIFFICULTY LEVEL

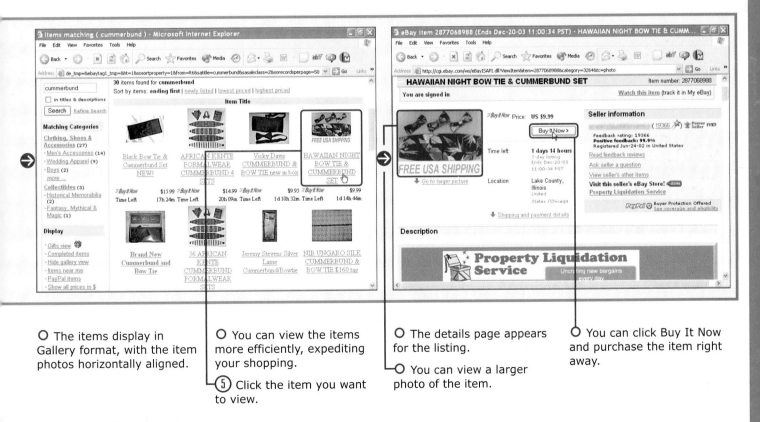

O The items display in
Gallery format, with the item
photos horizontally aligned.

O You can view the items
more efficiently, expediting
your shopping.

⑤ Click the item you want
to view.

O The details page appears
for the listing.

O You can view a larger
photo of the item.

O You can click Buy It Now
and purchase the item right
away.

# Buy multiple items to
# SAVE ON SHIPPING

You can save money on shipping costs by buying several items from the same seller. It is usually cheaper to mail two items in one envelope or box than it is to ship two separately packaged items so sellers usually offer to pass the savings to you.

Sellers try to get you to buy more from them by offering to combine shipping costs. If you need those other items anyway, it makes sense to buy them from the same seller and save money on postage.

For example, if you need both bubble wrap and padded mailers and the seller offers both, it makes

sense to buy both at the same time and save money on shipping fees.

You can use the View seller's other items link under the Seller information heading to view the other items the seller offers.

You can also search using the words "combine shipping" with the titles and descriptions option selected to find auctions where sellers offer savings on shipping.

For more information on using the title and description option, see task #2.

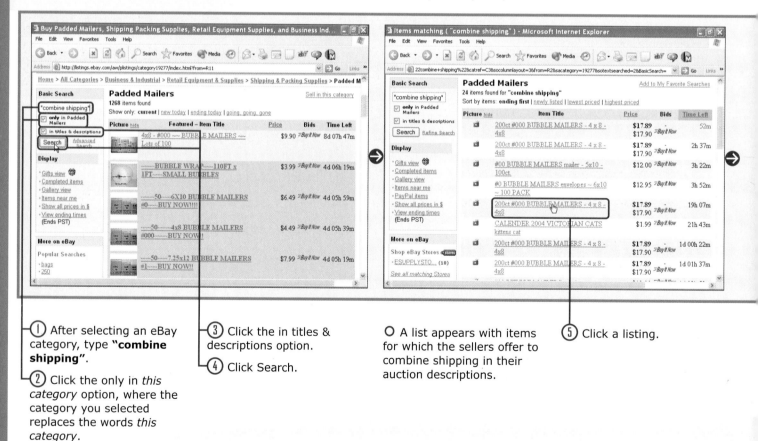

① After selecting an eBay category, type **"combine shipping"**.

② Click the only in *this category* option, where the category you selected replaces the words *this category*.

③ Click the in titles & descriptions option.

④ Click Search.

○ A list appears with items for which the sellers offer to combine shipping in their auction descriptions.

⑤ Click a listing.

# #20

## eBay Savvy! ※

Look for opportunities to combine shipping even on items you do not buy regularly. Consider buying other, similar things you need from sellers you use regularly. If a seller does not specify whether combine shipping is offered, you can use the Ask seller a question link, covered in task #13, to find out.

## Did You Know? ※

When you buy multiple items regularly from a seller, you can add that seller as a Favorite Seller in your My eBay page to save on shipping. In the eBay home page, click My eBay, click the Favorites tab, and then click Add new seller/store. Type the seller's user ID in the appropriate box, and then click Save Favorite.

○ A details page appears for the listing.

○ Scroll down through the auction description to confirm that the seller will combine shipping.

○ You can click the View seller's other items link under the Ask seller a question link to see if the seller offers other items you want to buy.

○ In this example, the seller allows you to buy multiple items to save money on shipping costs.

# Factor in
# HIDDEN COSTS

Although you can find many great deals on eBay, you should factor in hidden costs to determine if you really have a bargain. You can add up the less obvious fees associated with buying through an online auction, such as shipping, handling, and insurance.

On eBay, the buyer usually pays for the shipping costs. Some sellers also charge a handling fee, which is a value they place on their time to wrap, package, and send the item to you. Some sellers

may offer insurance, although this is usually optional for buyers.

It is a good idea to read an item's description carefully to ensure that you understand all of the fees the seller charges. For example, if you win an auction for a pair of shoes for twelve dollars, shipping and handling fees may bring the total cost to acquire those shoes up to twenty dollars. If you can buy the same shoes at a store for eighteen dollars, you may be better off buying them at a store.

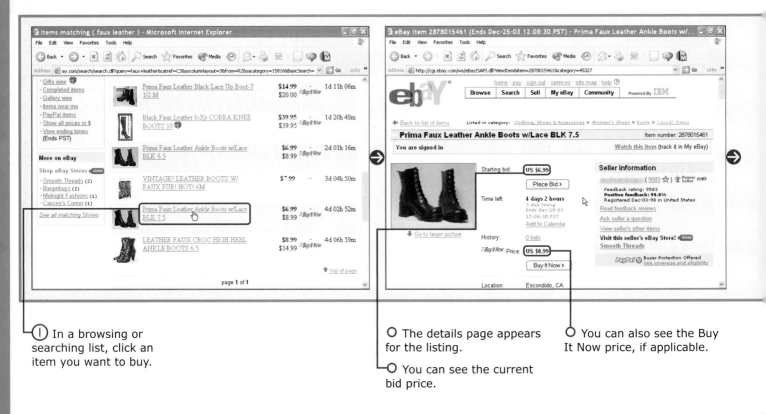

① In a browsing or searching list, click an item you want to buy.

○ The details page appears for the listing.

○ You can see the current bid price.

○ You can also see the Buy It Now price, if applicable.

# 21

## eBay Savvy! ☀

You can estimate shipping fees by using the United States Postal Service Web site at www. usps.com, the Federal Express Web site at www.fedex.com or the UPS Web site at www.ups.com. To calculate these fees, you need your ZIP code and the seller's ZIP code, which is usually included in the end-of-auction e-mail. This is only an estimate, because sellers set the shipping fees, which they determine in different ways. For more information about shipping, see Chapter 9.

## Buyer Beware! ☀

Be sure to find out the shipping charges before you bid, as some sellers inflate their shipping charges. If the seller does not state the shipping charges in the listing, you can use the Ask seller a question feature, as discussed in task #13.

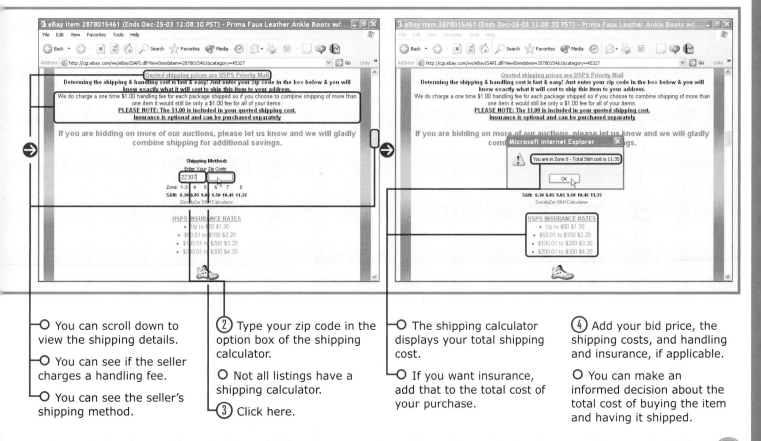

○ You can scroll down to view the shipping details.

○ You can see if the seller charges a handling fee.

○ You can see the seller's shipping method.

② Type your zip code in the option box of the shipping calculator.

○ Not all listings have a shipping calculator.

③ Click here.

○ The shipping calculator displays your total shipping cost.

○ If you want insurance, add that to the total cost of your purchase.

④ Add your bid price, the shipping costs, and handling and insurance, if applicable.

○ You can make an informed decision about the total cost of buying the item and having it shipped.

# CHAPTER 3

# Improve Your Bidding & Buying Strategies

Whether you intend to buy items at low cost through a Dutch Auction, or big-ticket items such as a house or car, the Advanced bidding strategies in this chapter show you how to soundly beat the competition.

Sniping techniques can mean the difference between winning and losing an auction. You can either snipe manually, or use a sniping service to snipe automatically. You can also take sniping to a new level by setting up bid groups that snipe similar types of items until you win. Another useful technique is to bid odd numbers to limit your chances of being outbid. You can also increase your chances of getting a low price by bidding on items in a Dutch Auction.

Not sure if a seller is offering you an item at a fair price? You have several options to research a particular item's price before bidding.

You can take advantage of the big-ticket items, such as cars and real estate, on eBay. eBay Motors offers an attractive alternative to the daunting negotiations that accompany buying a car at a dealership. You can use Blue Book pricing to educate yourself about your car deal and to get a lower price. eBay Real Estate listings can help you find that dream home or timeshare vacation deal.

The eBay Giving Works charity section and the Live Auctions offer some of the most exciting auction items — including celebrity-signed merchandise and unique opportunities, such as a walk-on part on a television show — while allowing you to help a worthy cause.

# TOP 100

**#22** Using Proxy Bidding to Your Advantage. . . . . . . . . . . . . . . . . . . 50

**#23** Snipe with Last-Second Bidding . . . . . . 52

**#24** Snipe While You Sleep . . . . . . . . . . . . . . . . 54

**#25** Out-Snipe Snipers with Advanced Techniques. . . . . . . . . . . . . . . . . . . . . . . . 56

**#26** Make Odd Numbers Work for You. . . . . . . . . . . . 58

**#27** Check Prices of Common Items. . . . . . . . . . . . . . 59

**#28** Get a Low Price with Dutch Auctions . . . . . . . . 60

**#29** Buy a Car with eBay Motors . . . . . . . . . . . . . 62

**#30** Find Real Estate Bargains . . . . . . . . . . . . . . 64

**#31** Support a Good Cause . . . . . . . . . . . . . 66

**#32** Join the Elite Fray of Live Auction Bidding. . . . . . . . . . . . . 68

# USING PROXY BIDDING
## to your advantage

You can avoid paying too much for an item by simply taking advantage of the eBay default bidding system, known as proxy bidding.

With *proxy bidding*, you set a price that is the most you want to pay for an item. The eBay software places a bid that is only high enough to outbid the current bidder by the auction's bid increment and no higher. If another bidder then outbids you, eBay places another bid that is only as high as it needs to be to outbid that bidder, given that your maximum

bid is high enough. eBay continues placing proxy bids until you are the high bidder or another bidder outbids your maximum bid.

eBay determines the bid increment by the current price of the auction. This means that you do not have to pay the most you may be willing to pay for an item, as long as another bidder does not bid as much as your maximum bid. For more information about advanced bidding strategies, see tasks #23, #24, and #25.

---

① Click on an item to view its details page.

*Note: For more on accessing the details page for an item, see tasks #1 and #2.*

○ You can view the Current bid price, the Time left in the auction, and the number of bids, if any.

② Click Place Bid.

○ The Place a Bid page appears.

○ eBay displays the Current bid.

○ eBay displays the minimum amount you need to bid.

③ Type the maximum amount you want to bid.

④ Click Continue.

## Did You Know? ☀

eBay's bid increments vary depending on the current price of an item. Below are the bid increments for various prices.

If the winning bidder's maximum bid beats the second-highest maximum bid by an amount that is less than the full bid increment, you can be outbid by less than a full bid increment.

### #22

**DIFFICULTY LEVEL**

| eBay Bid Increments | |
|---|---|
| *Current Price* | *Bid Increment* |
| $0.01 - $0.99 | $0.05 |
| $1.00 - $4.99 | $0.25 |
| $5.00 - $24.99 | $0.50 |
| $25.00 - $99.99 | $1.00 |
| $100.00 - $249.99 | $2.50 |
| $250.00 - $499.99 | $5.00 |
| $500.00 - $999.99 | $10.00 |
| $1,000.00 - $2,499.99 | $25.00 |
| $2,500.00 - $4,999.99 | $50.00 |
| $5,000.00 and up | $100.00 |

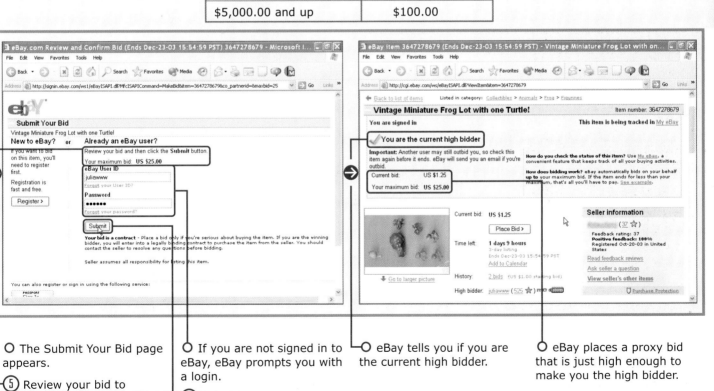

○ The Submit Your Bid page appears.

⑤ Review your bid to ensure that it is correct.

○ If you are not signed in to eBay, eBay prompts you with a login.

⑥ Click Submit.

○ eBay tells you if you are the current high bidder.

○ eBay places a proxy bid that is just high enough to make you the high bidder.

# Snipe with
# LAST-SECOND
# BIDDING

You can increase your chances of winning an item by bidding in the last seconds of the auction, a strategy known as sniping.

To snipe an item on eBay manually, you need to take note of the exact end time of the auction so that you can have your browser window open and be ready to bid.

The speed of your Internet connection determines how many seconds before the end of an auction you need to place your bid in order to successfully snipe. Some bidders with fast connections wait until only

five seconds before the end of an auction to place a bid. Others prefer more time and may wait until 20 seconds or more remain.

One strategy, shown in this task, is to open two browser windows and place them side by side to keep track of the time. You need to refresh one of the windows regularly. Then with the other window, you can quickly place your bid.

You can also use sniping software to place a snipe automatically. For more information on sniping software, see tasks #24 and #25.

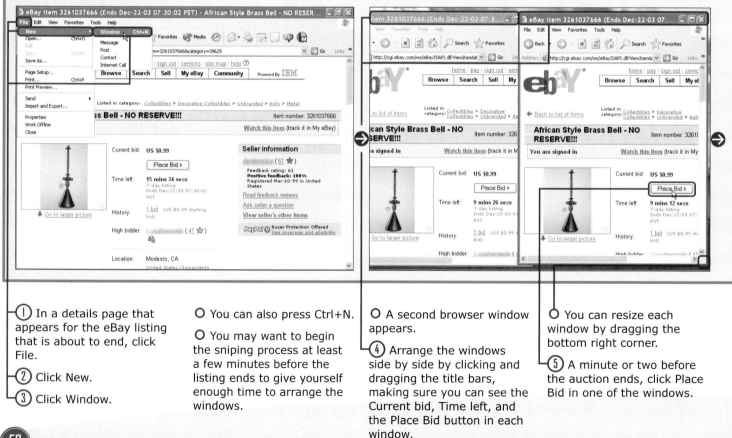

① In a details page that appears for the eBay listing that is about to end, click File.

② Click New.

③ Click Window.

○ You can also press Ctrl+N.

○ You may want to begin the sniping process at least a few minutes before the listing ends to give yourself enough time to arrange the windows.

○ A second browser window appears.

④ Arrange the windows side by side by clicking and dragging the title bars, making sure you can see the Current bid, Time left, and the Place Bid button in each window.

○ You can resize each window by dragging the bottom right corner.

⑤ A minute or two before the auction ends, click Place Bid in one of the windows.

# #23

DIFFICULTY LEVEL

## eBay Savvy! ※

To estimate the minimum time it takes your connection to snipe, refresh your browser and then note the Time left for the auction, which is in minutes and seconds. Refresh your browser again, and note the new Time left. The difference in seconds between the two numbers is the time it takes your connection to place a snipe.

## Caution! ※

It is possible, although unlikely, that both you and another bidder may snipe the same auction. In that case, the winner is whoever places the highest maximum bid. It is also possible that the hidden maximum bid of an earlier bidder is higher than your maximum bid. If two snipers place the exact same bid, the winner is whoever places the bid first.

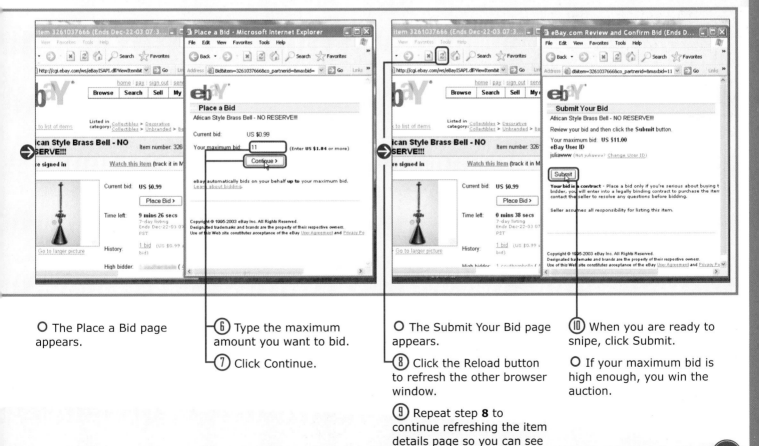

○ The Place a Bid page appears.

⑥ Type the maximum amount you want to bid.

⑦ Click Continue.

○ The Submit Your Bid page appears.

⑧ Click the Reload button to refresh the other browser window.

⑨ Repeat step **8** to continue refreshing the item details page so you can see how much time remains.

⑩ When you are ready to snipe, click Submit.

○ If your maximum bid is high enough, you win the auction.

# SNIPE
## while you sleep

You can snipe an item automatically with sniping software, such as Auction Sniper, which does the waiting for you. This prevents human error and lets you do other things besides sitting by the computer.

To use Auction Sniper, you must first set up an account at www.auctionsniper.com/register.aspx. To place a snipe, all you need is the item number of the eBay auction you want to snipe, and the maximum you want to spend on that item. You can also enter a *lead time* — the amount of time before the

auction ends, in seconds, that you want AuctionSniper to place your bid.

One sniping strategy involves just placing a snipe with your sniping software, but not bidding on the item first; if you place a bid and then place a snipe, you just drive up the bid price by that much more.

Auction Sniper displays a message that you have won, and reflects this in the status. You can also receive an e-mail message informing you of your win, or see all your wins by clicking the Wins tab.

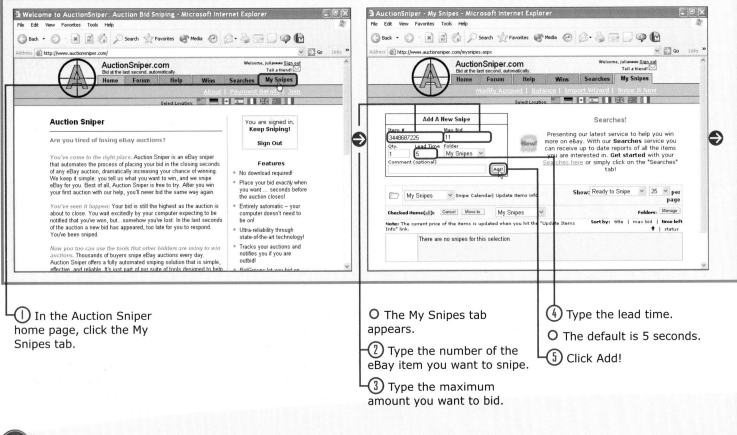

(1) In the Auction Sniper home page, click the My Snipes tab.

O The My Snipes tab appears.

(2) Type the number of the eBay item you want to snipe.

(3) Type the maximum amount you want to bid.

(4) Type the lead time.

O The default is 5 seconds.

(5) Click Add!

# #24

**DIFFICULTY LEVEL**

## More Options! ※

You can use other sniping services, including Bidnapper, Bidsage, eSnipe, EZsniper, Hammersnipe, Justsnipe, Powersnipe, and Snipeville. For a comparison in table format of 11 different auction services, including their pricing, see Auctionsbyte at www.auctionbytes.com/cab/pages/sniping.

## More Options! ※

You can keep track of your payments and feedback using the Auction Sniper Wins Tracker simply by signing in to Auction Sniper and clicking the Wins tab.

## Did You Know? ※

Although Auction Sniper offers a free trial, once the trial is up, they do charge for this service. For more information on costs for the service, go to www.auctionsniper.com/payment.aspx. You pay only for auctions you won.

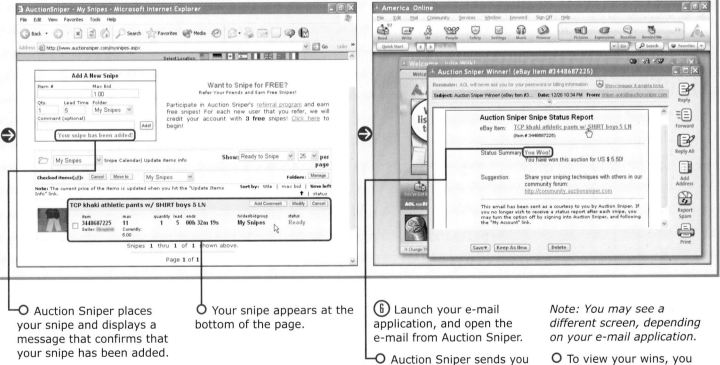

○ Auction Sniper places your snipe and displays a message that confirms that your snipe has been added.

○ Your snipe appears at the bottom of the page.

⑥ Launch your e-mail application, and open the e-mail from Auction Sniper.

○ Auction Sniper sends you an e-mail that tells you if you won the item.

*Note: You may see a different screen, depending on your e-mail application.*

○ To view your wins, you can also click the Wins tab, located at the Auction Sniper home page.

# OUT-SNIPE SNIPERS
## with Advanced Techniques

Rather than spend time sniping several auctions that you may lose, you can set up multiple bids at once. You can increase your odds of winning a certain type of item with Auction Sniper bid groups, which are specifically for several types of an item that is available simultaneously on eBay. This technique is not for a unique item. You use bid groups for items with a lot of competition, such as a popular laptop computer. Bid Groups are available as a feature from Auction Sniper's Web site at www.auctionsniper.com.

When numerous people bid on an item, they may try to snipe the item. Likewise, they may have a higher maximum bid set by eBay's proxy bidding system and unknown to you until the auction's end. For more on proxy bidding, see task #22. For more on sniping techniques, see tasks #23 and #24.

You can set up the software to bid until you win only one of that type of item, and then Auction Sniper cancels the other snipes so you do not buy items you do not want.

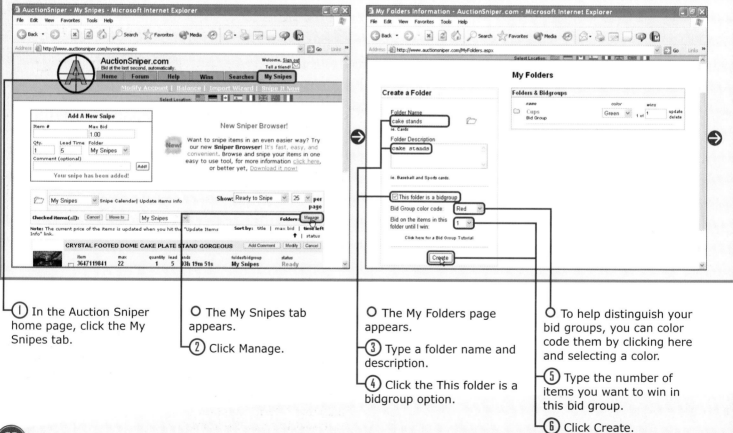

① In the Auction Sniper home page, click the My Snipes tab.

○ The My Snipes tab appears.

② Click Manage.

○ The My Folders page appears.

③ Type a folder name and description.

④ Click the This folder is a bidgroup option.

○ To help distinguish your bid groups, you can color code them by clicking here and selecting a color.

⑤ Type the number of items you want to win in this bid group.

⑥ Click Create.

## More Options! ☼

You can toggle between
the Auction Sniper and the eBay
interface and easily place snipes with
the click of a button by using Auction
Sniper's browser. For more information see
www.auctionsniper.com/sniperbrowser.aspx.
Download the browser at www.auctionsniper.
com/download/AuctionSniper100.exe.

## Did You Know? ☼

Bid groups are also available via BidSlammer at
www.bidslammer.com, and eSnipe at www.esnipe.com.
BidSlammer gives you three free snipes, after which you
pay $0.25 for every item you win under $10.00 and 1 percent
of the closing price for items over $10.00. eSnipe is free for
14 days, after which it costs $0.25 for items you won up to
$24.99, 1 percent of the winning amount for items up to
$1,000.00 — rounded down to the nearest penny — and a
maximum of $10.00 thereafter. See www.bidslammer.com/
help/?s=pricing for more information.

**DIFFICULTY LEVEL**

#25

○ Auction Sniper Bid Groups creates the folder.

⑦ Click the My Snipes tab.

○ You can see the list of items you are sniping.

⑧ Select the items you want to move into the bid group folder.

⑨ Click here, and select the bid group folder into which you want to move the items to snipe as a bid group.

⑩ Click Move to.

○ Auction Sniper moves your items into the bid group folder you specify and places snipes until you win an item.

# MAKE ODD NUMBERS
## work for you

If you bid odd amounts, you can increase your chances of winning auctions. Many buyers bid in simple, round, whole-dollar amounts. Others try to outsmart the system by adding one penny to their bids. If you regularly bid odd numbers, such as $13.39 or $23.17, you increase your chances of outbidding others who bid amounts like $13.01 or $23.00.

Because other bidders' maximum bids are hidden until the auction closes, you must make educated guesses as to what they are bidding to

try to outbid them. For example, if the current bid of an item with one bid is $28.99, you may guess a bidder's obvious maximum bid, such as $30.00 or $30.01, and place a bid of $31.05.

Of course, these strategies do not guarantee a win. If you prefer to keep your bid amount secret until the last few seconds of an auction, you can try sniping. For more information on sniping, see tasks #23, #24, and #25.

---

① In a Place a Bid screen for a listing, type an odd number of a maximum bid amount.

*Note: See task #4 to access this screen.*

○ eBay bases the minimum bid you must make on the Current bid.

② Click Continue.

○ eBay displays a message that you are the high bidder.

○ If no one outbids your odd number bid, you win the auction.

○ If you are outbid, you can place another odd number bid by following steps **1** and **2**.

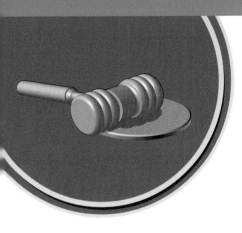

# CHECK PRICES

## of common items

## 27

**DIFFICULTY LEVEL**

You can ensure you do not pay too much for an item on eBay by using a price comparison Web site, such as Froogle.com. Froogle searches the Web to find products for sale online and presents you with the results in an easy-to-read format. You can go directly from Froogle's search results to a merchant's Web site to buy an item.

Froogle is owned by Internet search company Google, and uses Google's powerful search technology to find items from a wide range of online retailers.

You can find prices for items by browsing Froogle's categories or by using Froogle's

search. You can also search within a certain category or search the whole Froogle site.

When you check prices by combining both Froogle and eBay's Completed Items options in the Advanced Search, you have a powerful tool for educating yourself about the best deals you can get for a given type of item.

For more information on using the Completed Items option in eBay's Advanced Search, see task #3.

---

① Type **www.froogle.com** into the Address bar of your Web browser, and press Enter.

○ The Froogle home page appears.

② Type your search phrase into the box.

③ Click Search Froogle.

○ The search results appear.

○ You can see photos and sale prices of items.

○ The Sponsored Links on the right are ads.

○ You can click an item link to go to the retailer's web site and buy the item.

# Get a low price with
# DUTCH AUCTIONS

You can take advantage of the *Dutch Auction*, or *multiple item auction,* format to get a low price on an item because in a Dutch Auction, all winning bidders pay the same amount: the lowest successful bid. In a Dutch Auction, the seller offers multiple items that are identical. For example, if a seller has 100 party favors to sell, the seller may list a Dutch Auction of 10 lots of 10 party favors each. A Dutch Auction is a great way to buy things for which you need multiple quantities.

If you have more bids than available items in a Dutch Auction, bidders who offer the highest total bid price — which is the bid price times the number of items bid on — win the auction. Earlier successful bids beat later ones. However, you often find more available items than bids for a Dutch Auction, which means that all bidders pay the starting, and therefore the lower, price.

To identify a Dutch Auction, you look for a number in the Quantity field in the item description that is 2 or greater.

(1) In an eBay listing, look for a number of 2 or greater in the Quantity field, which indicates that this is a Dutch Auction.

O You can use the Advanced Search tab's Quantity greater than 1 option to find Dutch Auction items.

*Note: For more information about Advanced Search, see task #2.*

(2) Click Place Bid.

O The Place a Bid page appears.

(3) Type the maximum amount you want to bid.

O eBay displays the minimum bid you must make.

(4) Type the quantity of items you want.

(5) Click Continue.

# #28

DIFFICULTY LEVEL

## Did You Know? ※

Besides Dutch Auctions,
eBay offers other types of
auction formats, including regular
auctions; reserve price auctions, where
the seller designates a hidden minimum
price; Buy It Now auctions; Ads, as in the
Real Estate area; and Private Auctions, where
bidders, user IDs do not display on the listing.
For more on the various auction formats, go to
www.pages.ebay.com/help/buy/formats-ov.html.

## Did You Know? ※

If the seller offers you a partial quantity at the
auction's end, or fewer items than the number on
which you bid, you can refuse all of the items.

## Did You Know? ※

You can see all the item's bids — including
unsuccessful bids — at the end of the
auction by clicking the Winning bidders
list link in the item listing.

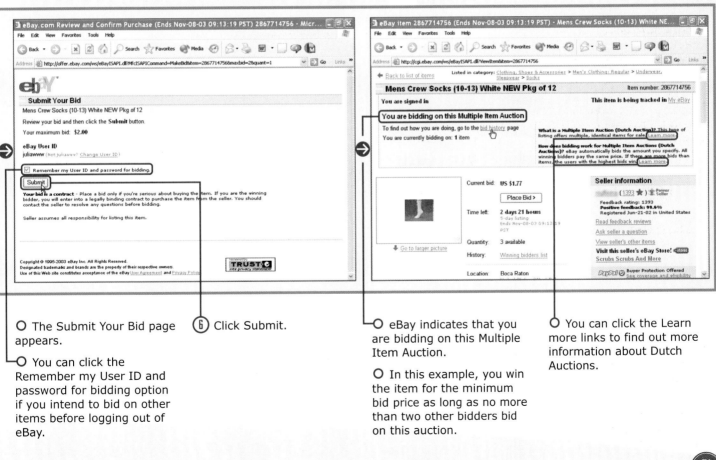

○ The Submit Your Bid page
appears.

○ You can click the
Remember my User ID and
password for bidding option
if you intend to bid on other
items before logging out of
eBay.

⑥ Click Submit.

○ eBay indicates that you
are bidding on this Multiple
Item Auction.

○ In this example, you win
the item for the minimum
bid price as long as no more
than two other bidders bid
on this auction.

○ You can click the Learn
more links to find out more
information about Dutch
Auctions.

# Buy a car with
# EBAY MOTORS

You can get a great deal on a car and avoid the stressful negotiation process of traditional car dealerships by buying a car on eBay Motors.

You can buy a car either with the traditional auction format or the fixed-price Buy It Now format.

You should look carefully at the car's description and assume the vehicle is being sold as is. Because of the higher dollar amount involved compared to most auctions, it is especially critical to check a seller's feedback. For more information on checking feedback, see task #14.

You should consider using an escrow service, like the one at www.escrow.com, to protect yourself from fraud. But be aware there are fake escrow sites targeting online auto buyers.

If you bid on any automobiles over $15,000, you need to provide background and credit verification. This means you must have your credit card on file with eBay. eBay notifies you when you place a bid, so allow yourself extra time for credit verification if you bid near the end time of an auction.

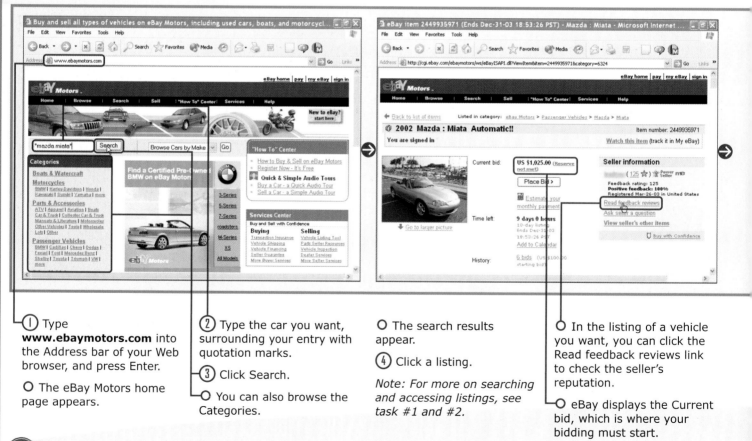

① Type **www.ebaymotors.com** into the Address bar of your Web browser, and press Enter.

○ The eBay Motors home page appears.

② Type the car you want, surrounding your entry with quotation marks.

③ Click Search.

○ You can also browse the Categories.

○ The search results appear.

④ Click a listing.

*Note: For more on searching and accessing listings, see task #1 and #2.*

○ In the listing of a vehicle you want, you can click the Read feedback reviews link to check the seller's reputation.

○ eBay displays the Current bid, which is where your bidding must start.

## eBay Savvy! ☀

If you are unable to pick
up the vehicle, you can use a
delivery service, such as Dependable
Auto Shippers, or DAS. DAS offers
free shipping quotes at pages.ebay.com/
ebaymotors/services/das-shipping.html.

## eBay Savvy! ☀

You can obtain a vehicle history report on any
used car to find out information such as the
accident history, or if the car has been in a flood.
To obtain a report, click the VIN link on the vehicle
description page. For eBay Motors users, a single
Vehicle History Report costs $4.99, or you can receive
ten reports for $9.99. You can view a sample vehicle
history report at pages.ebay.com/ebaymotors/
services/vehicle_history_report.html.

---

**⑤** Scroll down to see a
description of the vehicle.

**O** The seller should include
information such as the
transmission type and
mileage, as well as
vehicle options.

**O** Make sure you read the
entire description to find out
if the car has ever been in an
accident or had body work
done.

**⑥** Scroll down to see if the
seller included a report from
the Kelley Blue Book.

**O** You can go to
www.kbb.com and verify
the report yourself.

# Find
# REAL ESTATE BARGAINS

You can shop for a property anywhere in the world with eBay Real Estate. If you do your research and understand the listing details, you may find a good deal.

Different from the rest of the site, many eBay Real Estate listings are in an Ad format. With the Ad format, you provide your name, contact information, and any questions through the listing's Contact the Seller form to inform the seller of your interest.

In addition to residential homes, the other types of property for sale on eBay include land parcels and commercial real estate. You can also find timeshares and vacation rentals.

You can narrow your search by state or province, and by sale type, such as a foreclosed home or a new home. You can also select a number of bedrooms or bathrooms, and a price range.

Please note that eBay strongly recommends that you seek your attorney's advice before entering into any binding real estate transaction. For more information, see eBay's disclaimer page: pages.ebay.com/help/community/re_agreement.html.

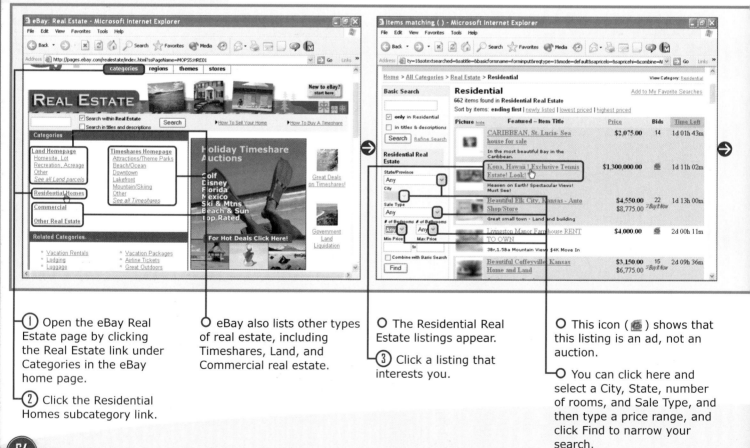

①  Open the eBay Real Estate page by clicking the Real Estate link under Categories in the eBay home page.

②  Click the Residential Homes subcategory link.

O  eBay also lists other types of real estate, including Timeshares, Land, and Commercial real estate.

O  The Residential Real Estate listings appear.

③  Click a listing that interests you.

O  This icon (🏠) shows that this listing is an ad, not an auction.

O  You can click here and select a City, State, number of rooms, and Sale Type, and then type a price range, and click Find to narrow your search.

## Did You Know? ※

eBay also displays Real Estate
listings in an Auction format, in
which you click Place Bid to bid. A
listing is in Auction format if it shows a
number of bids in the Bids column —
instead of the Ad icon — in the search or
browse results list.

eBay Real Estate Auctions offer non-binding
or binding bids. A note at the bottom of the
listing tells you if the auction is binding or
non-binding. With *non-binding auctions*, you
can view properties in the familiar, auction-style
format without committing to the seller to complete
the transaction. *Binding auctions* are more likely to
result in a sale because the buyer is expected to
complete the purchase in good faith.

**#30**

**DIFFICULTY LEVEL**

○ The details page appears
for the listing.

○ You can view the property
description.

○ You can click this link to
read the seller's feedback
reviews.

④ Scroll down to the Ready
to contact seller/agent?
section.

⑤ Type your personal
information.

⑥ Click Submit.

○ eBay transmits your
interest to the owner of the
property.

# Support a
# GOOD CAUSE

You can buy items on eBay and support a charity of your choice at the same time by shopping at Giving Works, eBay's charity section. Giving Works offers many wonderful items, as well as services, and even some unique experiences, such as being Redbook Magazine editor for a day, or attending Entertainment Weekly's Oscar Viewing Party.

You can also find many items signed by celebrities, such as a guitar signed by Nickelback and a signed CD from Clay Aiken.

You can search the eBay Giving Works section for items at www.pages.ebay.com/givingworks. You can also search for items benefiting a specific nonprofit organization by name, keyword, mission area, and geography, or browse the categories from that page.

You can bid on eBay Giving Works items the same way you bid on any other eBay items. Just find an item you like, sign in with your eBay account, and place a bid.

In the item description, you can see the percentage of the item's final price that the seller donates to the benefiting nonprofit organization.

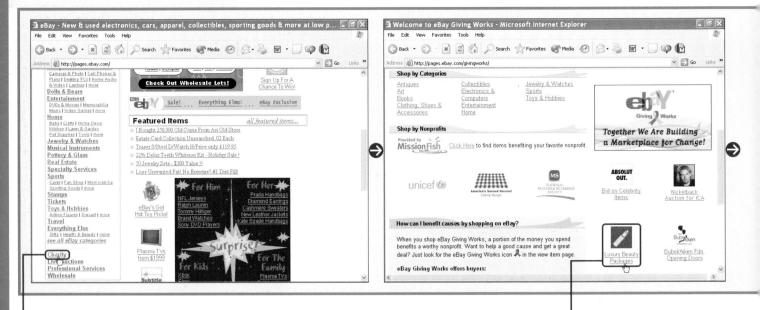

① In the eBay home page, click the Charity link.

○ The eBay Giving Works page appears.

○ eBay displays a list of nonprofit organizations and charity auctions.

② Click the charity icon of your choice.

## eBay Savvy! ☀

As an eBay seller, you can
donate your auction's proceeds
to a designated charity. eBay works
with MissionFish, a third-party nonprofit
organization, to facilitate transactions
between charities and sellers. To list an
eBay Giving Works item, you must first
register with MissionFish and list your items
using the MissionFish Giving Assistant. After
an auction ends, MissionFish forwards the funds
to the designated nonprofit organization. To register
with MissionFish, go to www.missionfish.org and click
the Register to sell or Register to benefit link.

**DIFFICULTY LEVEL**

## Did You Know? ☀

If you pay over fair market value for an item from a
nonprofit organization, the amount you overpaid
may be tax-deductible. However, fair market
value or below is not tax-deductible. Consult
your accountant or tax advisor for specific advice.

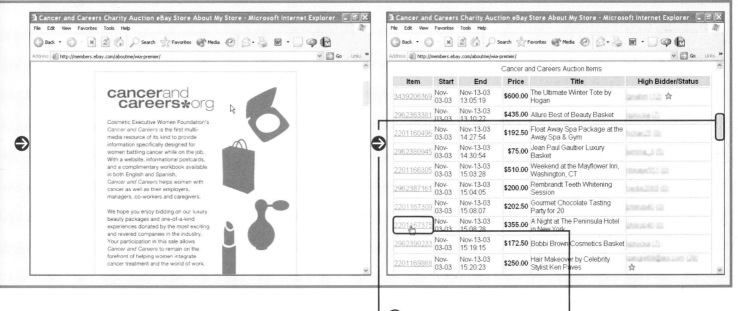

⊙ The charity listing page
appears.

⊙ You can read the
description of the charity
and whom it helps.

⊙ You can read about the
donated items.

③ Scroll down to see the
actual item listings.

⊙ You can click a listing that
interests you and bid on it,
thus donating money to the
charity.

# Join the elite fray of
# LIVE AUCTION BIDDING

You can bid in real-time auctions taking place in some of the world's most elite auction houses with eBay's Live Auctions.

In addition to offering exquisite and unique merchandise, Live Auction places you in contact with sellers that are highly reputable and experienced, so you can minimize your chances of having a bad transaction.

Before bidding in a live auction, you can prepare yourself by browsing live auctions either by the auction catalog or by categories. The catalog features all the lots available in a particular live auction. You can search both live auction lots and

categories at www.pages.liveauctions.ebay.com/search/items/search.html. Categories include Asian Arts, Books and Manuscripts, Furniture and Decorative Arts, Fine Arts, and Jewelry and Timepieces.

To participate in a live auction, you must first register, which you can do in the Browse tab at the top of any eBay Live Auctions page. Once you register, you can place absentee bids, or you can go to the live auction.

The Live Auction sellers each have their own terms and conditions of sale for each event, which usually include a satisfaction and authenticity guarantee.

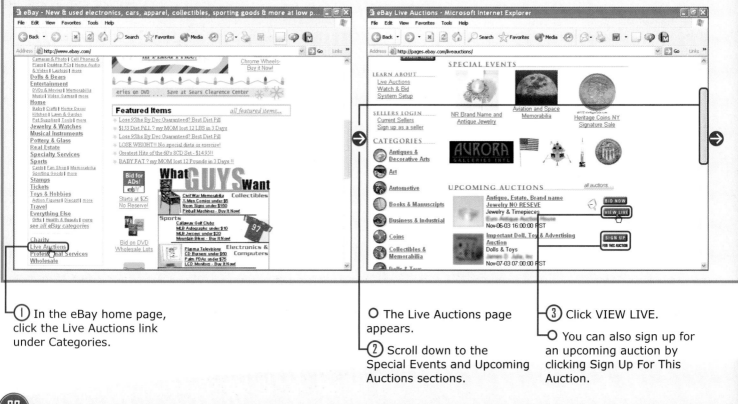

① In the eBay home page, click the Live Auctions link under Categories.

○ The Live Auctions page appears.

② Scroll down to the Special Events and Upcoming Auctions sections.

③ Click VIEW LIVE.

○ You can also sign up for an upcoming auction by clicking Sign Up For This Auction.

## Did You Know? ☀

When you sign up to bid in a live auction, eBay displays the seller's terms and conditions of sale. For example, the buyer may need to contact the seller within a certain number of business days, or the seller may have a disclaimer about the auction items, such as that items are all sold as is. You must click the option (☐ changes to ☑) to indicate that you have read and accept the terms and conditions of sale. You can also check an option (☐ changes to ☑) to have eBay send you a reminder e-mail about the auction. Click Continue. eBay then informs you that you have successfully signed up to participate in the upcoming live auction and displays the catalog name, auction dates, and seller name.

## DIFFICULTY LEVEL

○ The What you need to view a live auction! page appears.

○ eBay displays the Catalog and Seller name.

④ Click the View Live Now link.

○ The Live Auction page appears with bids showing in real time.

○ If you have signed up to bid, you can click the Bid now! link to place a bid.

○ If you have not signed up to bid, you can click the Sign up to bid now! link.

# CHAPTER 4

# Paying For Items Painlessly

You can save time and please both buyers and sellers on eBay by using the right payment services. The tasks in this chapter show several available payment options and the advantages of each.

You should familiarize yourself with the wide range of payment options that you can use, from money orders to eBay's integrated payment service, PayPal. Many eBay buyers and sellers prefer PayPal for its ease of use and because it allows sellers to accept credit card payments, as well as transfer funds into and out of a designated bank account.

You can also earn discounts and even get eBay items for free by earning Anything Points, a promotional currency that works with eBay and PayPal.

In some cases you may need to use alternate payment services. For example, if a seller only accepts money orders, you can save time by ordering a money order online with the Auction Payments service. For items priced over $500, where you have a much higher risk, you can use an escrow service.

Although most transactions on eBay go smoothly, you need to know what to do when you encounter a problem. For example, you should follow the recommended procedures if you receive a misrepresented item. The SquareTrade service offers a valuable, impartial way to work out a positive solution to a variety of transaction problems when the recommended procedures fail.

You can build your own feedback rating so both sellers and buyers implicitly trust you.

# TOP 100

**#33** Find the Right Payment Options... 72

**#34** Set Up a PayPal Account . . . . . . . . . . 74

**#35** Add PayPal Funds. . . . . . . . . . . . . 76

**#36** Withdraw Funds from PayPal. . . . . . . . . . 78

**#37** Save Time with Auction Payments. . . . . . . . . 80

**#38** Get Discounts with Anything Points . . . . . . . . . 82

**#39** Using Escrow to Buy Your Item . . . . . . . . . . . 84

**#40** Troubleshoot After-Sale Problems. . . . . . . . . 86

**#41** Resolve Payment Disputes with
SquareTrade . . . . . . . . . . . . . . . . . . . . 88

**#42** Using Feedback to Build Goodwill . . . 90

# PAYMENT OPTIONS

The payment options available for an item vary from seller to seller. You should know all these options so you can make a timely payment with as few problems as possible. Ideally, you should check the seller's payment instructions, which are usually in the Shipping and payment details section of the auction listing, before you place a bid. Consequently, if you win the item, you do not have to pay for the item with a payment method you do not prefer. To find

what type of payments the seller accepts, you view the Shipping and payment section of the auction listing, which you can access following the steps in task #1.

Although sellers usually state their payment instructions in detail, if they do not, you can use the Ask seller a question link in the auction listing for more information. For more information about the Ask seller a question link, see task #13.

## Western Union Auction Payments

Some sellers may only accept money orders or cashier's checks, in which case you may want to consider Western Union Auction Payments, formerly BidPay, an online money order service, located at www.auctionpayments.com. The service starts at $1.95 for transactions up to $10.00. For more information about Western Union Auction Payments, see task #37.

## CheckFree

An alternative to Paypal, CheckFree is located at www.checkfree.com and is free to buyers, although the seller pays 1.85 percent plus $0.30 per transaction. Sellers may prefer CheckFree to PayPal because the fees are lower. The only drawback is that both buyers and sellers must have an account to use the service. To open an account, go to www.checkfree.com, and specify your financial institution. Select it by specifying a state in the appropriate option box.

## Payingfast

You may want to use Payingfast to buy a money order for an item that cost $10.00 or less, because Payingfast's fee is lower than Western Union Auction Payments' for such items. You find this service at www.payingfast.com. It starts at $1.75 for transactions up to $10.00. To use Payingfast, go to www.payingfast.com and follow the instructions.

DIFFICULTY LEVEL

<table>
<tr><td colspan="2">Joseph McDonald<br/>322 South St.<br/>Berkley, IN 46576</td><td>313</td></tr>
</table>

Joseph McDonald
322 South St.
Berkley, IN 46576                                    313

Pay to the
Order of ___eBay merchant_____ $ _76.85_

_Seventy-six dollars and_ 85/100 _____ Dollars

Small Town Bank
Small Town Bank of Ohio
Berkley, Ohio

For _nehru jacket_                    Joseph McDonald

1080433367 833089361 8974

## PayPal

Many sellers and buyers prefer PayPal because it is integrated into the eBay Web site and allows buyers to make payments quickly and easily. With PayPal, you can send cash to anyone who has an e-mail address. Buyers can pay by simply clicking on a PayPal link in the e-mail they receive at an auction's end. Personal PayPal accounts are free, but Business and Premier accounts pay either a Standard rate of 2.9 percent of the transaction amount + $.30, or a Merchant rate of 2.2 percent of the transaction amount + $.30. For more information about PayPal, see tasks #34 to #36.

## Personal Check

You can pay with a personal check, but some sellers may require you to have a good feedback rating to do this. For more on feedback ratings, see task #14. If you do pay with a personal check, remember that it may take longer to receive your item because it takes time for the check to arrive at the seller's by U.S. mail, and because sellers sometimes hold personal checks until they clear. Read the seller's payment instructions in the auction listing carefully to find out their policy on personal checks and to whom you should make the check out.

## Other Payment Services

You can view a complete chart of the payment services, how they work, and their fees on the AuctionBytes Web site at www.auctionbytes.com/cab/pages/payment.

# Set up a
# PAYPAL ACCOUNT

You can make it easier for yourself and your customers to pay for items on eBay by having a PayPal account. PayPal allows buyers to make online payments from their designated bank account or a credit card. PayPal is owned by eBay and is seamlessly integrated into the Web site as a payment option.

With a PayPal Premier or Business account, you can accept credit card payments without paying the high overhead of a credit card merchant account. You can set up a PayPal account by going to the Web site at www.paypal.com and following the relatively simple steps to sign up for the account.

Once you have a PayPal account, you can pay for many auction items right away by simply using the Pay Now or PayPal link in the auction listing.

Not all sellers on eBay accept PayPal, so you may need to pay by personal check or money order. However, many sellers realize the value in accepting eBay buyers' favorite payment method. For more information on PayPal, see tasks #35 and #36. For more on the various payment options, see task #33.

---

① Type **www.paypal.com** into your Web browser address bar, and press Enter.

② In the PayPal home page, click the Sign Up link.

③ Click to select an account option.

④ Click here, and select the country.

⑤ Click Continue.

○ The Acccount Sign Up page appears.

⑥ Type your name, address, and phone number.

# Did You Know?

Personal accounts are free, but your buyers cannot pay with a credit card. However, personal accounts can use PayPal's Winning Buyer Notification feature, which automatically sends payment requests to your auction winner. PayPal Business and Premier accounts accept credit card payments, but they cost 2.9 percent plus $0.30 per transaction to receive funds. If you qualify, you may receive a reduced Merchant Rate of 2.2% + $.30 per transaction.

# eBay Savvy!

Premier PayPal accounts have access to PayPal's premium features, such as the ability to receive credit card payments. The cost is 2.9 percent plus $0.30. Sending payments is free. Sign in to PayPal, and click the Profile tab on PayPal's main screen to upgrade from a Personal to a Premier account.

⑦ Type your e-mail address and password.

○ You may need to scroll down the page.

⑧ Select a security question, and type an answer.

⑨ Select an account option.

⑩ Click Yes in the PayPal's User Agreement section.

⑪ Click Sign Up at the bottom of the page.

○ A page appears, asking you to confirm your e-mail address.

⑫ To confirm your e-mail address now, follow the steps on the screen.

○ You can confirm your e-mail address at a later time, if you prefer.

⑬ Click Continue.

○ PayPal creates your account.

# Add
# PAYPAL FUNDS

You can transfer money to your PayPal account from your bank account. You can also accept payments from other PayPal users to your PayPal account. To transfer funds to your PayPal account, you must first add your account to PayPal and then verify your bank account. Electronically-transferred funds become available in your PayPal account within three to four business days. PayPal sends you an e-mail confirming when you add funds to your account, as well as when eBay buyers pay you with PayPal for items they purchase from you.

If you receive an e-mail notification that a payment has been made to your PayPal account but the transaction does not appear on your History page, the sender may have typed an incorrect e-mail address. You should contact the sender and confirm that they have sent the payment to the correct address.

You should check your PayPal balance periodically to ensure that you have adequate funds to cover any eBay purchases. For more information on PayPal, see tasks #34 and #36.

① Type **www.paypal.com** into your Web browser address bar, and then press Enter.

*Note: You need to log in to the PayPal site if you have not already done so.*

② In the main PayPal page, click the Add Funds tab.

O The Add Funds tab appears.

③ Click the Transfer Funds from a Bank Account link.

# Did You Know?

After you sign up for PayPal, you need to add and then confirm your bank account. You also need to confirm your e-mail address. To add your bank account, click the My Account tab and then click the Add Checking Account link. Fill out the Add Bank Account form, and click Add Bank Account. PayPal e-mails you instructions on how to confirm your e-mail address and bank account. To confirm your e-mail address, simply launch your e-mail application, open PayPal's e-mail, and click the link. Type your PayPal password. To confirm your bank account, PayPal makes two small deposits into it and then asks you to confirm them by checking your bank balance after two to three days.

DIFFICULTY LEVEL

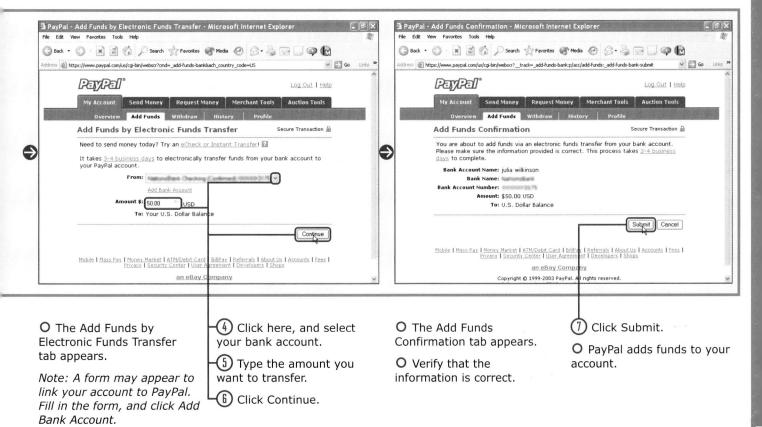

○ The Add Funds by Electronic Funds Transfer tab appears.

*Note: A form may appear to link your account to PayPal. Fill in the form, and click Add Bank Account.*

④ Click here, and select your bank account.

⑤ Type the amount you want to transfer.

⑥ Click Continue.

○ The Add Funds Confirmation tab appears.

○ Verify that the information is correct.

⑦ Click Submit.

○ PayPal adds funds to your account.

# WITHDRAW FUNDS
## from PayPal

You can use your PayPal funds in many different ways. For example, you can transfer the money you make from selling items on eBay into your bank account. PayPal does not charge for transferring funds into your bank account. You can also leave the funds in your PayPal account and use them to buy items on eBay.

Be aware that transfers from PayPal to your account are not instantaneous and that you may have a delay between the time you transfer funds and the time that they appear in your account. Although

PayPal shows the transaction as complete, your bank may not recognize the transfer, and as a result, may not reflect the transfer. PayPal cannot verify when funds transfer to your bank account. If your transfer request has a problem, your bank may take up to one week to notify PayPal. PayPal e-mails you if they learn of any problems.

You cannot cancel a withdrawal from your PayPal account, so be very sure you want to withdraw the funds before doing so. For more information about PayPal, see tasks #34 and #35.

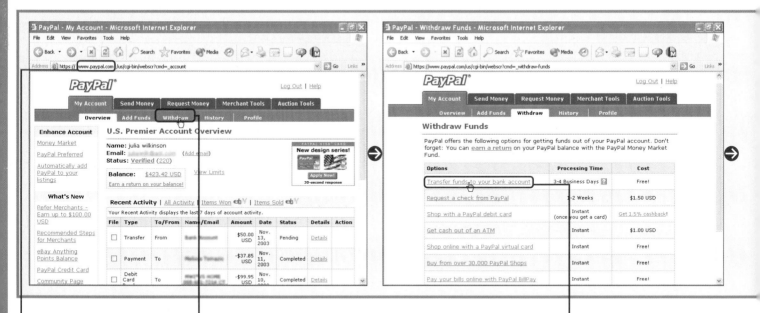

① Type **www.paypal.com** into your Web browser address bar, and then press Enter.

*Note: You need to log in to the PayPal site, if you have not already done so.*

② In the main PayPal page, click the Withdraw tab.

○ eBay displays your withdrawal options.

○ The processing time and cost appear for each option.

③ Click the Transfer funds to your bank account link.

# #36

DIFFICULTY LEVEL

## More Options!

You can also request a check from PayPal, which takes one to two weeks and costs $1.50. Another option is to use PayPal's debit card, which allows you to receive 1.5 percent cash back on your purchases. To request the card, click the ATM/Debit Card link on the bottom of any PayPal page.

## eBay Savvy!

You can use your PayPal funds to purchase items from over 30,000 PayPal shops through an online directory of businesses that accept PayPal. To access PayPal shops, click the Shops link in the lower right corner of any PayPal page. You can also pay your bills online with PayPal BillPay. To use BillPay, click the BillPay link that appears on the bottom of any PayPal page once you log in.

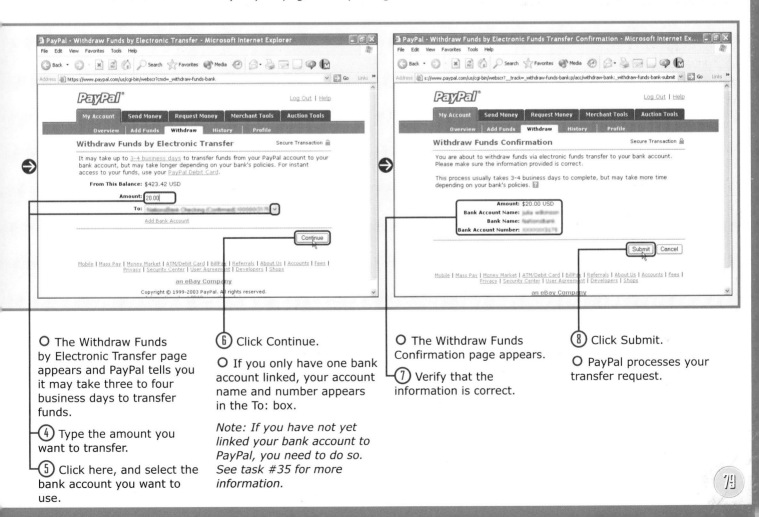

○ The Withdraw Funds by Electronic Transfer page appears and PayPal tells you it may take three to four business days to transfer funds.

④ Type the amount you want to transfer.

⑤ Click here, and select the bank account you want to use.

⑥ Click Continue.

○ If you only have one bank account linked, your account name and number appears in the To: box.

*Note: If you have not yet linked your bank account to PayPal, you need to do so. See task #35 for more information.*

○ The Withdraw Funds Confirmation page appears.

⑦ Verify that the information is correct.

⑧ Click Submit.

○ PayPal processes your transfer request.

# AUCTION PAYMENTS

You can avoid long, tedious waits at the bank or post office to purchase a money order by using Auction Payments, a Western Union service, to purchase it online with a credit, debit, or charge card. You can then purchase online auction items with the money orders. You access Auction Payments, which was formally BidPay, at www.auctionpayments.com. This service is especially useful if you win an auction for which the seller only accepts money orders instead of PayPal or personal checks. Auction Payments also allows both you and the seller to track the money order online.

You receive confirmations by e-mail when the money order ships. You also may receive your item more quickly when you use Auction Payments because many sellers ship items as soon as they receive e-mail confirmation that Auction Payments has sent your money order.

Auction Payments bases the cost of the service on the amount of the money order, with fees starting at $1.95 for a money order of up to $10.00. Auction Payments limits money orders to $700 per item purchased.

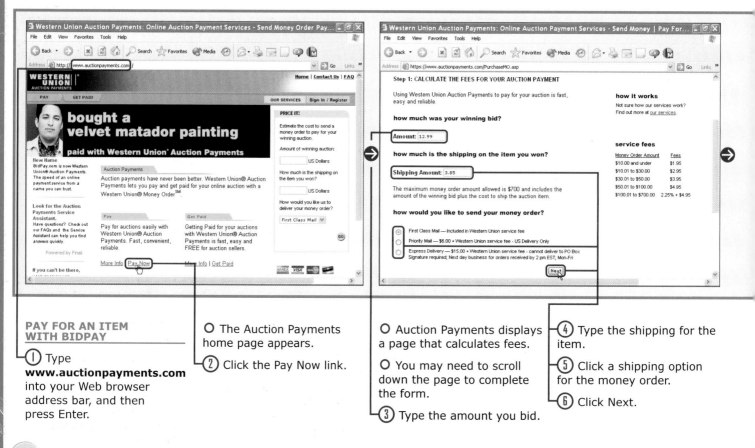

**PAY FOR AN ITEM WITH BIDPAY**

① Type **www.auctionpayments.com** into your Web browser address bar, and then press Enter.

○ The Auction Payments home page appears.

② Click the Pay Now link.

○ Auction Payments displays a page that calculates fees.

○ You may need to scroll down the page to complete the form.

③ Type the amount you bid.

④ Type the shipping for the item.

⑤ Click a shipping option for the money order.

⑥ Click Next.

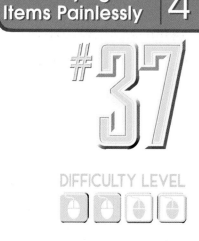

## eBay Savvy!

You can check the status of your orders online. Click the Buyer Login link, and type your e-mail address and password. You can then modify your information, see the history and status of your orders, or place new orders.

## Did You Know?

You need to include the seller's shipping fee and other fees in the principal amount of the money order. The principal is labeled Amount in US$ on the purchase money order form in the pay for your auction page. Remember that the delivery charge on the form in the pay for your auction page is for the shipment of the money order to the seller, and not for the shipment of the item you purchase from the seller.

○ Auction Payments displays a summary of your fees.

⑦ Review the Fee Summary information for accuracy.

─○ You can click Previous and edit the amounts you have typed.

⑧ Click Next.

○ The page to enter auction item and seller information displays.

⑨ Type the Item information, including the auction site, your user ID, the item number, and item description.

⑩ Type the seller's information.

⑪ Click Next at the bottom of the page.

○ Auction Payments prompts you for your billing information and confirms your order.

# ANYTHING POINTS

You can pay for eBay items and seller fees with eBay Anything Points when you use PayPal. eBay Anything Points are promotional currency that you can earn from designated eBay partners, such as Hilton, Netflix, and The New York Times. You can also earn points with the eBay Anything Points credit card, which you can sign up for at www.anythingpoints.ebay.com. Also, sellers can offer Anything Points to buyers who use PayPal to purchase items from them.

One eBay Anything Point equals $0.01 towards the payment of an eBay item, providing the seller accepts PayPal as a payment method. Anything Points apply only to the final price of an eBay item, and not to shipping, sales tax, or insurance fees.

If you do not have enough Anything Points to purchase an item, you can spend the points you have, and pay the remaining portion using PayPal.

To use Anything Points, you need to first sign up for the program at www.anythingpoints.ebay.com. At this site, you can also view or spend your points, or get a complete list of the details for Anything Points.

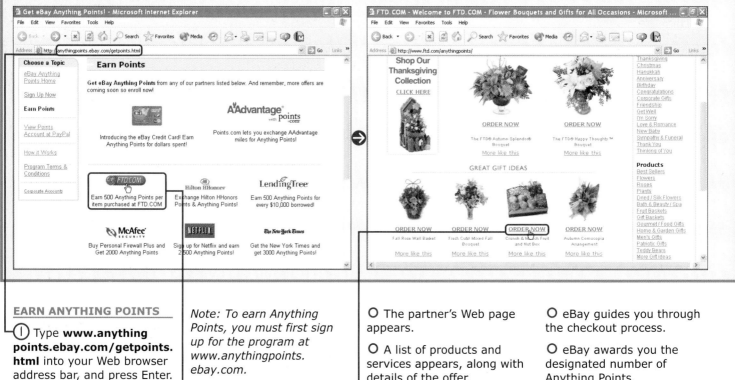

## EARN ANYTHING POINTS

① Type **www.anything points.ebay.com/getpoints. html** into your Web browser address bar, and press Enter.

O A list of eBay partners appears.

*Note: To earn Anything Points, you must first sign up for the program at www.anythingpoints. ebay.com.*

② Click the logo of the eBay partner whose points you want to earn.

O The partner's Web page appears.

O A list of products and services appears, along with details of the offer.

③ Click the ORDER NOW link to buy an item.

O eBay guides you through the checkout process.

O eBay awards you the designated number of Anything Points.

## Apply it!

To pay for an eBay item using your Anything Points, click Pay Now on the eBay won item page, and then click the PayPal option. Click Continue, and follow the PayPal login process. On the Confirm Your Payment page, click Add/Select in the Redemption Code (Optional) section, which allows you to designate that the payment uses your Anything Points.

## Did You Know?

To pay your eBay seller fees with Anything Points, click the My eBay tab, and then click Accounts. Type the amount in the PayPal payment text box, and click Pay. Click the Redemption Code link, and your Anything Points balance appears. Select the option to use your Anything Points for the payment, and click Continue.

Redemption Code (Optional)
To use your **eBay Gift Certificate or Anything Points** for this purchase, click the 'Add / Select' button to add or select a redemption code.    [ Add / Select ]

# ＃38

DIFFICULTY LEVEL

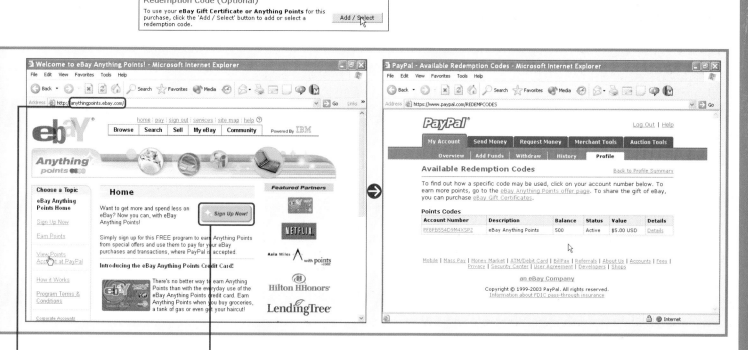

### VIEW YOUR ANYTHING POINTS

① Type **www.anything points.ebay.com/ getpoints.html** into your Web browser address bar, and then press Enter.

○ You can sign up for Anything Points by clicking the Sign Up Now link or button.

② Click the View Points Account at PayPal link.

*Note: If you have not already logged in to PayPal, a prompt appears asking you to do so.*

○ The PayPal Available Redemption Codes page appears.

○ PayPal displays your Anything Points balance.

# USING ESCROW
## to buy your item

You can protect yourself from seller fraud and ensure the quality of your purchase using an escrow service. An *escrow service* is one that both buyer and seller trust to hold the buyer's payment until the buyer receives, inspects, and approves the item.

Both buyer and seller must agree to use escrow before the auction ends. You can check the seller's payment terms in the listing to see if they accept escrow. If you have any doubt, use the Ask seller a question link, discussed in task #13, to ask if they accept escrow.

Although you can use escrow for any type of item once the seller agrees, you generally use escrow for items worth $500 or more because of the level of risk involved and because the escrow service generally charges you for using the service.

Make sure you research the escrow company you use. There have been cases of fraudulent Web sites made to look like real escrow services. eBay recommends that U.S. and Canadian users use escrow.com and recommends other escrow sites for users in other countries.

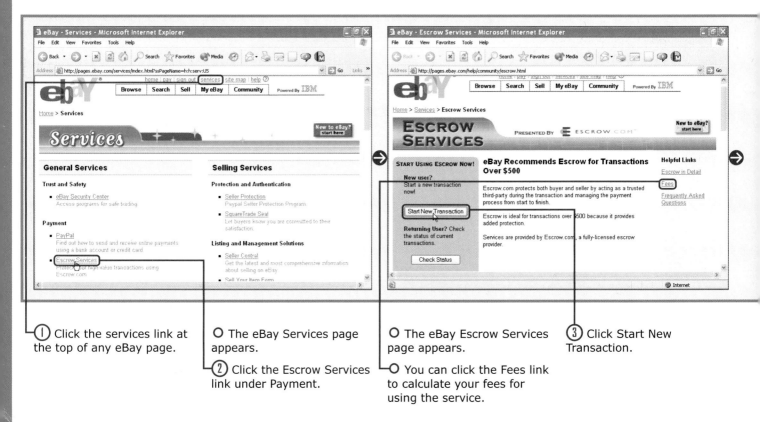

① Click the services link at the top of any eBay page.

○ The eBay Services page appears.

② Click the Escrow Services link under Payment.

○ The eBay Escrow Services page appears.

○ You can click the Fees link to calculate your fees for using the service.

③ Click Start New Transaction.

# Apply It!

To calculate your escrow fee, go to www.pages.ebay.com/ help/community/escrow.html, and click the Fees link. In the Rates for eBay Customers page that appears, type the transaction value, indicate your method of payment, and then click Calculate Your Fee. Your escrow fee appears for this transaction. Fees for escrow vary, depending on the price of the item. For example, the escrow fee for a $500 item using a credit card is $37.

# Did You Know?

Both seller and buyer must agree to the inspection period and the length of time the buyer has to examine the item, which can be from 1 to 30 days. If the buyer rejects the item, the seller has five days to examine the merchandise after the buyer returns it.

**DIFFICULTY LEVEL**

○ The Escrow Services: Enter your eBay Item Number page appears.

④ Type your eBay item number.

⑤ Click Continue.

○ Your bid and contact information appear.

⑥ Click I Agree.

○ escrow.com initiates the escrow process.

# AFTER-SALE PROBLEMS

Although most transactions on eBay go smoothly, some unfortunately do have problems. To protect your important feedback rating, you need to handle problems carefully by following eBay's procedures.

Many sellers send a confirmation e-mail right away, including shipping fees, if necessary. If they do not, you can request the total amount using the Ask seller a question link in the item's listing page.

If the seller does not contact you within three days, as stipulated in eBay's Item Won e-mail, you can use eBay's Request a member's contact info form to get

the seller's phone number. For information about how to contact a seller, see task #13.

If you get into a disagreement, you can try to resolve the problem with the SquareTrade service. For more information about SquareTrade, see task #41.

If your attempts to resolve a problem do not work, you can file a fraud alert between 30 and 60 days after the auction ends. eBay then gives you instructions as to how to file a protection claim, which you must file within 90 days after the auction ends.

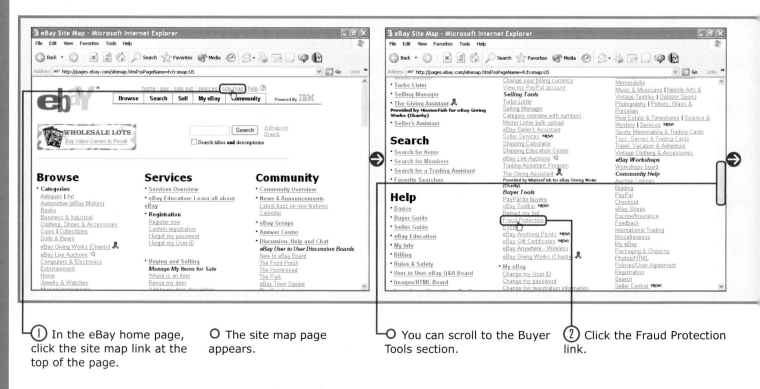

① In the eBay home page, click the site map link at the top of the page.

○ The site map page appears.

○ You can scroll to the Buyer Tools section.

② Click the Fraud Protection link.

# #40

## Did You Know?

Most credit card companies offer 100 percent consumer protection for online fraud or misrepresentation. eBay also offers buyer protection on items up to $200, minus a $25 processing fee. If you pay with PayPal, you are eligible for up to $500 of coverage through PayPal's Buyer Protection program. To check if you are covered, look for the PayPal Buyer Protection icon in the Seller Information box on an eBay View Item page.

## eBay Savvy!

Some eBay buyers complain that sellers give retaliatory negative feedback when they receive negative feedback. To protect your own feedback rating, leave negative or neutral feedback only as a last resort. For more information about the proper use of feedback, see tasks #14 and #42.

---

**Buyer Protection Program - Microsoft Internet Explorer**

File   Edit   View   Favorites   Tools   Help

Back · · Search Favorites Media

Address http://pages.ebay.com/help/confidence/isgw-fraud-protection.html   Go   Links

Contact Us

**Related Links**

Learning Center
eBay University
Security Center
About Customer Support

### Buyer Protection Program

eBay pledges to work with our community members to ensure a safe trading environment. Most issues can usually be resolved through communicating directly with the other eBay members involved. eBay recommends the following steps:

#### 1) Initial Steps For Buyer:

| Step | Explanation | Time Frame |
|------|-------------|------------|
| 1. Call your Seller | Request your seller's contact information and give him or her a phone call. Many issues are just simple misunderstandings that can be resolved with a single phone call. | First 15 days after the listing ends |
| 2. Report suspicious activity | Notify eBay in the following cases:<br>You paid but received a significantly misrepresented item<br>You paid but did not receive the item<br><br>If the issue remains unresolved after calling the seller and then seeking outside resolution, here are some additional steps eBay offers to assist buyers: | Any time |
| 3. Try dispute resolution through a third party. | Try FREE online dispute resolution through SquareTrade. | First 30 days after the listing ends |
| 4. Contact your payment provider. | A. If you paid with PayPal, your item may have enhanced protection through PayPal Buyer Protection. | First 30 days after the |

---

**Buyer Protection Program - Microsoft Internet Explorer**

File   Edit   View   Favorites   Tools   Help

Back · · Search Favorites Media

Address http://pages.ebay.com/help/confidence/isgw-fraud-protection.html   Go   Links

#### 2) Using the Buyer Protection Program

If you've followed the above steps and have not been able to resolve the issue, you may be entitled to partial reimbursement through our Buyer Protection Program.

| Step | Explanation | Time Frame |
|------|-------------|------------|
| 1. File a fraud alert. | The buyer protection program covers provides partial reimbursement for losses resulting from non-delivery or misrepresentation of most items up to $200 (minus $25 processing cost). Learn more.<br><br>Filing a fraud alert is the **initial step** toward potential reimbursement through the program.<br><br>File a fraud alert now, to initiate a buyer protection claim. | Between 30 and 60 days after the listing ends |
| 2. File a protection claim. | Once the fraud alert you have filed is processed, you'll be given instructions to file a protection claim.<br><br>**Note:**<br>You **must** file a claim with your credit card issuer prior to filing a claim with eBay (if applicable). | After filing a fraud alert, but within 90 days of the end of the listing. |

**Note:** In order to be eligible for reimbursement through eBay, you must submit a claim postmarked within 90 days of the end of the listing.

---

○ The Buyer Protection Program window appears.

○ You can click the You paid but received a significantly misrepresented item link in the Report suspicious activity section.

○ You can click the You paid but did not receive the item link in the Report suspicious activity section.

③ Scroll down to the Using the Buyer Protection Program section.

④ Click the File a fraud alert link to report non-delivery or misrepresentation of an item between 30 and 60 days after the auction ends.

○ eBay steps you through the complaint process.

# CHAPTER 5

# Smart Selling on eBay

Selling items on eBay can be just as exciting as bidding on them because it brings a great deal of satisfaction — as well as extra cash. You can become a savvy seller by knowing what length to make your auction, the various listing options, and what to do when your highest bidder falls through. Adding pizzazz to your listing with a different design or color gives you an edge over the competition. Understanding listing fees and the pre-filled information feature saves you time and money.

Knowing how to list an item to match your situation is extremely important because listing formats determine how you conduct an auction. Regular auctions let buyers bid on an item until time runs out and the best bid wins. But if you want to set the price of your item, you can use a Fixed Price auction. To allow bidding as well as the option of a set price, you can add a Buy It Now feature. If you have multiple identical items to sell, you can offer them in a single listing using a Dutch Auction.

To start your path as a smart seller, register on your My eBay page and become familiar with the eBay policies page, which lists legal standards you must follow. You can also ensure that eBay allows your item by checking it against the Prohibited and Restricted Items list. As the seller, you must follow the law as well as eBay rules and guidelines. Failing to do so can lead to legal problems.

# TOP 100

**#43** Avoid Problems with Trademark Protection . . . . . . . . . . . . . . . . . . . 94

**#44** Check That eBay Allows Your Item . . . . 96

**#45** Set an Auction Length . . . . . . . . . . . . . . . . . . 97

**#46** Determine When to Use Buy It Now . . . . . . . . 98

**#47** Create a Fixed-Price Listing . . . . . . . . . . . . . . . . 99

**#48** Sell in Bulk with Dutch Auctions. . . . . . . . . . . . 100

**#49** Protect Your Item with a Reserve. . . . . . . . . . . . 101

**#50** Save Money on Listing Fees . . . . . . . . . . . . . . 102

**#51** Give Your Listing a Background Color . . . . . 103

**#52** Jazz Up Your Listing with Listing Designer Graphics . . . . . . . . . . . . . . . . . 104

**#53** Save Time with Pre-filled Information. . . . . . . . . . . . . . . . . . . . . 106

**#54** Make a Second-Chance Offer . . . . . . . . . . . . . . . . . . 108

# Avoid problems with
# TRADEMARK PROTECTION

When you sell items on eBay, you must consider trademark and copyright protection. eBay prohibits infringing materials, which can include copyrighted items, such as written works, music, movies, television shows, software, games, artwork, and other images.

Intellectual property rights generally belong to the creator of the material. If you hold a copyright to materials being sold illegally on eBay, you can join the Verified Rights Owner, or VeRO, Program to help keep illegal copies of your work from circulating. Because eBay cannot verify if an item is auctioned illegally, the owners of such properties must be vigilant.

In 1997, eBay created the VeRO Program to enlist owners of intellectual property rights to help keep eBay safe from trademark and copyright violations. As a member of VeRO, you can report and request the removal of listings that infringe on your ownership rights.

As a seller, it is your responsibility to make sure that the item you auction does not infringe upon the rights of the owners. If you are unsure, you can check the VeRO Program participant's About Me pages.

① In the eBay Policies page, scroll to the bottom of the page, and click the Protecting Intellectual Property link.

*Note: See task #44 to learn how to view the eBay Policies page.*

O The Protecting Intellectual Property page appears.

② Click the VeRO Program link.

## eBay Savvy! ※

When you find it confusing to determine what constitutes illegal use, let common sense guide you. For example, if an eBay auction offers a DVD and that movie is still in theaters, the DVD is clearly an illegal copy. Another example is a photograph, which is copyrighted, from a catalog being used to describe an item in a listing.

## Caution! ※

If eBay removes your listing through VeRO, you receive an e-mail explaining why. To find out what you did wrong, consult the VeRO About Me pages. If you believe the rights owner is in error and the item was legal for trade, you can contact the owner directly and ask about the problem. The notification e-mail includes the rights owner's e-mail address.

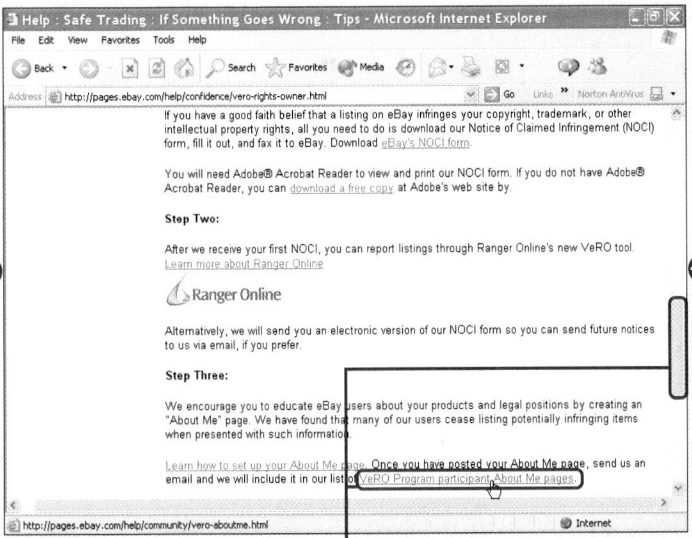

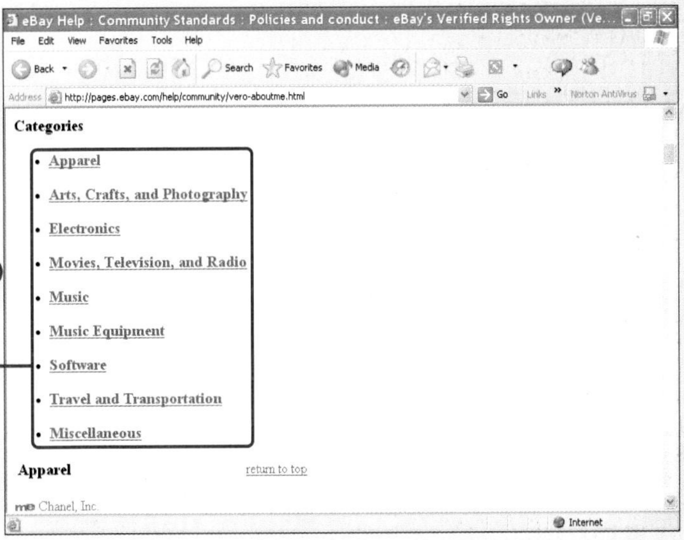

---

**Screenshot 1 (left):**

Help : Safe Trading : If Something Goes Wrong : Tips - Microsoft Internet Explorer

File  Edit  View  Favorites  Tools  Help

Address http://pages.ebay.com/help/confidence/vero-rights-owner.html

If you have a good faith belief that a listing on eBay infringes your copyright, trademark, or other intellectual property rights, all you need to do is download our Notice of Claimed Infringement (NOCI) form, fill it out, and fax it to eBay. Download eBay's NOCI form.

You will need Adobe® Acrobat Reader to view and print our NOCI form. If you do not have Adobe® Acrobat Reader, you can download a free copy at Adobe's web site by.

**Step Two:**

After we receive your first NOCI, you can report listings through Ranger Online's new VeRO tool. Learn more about Ranger Online

Ranger Online

Alternatively, we will send you an electronic version of our NOCI form so you can send future notices to us via email, if you prefer.

**Step Three:**

We encourage you to educate eBay users about your products and legal positions by creating an "About Me" page. We have found that many of our users cease listing potentially infringing items when presented with such information.

Learn how to set up your About Me page. Once you have posted your About Me page, send us an email and we will include it in our list of VeRO Program participant About Me pages.

http://pages.ebay.com/help/community/vero-aboutme.html

**Screenshot 2 (right):**

eBay Help : Community Standards : Policies and conduct : eBay's Verified Rights Owner (Ve...

File  Edit  View  Favorites  Tools  Help

Address http://pages.ebay.com/help/community/vero-aboutme.html

**Categories**

- Apparel
- Arts, Crafts, and Photography
- Electronics
- Movies, Television, and Radio
- Music
- Music Equipment
- Software
- Travel and Transportation
- Miscellaneous

**Apparel**                                    return to top

m⊕ Chanel, Inc.

---

○ The eBay Verified Rights Owner (VeRO) Program page appears in a new browser window.

○ You can read more about the program.

③ Scroll down the page and click the VeRO Program participant About Me pages link.

○ A list of categories appears.

④ Click a category.

○ eBay displays individual policies regarding copyrights and trademarks.

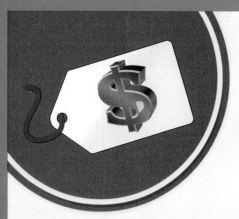

# Determine when to use BUY IT NOW

**DIFFICULTY LEVEL**

The Buy It Now option allows buyers to purchase an item without going through the actual bidding process, so that your bidder can end an auction early by paying the listed price. Essentially, your item becomes a real time-saver for impatient buyers, but still displays as a regular auction item.

When you add the Buy It Now option, a special button appears on the auction page. The option is only available until someone makes a bid on the item, at which time the button disappears.

When determining a reasonable price for your Buy It Now auction, you need to do some research. Setting the price too high drives off potential bidders who find that the price exceeds what they want to bid. If you set the price too low, you risk selling the item for less than it is worth. For more information about researching prices for your items, see task #3.

eBay charges five cents for using Buy It Now for auction listings, but not for Buy It Now fixed price listings. For more on fixed price listings, see task #47.

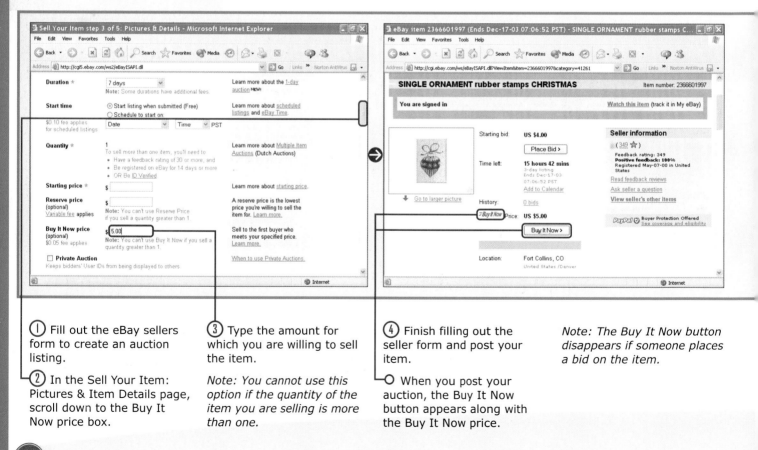

① Fill out the eBay sellers form to create an auction listing.

② In the Sell Your Item: Pictures & Item Details page, scroll down to the Buy It Now price box.

③ Type the amount for which you are willing to sell the item.

*Note: You cannot use this option if the quantity of the item you are selling is more than one.*

④ Finish filling out the seller form and post your item.

○ When you post your auction, the Buy It Now button appears along with the Buy It Now price.

*Note: The Buy It Now button disappears if someone places a bid on the item.*

# Create a
# FIXED-PRICE
# LISTING

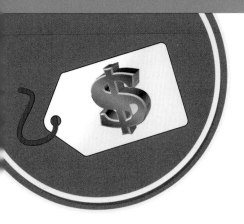

## DIFFICULTY LEVEL

You can use the new eBay Fixed-Price listing option to bypass all the bidding and offer a set price to anyone who looks at the item listing. Fixed-Price listings allow for an immediate transaction for both the buyer and seller without waiting for an auction to end. You use this listing to ensure that your item does not sell for less than its value, or to sell multiple items at the same price.

When you use the Fixed-Price listing, eBay lists the item with the Buy It Now feature, a button that appears on the item description page that

lets buyers purchase the item with a single click. To use the new Fixed-Price listing option, you must be an established eBay seller, with a feedback rating of 30 or more.

Although both Fixed-Price listings and Buy It Now auctions show the Buy It Now button, a Fixed-Price listing shows only the Buy It Now button, whereas a Buy It Now listing offers both a Place Bid and a Buy It Now option. For more information about the Buy It Now feature, see tasks #19 and #46.

---

① Fill out the eBay Sell Your Item form to create an auction listing.

② In the Sell Your Item: Choose Selling Format page, click the Sell at a Fixed Price option.

③ Click Continue, and resume setting up your item listing.

④ In the Sell Your Item: Provide Pictures & Item Details page, scroll down to the Buy It Now price box.

⑤ Type the amount for which you are willing to sell the item.

○ eBay assigns the fixed price to your auction.

⑥ Finish filling out the seller form, and post your item.

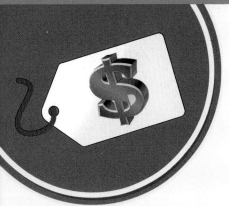

# SELL IN BULK
## with Dutch Auctions

**DIFFICULTY LEVEL**

To sell a quantity of the same item quickly, consider offering a Dutch Auction — also called *multiple item auctions* — a format that allows multiple bidders to bid on a set quantity of identical items. For example, to sell ten tape measures without the Dutch Auction feature, you must sell them as a lot using a regular auction and hope for a good price, or set up ten different auctions for each item. However, if you offer the ten tape measures in a Dutch Auction with a minimum price, you leverage your selling potential and only have to set up one auction listing.

What makes Dutch Auctions unique is the winning bid price — all winning bidders pay the lowest successful bid. If you have more buyers than goods, the earliest successful bidders win the auction.

eBay does not allow a seller to list more than 10 identical items as regular auctions, so in the example, you must use a Dutch Auction format. You can also use a Fixed-Price format or sell through your eBay Store, if you have one.

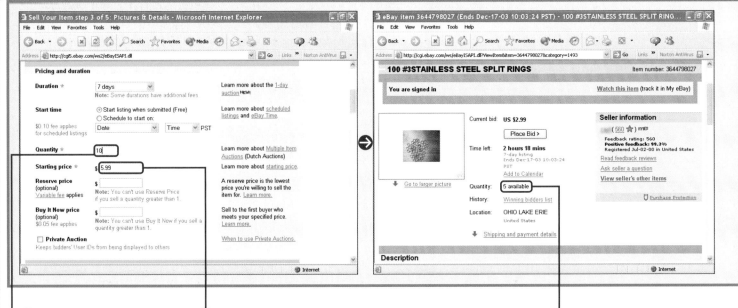

① Fill out the eBay Sell Your Item form to create an auction listing.

② When you get to the Quantity box in the Sell Your Item: Provide Pictures & Item Details page, type an amount.

③ Type a starting price.

○ eBay assigns Dutch Auction status.

④ Finish filling out the seller form, and post your Dutch Auction.

*Note: In order to sell items in a Dutch Auction, you must have a feedback rating of 30 or more or be ID-Verified. See task #14 for more on feedback.*

○ The auction listing displays the quantity available.

○ The quantity being more than one item identifies this listing as a Dutch auction.

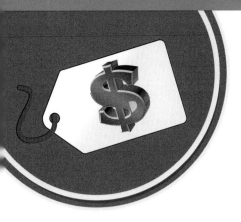

# Protect your item with a RESERVE

## DIFFICULTY LEVEL

If you do not want to sell your auction item below a particular price, you can assign a reserve price to the item. A *reserve price* is the lowest price for which you are willing to sell the item and is hidden from the bidder in the auction listing. You must make this price higher than the minimum bid price. Keep in mind, that setting the reserve price too high may discourage buyers from continuing to bid for the item.

When you assign a reserve, eBay displays the phrase "Reserve Not Met" on the auction page.

When the bidding reaches the reserve price, the phrase disappears. If none of the bidders meet the reserve price by the end of the auction, you reserve the right not to sell the item below the reserve price.

Be warned, however, that adding a reserve price to an auction incurs an additional listing fee. If your item sells above the reserve price, eBay refunds the fee. If the item fails to sell, eBay does not refund the fee.

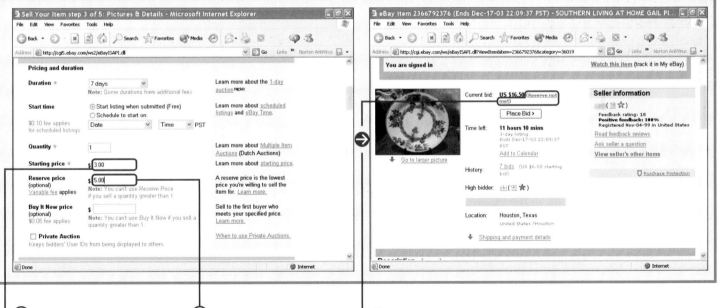

① Begin filling out the eBay Sell Your Item form to create an auction listing.

② When you get to the Starting price box, type a minimum price.

③ In the Reserve price box, type the minimum amount you will accept as a final sale price.

○ eBay assigns the reserve status to your listing.

④ Finish filling out the seller form, and post your reserve price Auction.

─○ The reserve phrase displays in your auction listing until the reserve price is met.

# Save money on
# LISTING FEES

If you incur extra fees by adding too many extra features to your auctions, you may reduce your profits by spending more than you intended. To help you limit your costs, evaluate the effectiveness of a feature before adding it to your listing.

You can save some money on your eBay listing fees by thinking creatively. For example, if you decide you really must add a starting price or reserve price to an item, first check out the insertion fees chart on eBay to see a breakdown

of fee prices. If you planned to sell the item in the $10.00 price range, you may save money if you pay attention to how eBay defines its insertion fee brackets. Items priced from $1.00 to $9.99 cost $0.35 to list. Items priced from $10.00 to $24.99 cost $0.60 to list. As a result, by listing your item at $9.99 instead of $10.00, you save $0.25.

It is a good idea to regularly check the Fees Overview page on eBay to keep up with any fee changes.

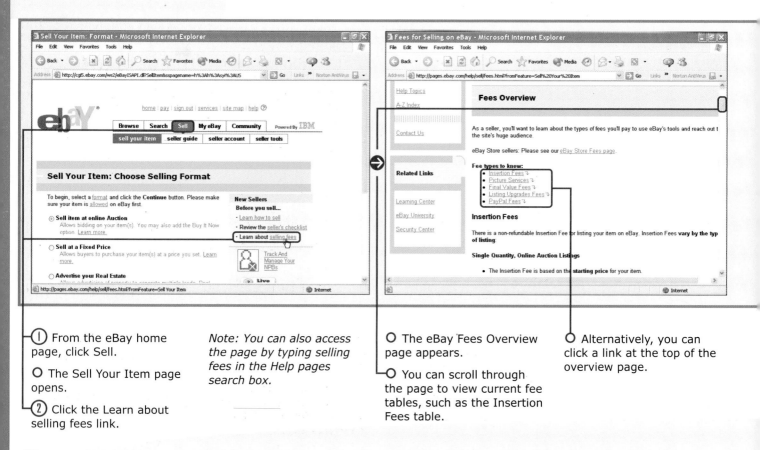

① From the eBay home page, click Sell.

○ The Sell Your Item page opens.

② Click the Learn about selling fees link.

*Note: You can also access the page by typing selling fees in the Help pages search box.*

○ The eBay Fees Overview page appears.

○ You can scroll through the page to view current fee tables, such as the Insertion Fees table.

○ Alternatively, you can click a link at the top of the overview page.

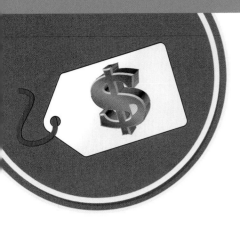

# Give your listing a
# BACKGROUND COLOR

## DIFFICULTY LEVEL

By default, eBay auction pages use a white background. With some HTML and JavaScript coding, you can add extra interest to your auction by assigning a unique color background to your page. Anything you can do to make your auction seem more distinct can draw a buyer's attention. Color backgrounds can also display your personal style.

To designate a background color, you can enter HTML coding into the auction description text box when you fill out the sellers form. Valid HTML colors include teal, blue, aqua, fuchsia,

green, lime, maroon, red, purple, yellow, olive, and silver. Type any of these color names in your HTML code to specify the corresponding background color. If you are familiar with hexadecimal numbers, you can also use six-digit color codes that mix varying amounts of red, green, and blue.

When adding a background color, be careful that the color does not interfere with the buyer's ability to read your item description and instructions.

---

① Begin filling out the eBay seller's form to create an auction listing.

② Scroll down the Sell Your Item: Title & Description page to the description text box.

③ Type **<script language=javascript><!--document.bgColor='X';--></script>**, where *X* is the color you want to use.

○ This example uses olive.

④ Scroll down the page to click the Preview your description link.

○ A separate browser window appears displaying your description with the background color.

⑤ Click Close Window.

○ The browser window disappears.

⑥ Continue filling out the information for your auction.

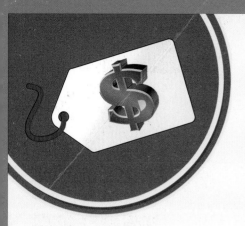

# Jazz up your listing with
# LISTING DESIGNER GRAPHICS

You can add interest to your auction listing by using graphics with the eBay Listing Designer feature. For an extra fee, you can add a graphical theme to make your listing more attractive to potential buyers. A Listing Designer theme sets a default font and background color for your listing that controls the appearance of the description area.

eBay's Listing Designer themes include holiday themes, themes related to collectible items — such as clothing — and generic graphical themes that add color and liveliness to your description area. The Listing Designer also lets you choose from a variety of layouts to customize the appearance of any photos that you display in the auction. For example, you can select a layout that displays your item photo prominently in the description area.

As with all features that enhance your listing, remember to consider if the price of your item justifies the fee for a design.

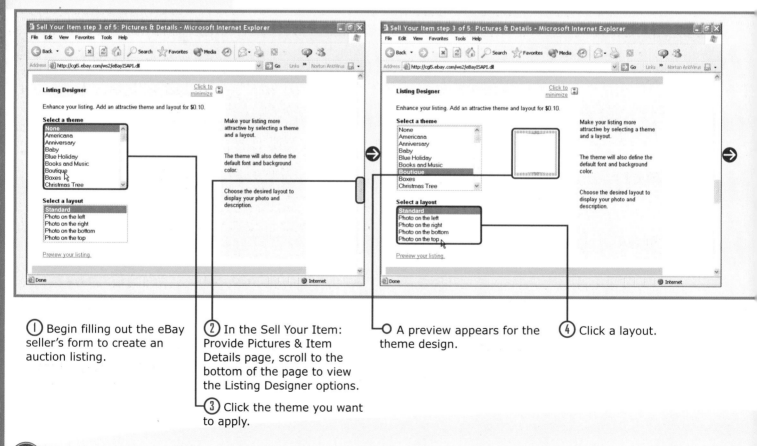

① Begin filling out the eBay seller's form to create an auction listing.

② In the Sell Your Item: Provide Pictures & Item Details page, scroll to the bottom of the page to view the Listing Designer options.

③ Click the theme you want to apply.

○ A preview appears for the theme design.

④ Click a layout.

## Did You Know? ☀

If you include HTML tags and JavaScript in your auction listing description, you can still use the Listing Designer themes and layouts. Keep in mind, however, that if you set font color tags, you should make sure that the colors do not conflict with the theme colors. For more on using HTML tags with your listing, see task #68.

# #52

## DIFFICULTY LEVEL

## Did You Know? ☀

You can also add your own graphics to an auction description. Graphic elements should never replace a photo of an item, but if you do not mind paying the extrafees to list them, you can graphic files just like you can add photo files.

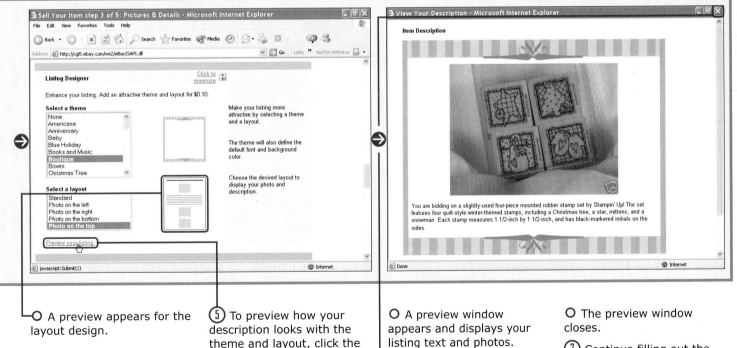

○ A preview appears for the layout design.

⑤ To preview how your description looks with the theme and layout, click the Preview your listing link.

○ A preview window appears and displays your listing text and photos.

⑥ Click the Close button.

○ The preview window closes.

⑦ Continue filling out the information for your auction.

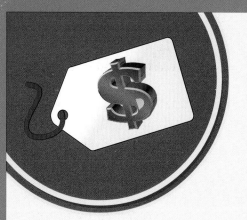

# Make a SECOND-CHANCE OFFER

If your winning bidder fails to complete a sale, you can make a second-chance offer to the next-highest bidder, if you have one. You can also offer the item to any under-bidder if you have duplicate items available. This allows you to sell more than one item for one listing fee. A second-chance offer allows you to leverage the bidders in an auction and sell an item without having to relist the item, or pay additional listing fees. You pay only a Final Value Fee if the bidder accepts the offer.

You can create a second-chance offer immediately after a listing ends, and for up to 60 days afterwards. However, bidders can opt not to receive

the offer. For this reason, you should first attempt to complete the sale with the original winning bidder before making a second-chance offer.

You can create a Second-Chance offer from your closed listing's page. A Second Chance Offer link is only available for closed items with at least one under-bidder.

Second-Chance offers are not available for Multiple Item Auctions, also known as Dutch Auctions.

① From your item's closed listing page, click the Second Chance Offer link.

○ This link only appears for closed listings that had at least one under-bidder.

○ The Second Chance Offer page appears.

○ You can read the rules for using a Second Chance Offer.

② Type the item number.

③ Click Continue.

# Did You Know? ☀

You can make a second-chance offer to under-bidders in a reserve price auction that ends without the reserve price being met. In addition, eBay refunds the reserve fee to you if the bidder accepts your second-chance offer. For more information about eBay's Second Chance Offer, go to www.pages.ebay.com/help/sell/second_chance_offer.html.

# Did You Know? ☀

You can leave feedback for your original winning bidder as well as for the buyer or buyers in your second-chance offer sale. Your buyers can also leave feedback for you. eBay protection services covers second-chance offer sales. For more on eBay's fraud protection and related programs, see task #40. For more on giving and receiving feedback, see tasks #14 and #42.

## #54

**DIFFICULTY LEVEL**

---

**eBay Second Chance Offer SetUp - Microsoft Internet Explorer**

File Edit View Favorites Tools Help

Address http://cgi3.ebay.com/aw-cgi/eBayISAPI.dll

### Second Chance Offer

Original item number: 3577551295

Title: What Sells on eBay for What

Duration: 3 days

**Select who will receive your offer**

Below is a list of eBay users who did not win your item. Remember: The number of eBay users you select can't be more than the number of items you have.

| Select | User ID | Buy It Now price |
|--------|---------|------------------|
| ☑ | chgcosmicmg (12) | $10.00 |
| ☑ | waterman1946 (5) | $6.95 |

**Note:** Users who have chosen not to receive Second Chance Offers or who have already been sent one will not appear above.

**Receive a copy of your Second Chance Offer**

☑ Send me a copy at:
Change my email address

< Back   Review >

---

**eBay Second Chance Offer Verify - Microsoft Internet Explorer**

File Edit View Favorites Tools Help

Address http://cgi3.ebay.com/aw-cgi/eBayISAPI.dll

### Second Chance Offer: Review and Submit

To make corrections, click the Back button at the bottom of this page.

| | |
|---|---|
| Title: | What Sells on eBay for What |
| Your User ID: | juliawww |
| Second Chance Offer duration: | 3 Days |
| Send me a copy: | Yes |

| eBay users selected | Price offered |
|---------------------|---------------|
| virgomommy | $10.00 |
| waterman1946 | $6.95 |

All other listing details will be the same as the original item

**Note:** If your item sells, you will be charged a Final Value Fee based on a percentage of the final sale price. For more information, view the Fees and Credits page. There is no fee for sending a Second Chance Offer.

< Back   Submit

---

○ The Second Chance Offer setup page appears.

④ Click here, and select how long you want the offer to last.

⑤ Click to select the bidders to whom you want to make the offer.

⑥ You can click this option to receive an e-mail copy of your offer.

⑦ Click Review.

○ The Second Chance Offer: Review and Submit screen appears.

⑧ Review your offer details for accuracy.

○ eBay charges a Final Value Fee if your item sells.

⑨ Click Submit.

○ eBay sends a Second Chance Offer to the designated under-bidders.

# CHAPTER 6

# Using Effective Seller Tools

When you use the eBay marketplace as a seller, you gain access to a whole new world of eBay areas and expertise. To help you gain more experience, this chapter shows you some practical ways to sell more efficiently online.

Savvy eBay sellers know that it pays to invest in a quality image-editing program. Whether you take a snapshot of your item with a digital camera and download it to your computer, or scan a picture, you should edit the picture in an image-editing program to make your item look its best. Most image-editing programs offer features to cover up imperfections in a photo's quality, to improve tone and contrast, and to crop out parts of the picture that detract from the subject.

Another way to optimize your selling potential is to take advantage of eBay's tools, such as the auction scheduler, and the free counters that track how many people visit your listing page. These tools are available on the seller's form when you create a new auction listing.

eBay also offers several additional tools that you can download, such as the popular Turbo Lister, which enable you to prepare listings offline.

Another way to sell more efficiently is to take advantage of the many third-party auction tools available on the Web, such as DeepAnalysis and andale. These tools help you examine eBay data, for example, to find hot items, and marketing values for various items.

# TOP 100

**#55**  Using Photoshop Elements to
Edit a Picture . . . . . . . . . . . . . . . . . . 112

**#56**  Copyright Your Auction Photographs . . . . 114

**#57**  Track Listing Visits with a Free Counter . . . . 116

**#58**  Start an Auction with the Scheduler . . . . . . . . 117

**#59**  Create Auction Listings with Turbo Lister . . . . . . 118

**#60**  Research Auctions with DeepAnalysis. . . . . . . . . 122

**#61**  Determine the Best Auction Days . . . . . . . . . . . 124

**#62**  View eBay Seller Newsletters . . . . . . . . . . . . . 125

# Using Photoshop Elements to
# EDIT A PICTURE

Because photos show the buyer exactly on what they are bidding, a good photograph of your item is your most powerful selling tool on eBay. To show an accurate representation of your item, take clear and well-lit color photographs. You can then use a photo-editing program to improve your photo's quality before posting it in your auction listing. To avoid after-sale problems, the photo should clearly show any flaws in the item.

Photoshop Elements 2.0 is one of the best photo-editing programs on the market today. Retailing for less than $90, the program can handle all of your

photo-editing needs for eBay auctions. For example, you can use Elements to edit picture size, and improve focus, brightness, and contrast. You can also use the Auto Levels feature to quickly adjust tone and contrast. Finally, you can crop your image to eliminate extra background, and to minimize the file size, making the photo faster to load in your auction.

When you finish editing the picture, you must then save it as a GIF, JPEG, or PNG file to upload to the eBay Web site.

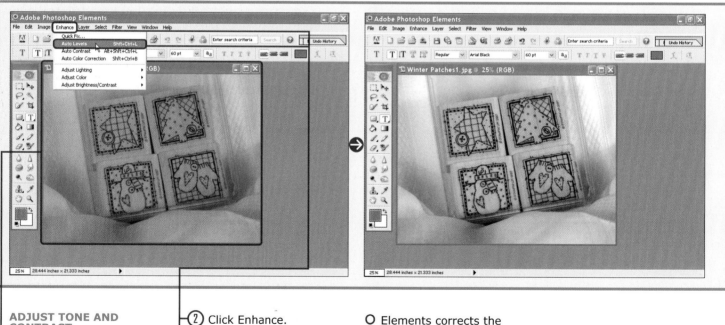

**ADJUST TONE AND CONTRAST**

① Launch Photoshop Elements, and open the image file that you want to edit.

② Click Enhance.

③ Click Auto Levels.

*Note: You can use similar commands in other image-editing programs.*

⬤ Elements corrects the shadows, midtones, and highlights of the image.

# eBay Savvy! ※

You should use a neutral background when taking a picture of an eBay auction item. A busy background, such as a pattern, distracts the viewer's focus from the item. It is also a good practice to shoot an item from a flattering angle instead of straight-on so the viewer can see more than one side of the item. If you are selling a collection of items, include at least one photo of all the items together. Be sure to take several snapshots so you can choose from among the best for posting in the auction listing.

## More Options! ※

Some other popular image-editing programs include IrfanView, free at www.irfanview.com; Jasc Paint Shop Pro, $79.00 at www.jasc.com; and Ulead PhotoImpact, $89.95 at www.ulead.com/pi.

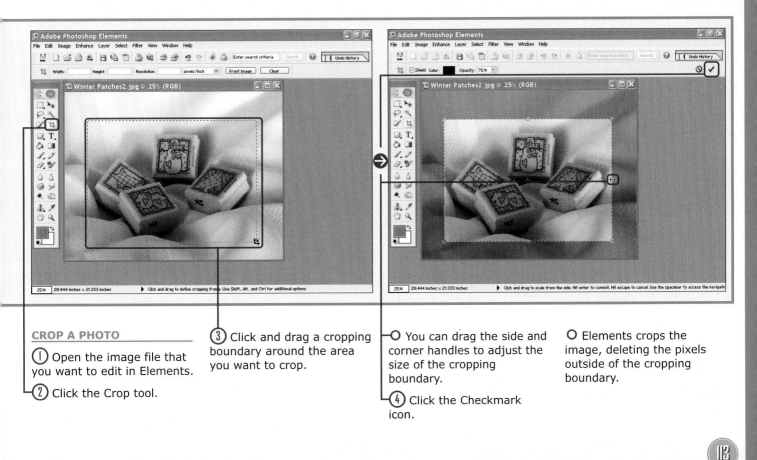

### CROP A PHOTO

① Open the image file that you want to edit in Elements.

② Click the Crop tool.

③ Click and drag a cropping boundary around the area you want to crop.

④ Click the Checkmark icon.

○ You can drag the side and corner handles to adjust the size of the cropping boundary.

○ Elements crops the image, deleting the pixels outside of the cropping boundary.

# COPYRIGHT
## your auction photographs

If you take a good photograph of your auction item, other eBay users may use your photograph in their own auctions. Although eBay disapproves of this behavior, which infringes on copyright laws, it is not uncommon to see photographs used in other sellers' auctions. To prevent this, you can place a text line discreetly in the image.

Most photo-editing programs, including Photoshop Elements, offer a text-editing feature that you can use to add your user ID number and a superimposed

copyright symbol to the photo. If someone co-opts your image for use on their site, bidders can clearly see that the image does not belong to the seller.

If someone does use your image without your permission, you can contact eBay and report the infringement, including the auction item number as well as your original auction item number. However, you must enroll in eBay's VeRO program for eBay to take action on your behalf. For more information about VeRO, see task #44. eBay may take a few days to investigate, at which point they may remove the auction and notify the seller of the offense.

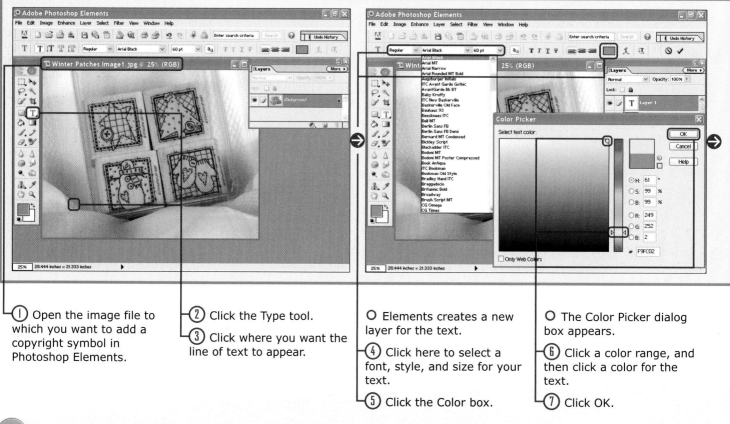

① Open the image file to which you want to add a copyright symbol in Photoshop Elements.

② Click the Type tool.

③ Click where you want the line of text to appear.

○ Elements creates a new layer for the text.

④ Click here to select a font, style, and size for your text.

⑤ Click the Color box.

○ The Color Picker dialog box appears.

⑥ Click a color range, and then click a color for the text.

⑦ Click OK.

# 56

DIFFICULTY LEVEL

## Caution! ⁕

When selecting a color for
text, be sure to make it a color
that does not conflict with the
image or distract the buyer
from viewing from the item.

## Did You Know? ⁕

You can change the opacity level of
a text layer in Photoshop Elements to
create a more transparent copyright
line of text in your photo. Click the text
layer in the Layer palette, click the Opacity
slider at the top of the palette, and then
drag to a new opacity setting; a setting
of 50% makes the text half as opaque
as the 100% setting. This lower opacity
setting allows the photo layer beneath
the text layer to show through, yet still
displays legible text over the image.

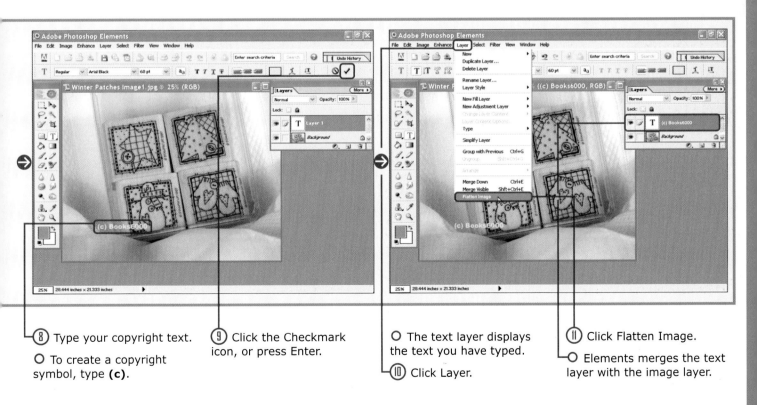

⑧ Type your copyright text.

O To create a copyright
symbol, type **(c)**.

⑨ Click the Checkmark
icon, or press Enter.

O The text layer displays
the text you have typed.

⑩ Click Layer.

⑪ Click Flatten Image.

O Elements merges the text
layer with the image layer.

# Track listing visits with a
# FREE COUNTER

## 57

DIFFICULTY LEVEL

You can use a counter on your auction listing page to keep track of how many people view your listing. Counting the number of visits can help you determine the marketability of your item, as well as how popular or unpopular your item is with other eBay bidders. You can use counters from third-party sources, or you can use a free counter from andale.

andale counters count every visit to your item listing, even if a person looks at your item more than once. The andale counter has two different

designs from which you can choose. You can also keep the counter hidden from the bidder's view. Counters appear as graphics at the bottom of your auction listing page.

If you want to hide your counter, visitors see only a Thanks for Looking graphic instead of the usual counter graphic. With a hidden counter, only you, the seller, can see how many people visit your listing.

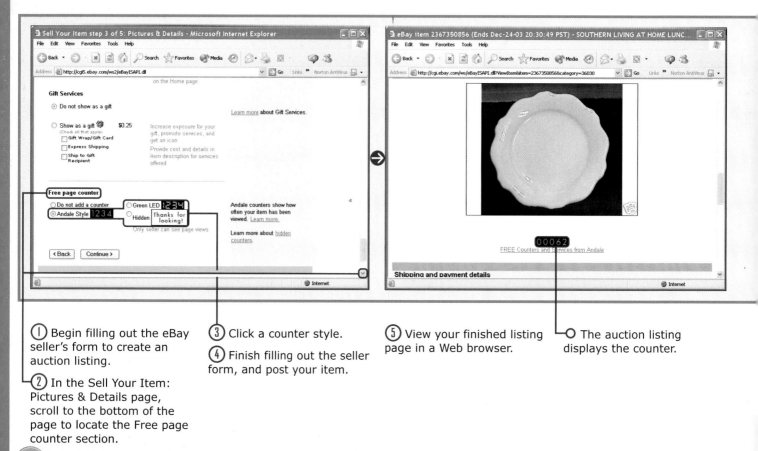

① Begin filling out the eBay seller's form to create an auction listing.

② In the Sell Your Item: Pictures & Details page, scroll to the bottom of the page to locate the Free page counter section.

③ Click a counter style.

④ Finish filling out the seller form, and post your item.

⑤ View your finished listing page in a Web browser.

○ The auction listing displays the counter.

# Start an auction with the SCHEDULER

 #58

You can use eBay's built-in scheduling feature to help you schedule auctions for the best times, even when you are not around to post your listings. For a small fee, the eBay scheduler allows you to pick a day and time to start the auction. You can use the scheduler to schedule up to 3,000 auction listings up to three weeks in advance.

For example, if you know you are going to be out of town when you want to begin a seven-day auction, you can use the scheduler to

designate the date and time for you. You may find that your item sells best when you start an auction on a particular day of the week, or that your item gets more bids when an auction closes at the end of the day rather than earlier. The scheduler allows you to select the date and time that works best for your particular item.

In addition to the eBay scheduler, you can also find third-party schedulers that you can use to list your items.

**DIFFICULTY LEVEL**

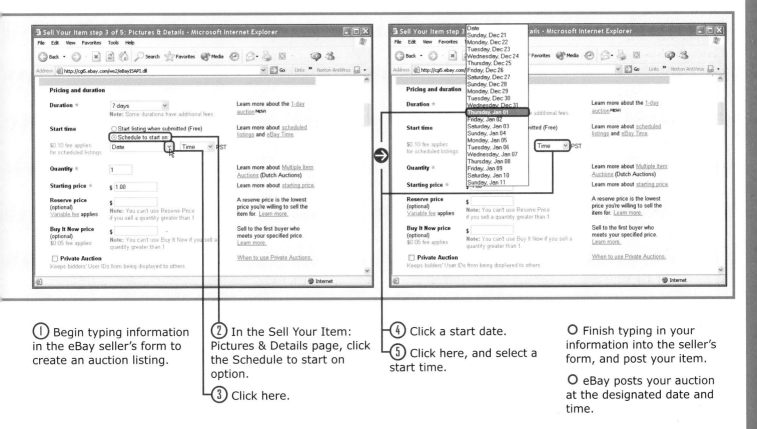

① Begin typing information in the eBay seller's form to create an auction listing.

② In the Sell Your Item: Pictures & Details page, click the Schedule to start on option.

③ Click here.

④ Click a start date.

⑤ Click here, and select a start time.

○ Finish typing in your information into the seller's form, and post your item.

○ eBay posts your auction at the designated date and time.

# Create auction listings with
# TURBO LISTER

You can use the eBay Turbo Lister program to give your eBay auction listings a more uniform and professional appearance. You can download Turbo Lister for free from eBay, and build your auction listings offline. When you are ready to post the auctions on eBay, Turbo Lister posts the listings for you.

Turbo Lister offers you a choice of several themes. You can also select from several layouts for photo placement in your listing. You can add your description text and format it just as you would

format text with a word-processing program. You can also view your listing in HTML format and add HTML tags to your text.

One of the most attractive features in Turbo Lister is the ability to duplicate listings for similar items without having to retype your information. For example, after you design and type a listing for a collectible item, you can duplicate that same listing for a second, similar item and then make small changes to describe the second item.

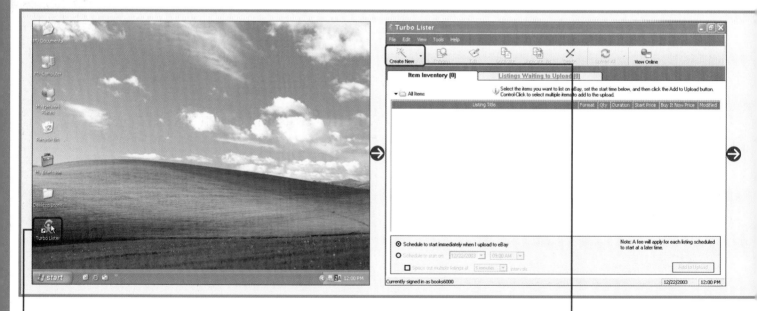

① Double-click the Turbo Lister shortcut icon.

*Note: A Turbo Lister shortcut icon appears on the Windows XP desktop after you install the free Turbo Lister program, which you can download from eBay.*

○ The Turbo Lister program window appears.

*Note: At first use, you must set up your eBay account to work with Turbo Lister by following the onscreen prompts.*

② Click the Create New button.

## Did You Know? ※

You can download a copy of Turbo Lister for free from eBay. Click the Community tab on any eBay page, and then click the eBay Downloads link at the bottom of the eBay Community page. Click the eBay Turbo Lister link, and follow the prompts for downloading the software onto your computer. After installing the software, a shortcut icon for Turbo Lister appears on the Windows desktop — Turbo Lister does not currently support the Macintosh platform. You can double-click the icon to open the program.

**DIFFICULTY LEVEL**

## eBay Savvy! ※

Turbo Lister can also import delimited data files, which means that you can use database core programs, such as inventory-management programs or order-accounting programs, with Turbo Lister.

**CONTINUED ▶**

O The Create a New Item page appears.

③ Click the type of auction you want to create.

─O To post your auction on another eBay site, you can click here and select the location.

④ Click Next.

O The next Create a New Item page appears.

⑤ Type a title that describes your item.

⑥ Type a category number.

─O You can also click Find Category and select your category.

⑦ Click Next.

# Create auction listings with
# TURBO LISTER

If you plan to sell items frequently on eBay, you can definitely benefit from downloading Turbo Lister. Turbo Lister helps you sell your items more efficiently, and you always have a list of your auctions ready to view or edit.

Turbo Lister presents a sellers' form similar to the one on the eBay site; however, creating your listing with Turbo Lister is much faster than creating an online eBay listing. You can relax and check your

work for errors without the pressure to complete your listing online. You can also save your work and edit it later before posting the auction on eBay.

Turbo Lister's themes and photo layouts are the same as those available with the Listing Designer feature on eBay's online sellers' form. You are charged a small fee per auction for using Listing Designer with Turbo Lister. Other items that you apply in Turbo Lister still incur a fee on eBay, such as adding a second category, adding a Bid Now option, or including more than one photo with the listing.

**CONTINUED ▶**

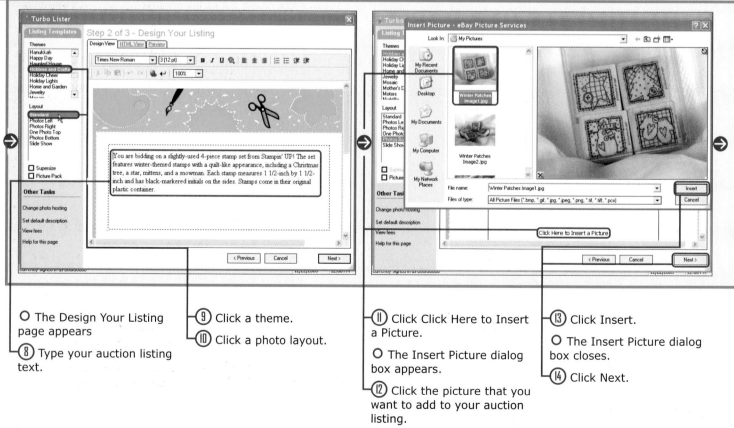

○ The Design Your Listing page appears

⑧ Type your auction listing text.

⑨ Click a theme.

⑩ Click a photo layout.

⑪ Click Click Here to Insert a Picture.

○ The Insert Picture dialog box appears.

⑫ Click the picture that you want to add to your auction listing.

⑬ Click Insert.

○ The Insert Picture dialog box closes.

⑭ Click Next.

When you upload your auction listings from Turbo Lister to eBay, eBay schedules the auction to start at the time you upload. If you prefer to start an auction at a later time, you must use the scheduler, which incurs a listing fee. For that reason, you may prefer to log onto your Internet connection and upload the listings at the most convenient time for your auctions. Remember that the start time on eBay's listing form is in PST — Pacific Standard Time.

## Did You Know? ※

Every time you upload listings to eBay from Turbo Lister, the program also checks for system updates. Any updates display in an update status message.

---

○ The Format Specifics page appears.

⑮ Type information in the form just as you would the eBay sellers' form, specifying auction duration, price, and payment methods.

—○ You can click Change to edit information.

⑯ Click Save.

—○ Turbo Lister saves the listing to your Item Inventory list.

○ You can continue adding more auction listings to your inventory.

⑰ When you are ready to post the listings, select the listings, click Add to Upload, log onto the Internet, and upload your auction to eBay.

# Research auctions with
# DEEPANALYSIS

You can use a variety of third-party auction tools to research the eBay marketplace. For example, a search for the keywords "auction tools" using a Web search engine such as google.com displays a variety of shareware and freeware tools that you can download and use, including the popular DeepAnalysis program from HammerTap.

DeepAnalysis is an eBay market research program that you can use to analyze and extract auction sales information and eBay statistics. You can download a trial version of the program. Once you install the program, you can specify what sort of auction data

you want to research. DeepAnalysis helps you to log onto eBay and extract the data. DeepAnalysis then displays the data by seller and item.

The program also features a Statistics tab for viewing eBay statistics about the item that you are researching; however, this feature is only available to registered users of the program.

You can use the full version of DeepAnalysis to view sell-through rates, see the average sale price per item, view average bids per item, and create reports about the data you analyze.

① Double-click the DeepAnalysis shortcut icon.

*Note: A DeepAnalysis shortcut icon appears on your desktop after you download and install the trial version of the program from www.hammertap.com.*

O The DeepAnalysis program window appears.

*Note: If a prompt appears asking you to register the trial version before proceeding, click Evaluate to continue.*

② Click the type of analysis you want to perform.

③ Type the keywords.

④ Click here, and select an auction type.

⑤ Click Start Analysis.

## eBay Savvy! ※

With a tool like DeepAnalysis,
you can quickly see which
eBay sellers are doing well in
the marketplace and examine their
techniques and product lines. You can also
use the data you research to find out which
categories work best for your own items and
find out which items receive the most bids.

## Did You Know? ※

Growing along with eBay are numerous eBay
industries, people, and companies dedicated
to improving and developing products that help
eBay users. Auction management software, also
a growing industry, helps users to track inventory,
maintain customer communication, and simplify
transaction checkout. Online auction management
service providers are also growing in popularity,
and allow sellers to manage their auctions from
a Web site rather than their own computers.

DIFFICULTY LEVEL

---

**O** DeepAnalysis displays a
window with the eBay login.

**⑥** Type your user ID and
password.

**⑦** Click I have logged in.
Continue the search.

**O** DeepAnalysis analyzes
the site.

**O** This process may take a
few minutes.

**O** The results appear in the
Items and Sellers tabs.

**O** After viewing the results
of the analysis, you can click
the Close button to exit
DeepAnalysis.

# Determine the
# BEST AUCTION DAYS

DIFFICULTY LEVEL

Although there is no magic formula for determining what times and days are the best for online auctions, some users argue that certain days are better than others. For example, the AuctionBytes Web site offers a useful calendar that you can reference when determining which days are best to start your auctions, with weather-related icons that identify good days and bad days.

The AuctionBytes calendar lists optimum days to end auctions, based on the number of days you set for your auction listing. For example, starting

a three-day auction on a Monday is good because Thursday is considered a good day to end your auction.

However, be aware that anomalies exist with any eBay formula; no one can predict with any certainty when a bidder may bid on an item. Trial and error is best gauged from your own experiences when selling items online. You may find that the market for your item contradicts popular eBay listing theories completely.

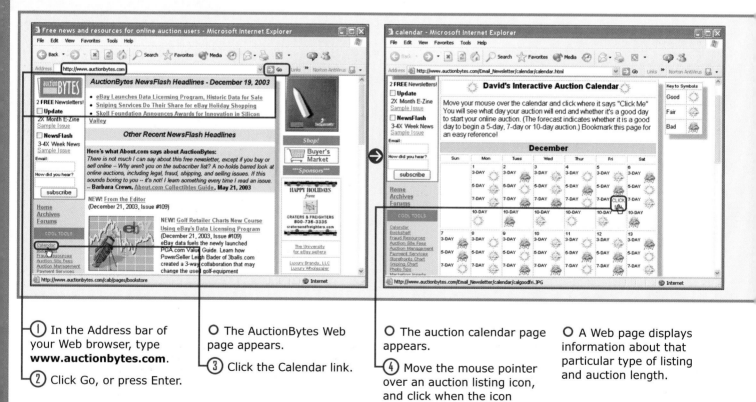

① In the Address bar of your Web browser, type **www.auctionbytes.com**.

② Click Go, or press Enter.

○ The AuctionBytes Web page appears.

③ Click the Calendar link.

○ The auction calendar page appears.

④ Move the mouse pointer over an auction listing icon, and click when the icon changes to text Click Me.

○ A Web page displays information about that particular type of listing and auction length.

This site has been visited **1150** times

# View eBay SELLER NEWSLETTERS

**DIFFICULTY LEVEL**

A great way to stay current with the latest news about any particular eBay auction category is to view the online category newsletter. Called *newsflashes*, the electronic newsletters offer information about upcoming events, seller tips, and special offers.

Published monthly, eBay newsletters are made for a variety of unique categories. For example, the Antiques Seller Newsflash is specific to online antique sellers, while the Entertainment Seller Newsflash is specific to entertainment products. Each newsflash lists the hottest-selling

items for that particular category as well as links to useful eBay tools and information. Be sure to look at the newsflash each month to find out the latest news about your category of interest.

You can sign up to have the newsletter delivered to your e-mail address. You can also subscribe to more than one newsletter. If you are new to selling items on eBay, start by subscribing to just one or two newsletters until you are ready to explore other categories. For information on various industry newsletters, see task #100.

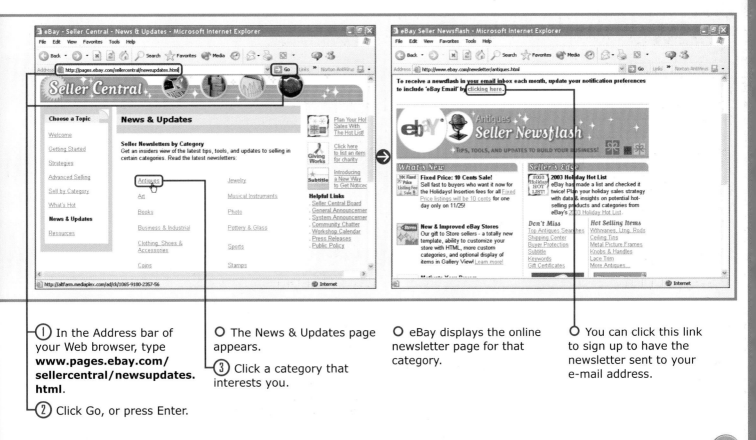

① In the Address bar of your Web browser, type **www.pages.ebay.com/ sellercentral/newsupdates. html**.

② Click Go, or press Enter.

○ The News & Updates page appears.

③ Click a category that interests you.

○ eBay displays the online newsletter page for that category.

○ You can click this link to sign up to have the newsletter sent to your e-mail address.

# CHAPTER 7

# Boost Your Sales with Advanced Selling Techniques

Once you master the basics of selling on eBay, you can learn new skills to manage and increase your sales.

If you consistently sell enough items on eBay, you can earn the prestigious title of PowerSeller which brings many benefits, such as icons that you can use in your auctions, a dedicated message board, and a health care program.

As you sell more items, your image fees may add up, especially if you list multiple images of each item. You can save money by using third-party image-hosting companies, such as inkFrog.com. You may also want to display multiple images of your items in a slideshow format.

eBay's tools, such as Selling Manager, can help you keep track of sales, archive sales records, and download statistics into a format that you can read with accounting applications, such as Microsoft Excel. Selling Manager also enables you to expedite the many chores associated with eBay sales, such as contacting buyers, managing payments, and tracking shipments.

You can improve the appearance of your auctions by using basic HTML tags to make your auction look much more professional.

You can create an even more professional image by opening your own eBay Store, which enables you to use listing management tools and many cross-promotion features.

Another option you have is to create a store using Vendio's tools, which allows you to sell items on eBay as well as other online marketplaces.

# TOP 100

**#63**  Benefit from PowerSellers . . . . . . . 128

**#64**  Save Money with Image-Hosting . . . . . . 130

**#65**  Add Multiple Images in Slideshow Format . . . . 132

**#66**  Using Statistics to Measure Sales . . . . . . . . . . 134

**#67**  Get Organized with Selling Manager . . . . . . . . . 136

**#68**  Improve Your Listings with eBay's HTML Editor . . . 138

**#69**  Market Your Goods with an eBay Store . . . . . . 140

**#70**  Create Your Own Store with Vendio . . . . . . . 142

**#71**  Cross-Promote Your eBay Store Items . . . . 144

**#72**  Manage Cross-Promoted Item Categories . . . . . . . . . . . . . . . . . . 146

# Benefit from
# POWERSELLERS

You can benefit from PowerSellers as both a buyer and a seller. As a buyer, when you bid on a PowerSeller's listing, you know you can trust the experienced PowerSeller to handle the transaction professionally. You find PowerSeller listings by adding the word "powerseller" to your other search words. See Chapter 1 for more on performing searches. As a seller, if you earn the PowerSeller title, you can enjoy benefits such as a health care program, enhanced customer service, and an exclusive discussion board.

eBay grants the title of *PowerSeller* to users who sell at least $1,000 worth of merchandise, with a minimum of four average total listings, for three consecutive months. A PowerSeller's feedback rating is at least 100, of which 98 percent is positive. eBay designates a PowerSeller with a special icon next to the user's ID, in the user's item listings, and on the user's About Me page.

You can read about how others became PowerSellers, and find out their success secrets, in eBay's PowerSeller of the Month story, located in eBay's Community Discussion Board areas.

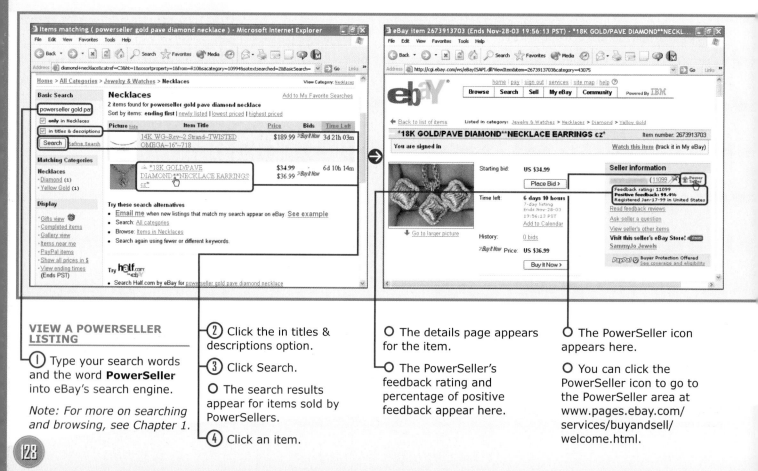

**VIEW A POWERSELLER LISTING**

① Type your search words and the word **PowerSeller** into eBay's search engine.

*Note: For more on searching and browsing, see Chapter 1.*

② Click the in titles & descriptions option.

③ Click Search.

O The search results appear for items sold by PowerSellers.

④ Click an item.

O The details page appears for the item.

O The PowerSeller's feedback rating and percentage of positive feedback appear here.

O The PowerSeller icon appears here.

O You can click the PowerSeller icon to go to the PowerSeller area at www.pages.ebay.com/ services/buyandsell/ welcome.html.

# #63

## DIFFICULTY LEVEL

## Did You Know? ※

eBay has five different types,
or tiers, of PowerSellers, based
on gross monthly sales. eBay notifies
eligible members each month by e-mail.

| PowerSeller Tiers | |
|---|---|
| *Tier Name* | *Qualifying Gross Monthly Sales* |
| Bronze | $1,000 |
| Silver | $3,000 |
| Gold | $10,000 |
| Platinum | $25,000 |
| Titanium | $150,000 |

## Did You Know? ※

If you no longer meet the criteria to keep your PowerSeller
status, eBay alerts you via e-mail. You have 30 days to
get your account back to the PowerSeller level, after
which eBay disqualifies your account from the
program. However, you can still attain
PowerSeller status in the future.

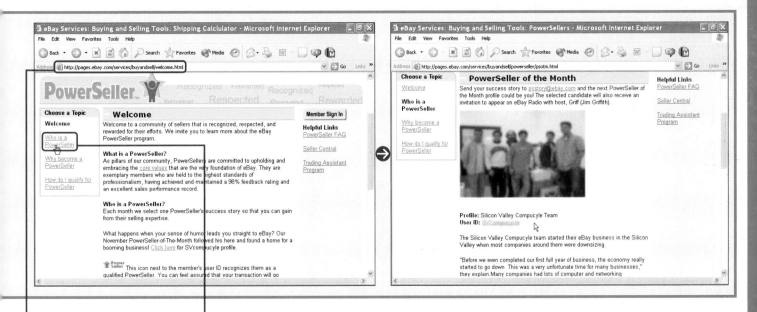

**READ A POWERSELLER
SUCCESS STORY**

① Type **www.pages.ebay.
com/services/buyandsell/
welcome.html** into the
address bar of your Web
browser, and press Enter.

○ The PowerSeller page
appears.

② Click the Who is a
PowerSeller link.

○ The PowerSeller of the
Month page appears.

○ The page displays the
PowerSeller of the Month
success story.

# Save money with
# IMAGE-HOSTING

Because eBay charges for each picture you upload to host auction images, you can save money on eBay's image-hosting fees by using a third-party image-hosting service. The first image on eBay's image-hosting service is free, but each subsequent image costs $0.15. Thus, your picture fees can add up to a significant amount of money. For example, if you upload four images for each auction, and you list ten auctions each week, your image-hosting fees on eBay are $4.50 each week, or about $18.00 every month.

With the same number of images, you can have a service, such as inkFrog.com, host your images for one flat monthly rate of $4.95 — a savings of $13.00 each month, or more, depending on how many auctions you list. inkFrog also offers other pricing plans.

Remember not to make your photo files too large — ideally under 50 kilobytes — or they load slowly on eBay. See task #55 to crop your image.

Before you can perform the steps in this task, you must first register at inkfrog.com. For more information on slideshows, see task #65.

① Log onto the inkfrog.com Web site.

O The inkFrog picture & auction management page appears.

② Click the Upload Images link.

O The Images Section appears.

③ Type the filename and pathname of the image you want to upload.

O You can also click Browse and then select the image from the appropriate folder on your hard drive.

*Note: To make sure that your image is eBay-ready, see task #55.*

④ Click Upload Images.

## More Options! ☀

You can use other third-party image-hosting services, such as SpareDollar, Vendio, or andale. SpareDollar offers 50MB of image storage space that holds approximately 1,000 images for $4.95 a month. andale offers a $3.00 monthly plan for up to 50 images. You can read about their pricing plans at www.sparedollar.com/corp/pricing.asp, www.vendio.com/pricing.html, and www.andale.com/corp/pricing_corp.jsp. Shop around and decide which is best for you. Consider the volume and size of images you host each week or month.

## More Options! ☀

inkFrog offers a premium plan at $7.95 each month, which includes 400 images and auction listing tools, such as professional-looking templates. It also offers a pro plan at $12.95 each month, which includes 1,000 images, thumbnails, cropping, and bulk listing tools.

**DIFFICULTY LEVEL**

○ inkFrog tells you that your image is uploaded.

○ The file size appears here.

○ Remember that if your file size is larger than 50KB, the image loads slowly on eBay.

⑤ Click the filename link.

○ inkFrog displays the image location, or URL.

○ inkFrog hosts your picture.

○ You can type the URL into the Picture URL box on eBay's listing page to add the picture to your eBay auction.

# Add multiple images in
# SLIDESHOW FORMAT

Using eBay's image-listing options, you can increase your sales by showing your prospective buyers different angles of an item using multiple images in a slideshow format. eBay buyers are savvy and like to know exactly what they are getting. For example, they bid more confidently if they can view both sides of a garment instead of only the front view.

You can upload up to a total of six images with eBay's image-hosting service. The first image for an auction is free. Each additional image is $0.15. Rotating the images in slideshow format costs an additional $0.75.

Because costs for images and a slideshow add up, you should make sure that the estimated final price of the auction item justifies adding them. For example, you may decide that it makes sense to post multiple images and a slideshow for an item worth $50.00, but not for an item worth only $10.00.

For more information about image-hosting, see task #64.

① In the eBay home page, click the Sell tab.

○ eBay guides you through the Sell Your Item process.

② In the Sell Your Item: Pictures & Item Details page, scroll to the eBay Picture Services tab.

③ Click Browse.

*Note: If this is the first time you use eBay Picture Services, a pop-up box appears prompting you to download software.*

○ The Choose file window appears.

④ Double-click the folder that contains your photo file.

## Did You Know? ※

You can use between two and
six images to create an animated
effect with a slideshow. Keep in mind
that you cannot have still pictures and a
slideshow in the same listing with eBay's
picture services. You can also increase the
size of your pictures — or *supersize* them —
up to 880 pixels wide by 600 pixels high for $0.75.
Images must be at least 440 pixels wide by 330 pixels
high to qualify for the Supersize Picture option.

**DIFFICULTY LEVEL**

## More Options! ※

You can create slideshows with third-party
image-hosting companies, such as WebShots
at auctions.webshots.com. WebShots offers
a range of plans from $9.99 a year for 20
photos to $249.99 a year for 1,000 photos.
For more information about third-party
image hosting, see task #64.

---

O The folder displays the
files.

⑤ Click the file you want to
upload.

⑥ Click Open.

O The photo appears in the
Picture 1 box.

⑦ Repeat steps **4** and **5** for
each additional photo you
want to add.

⑧ Select the Slide Show
option.

⑨ Continue the listing
process by completing the
Sell Your Item form.

O eBay adds a slideshow of
the selected images to your
listing.

# Using statistics to
# MEASURE SALES

If you sell items regularly on eBay, you may find keeping track of all your sales records for business and tax purposes time-consuming and difficult. The Selling Manager tool makes this tedious chore a lot easier.

You can download your sales records with eBay's Selling Manager tool in a comma-delimited file format, so that you can read them in a software application, such as Microsoft Excel. You can also retrieve an immediate estimate of your total active and past sales with Selling Manager's Quick Stats, which measures weekly or monthly profits, as well as tax records.

You can download sales records for periods ranging from yesterday to the last 90 days, or select a specific date. Because eBay only retains sales records for four months, you should download them at least that often to ensure that you have all the information you need for the entire tax year.

Selling Manager costs $4.99 per month. For more information about Selling Manager, see task #67. For a tour of Selling Manager, go to Selling Manager Tour at www.pages.ebay.com/selling_manager/tour.html.

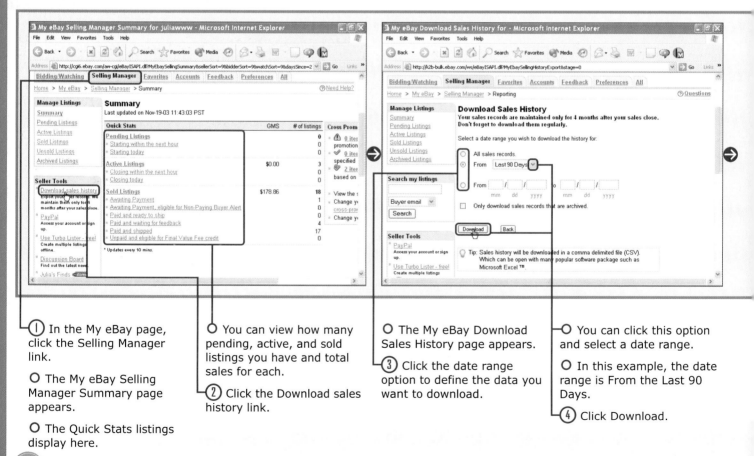

① In the My eBay page, click the Selling Manager link.

○ The My eBay Selling Manager Summary page appears.

○ The Quick Stats listings display here.

○ You can view how many pending, active, and sold listings you have and total sales for each.

② Click the Download sales history link.

○ The My eBay Download Sales History page appears.

③ Click the date range option to define the data you want to download.

○ You can click this option and select a date range.

○ In this example, the date range is From the Last 90 Days.

④ Click Download.

## More Options! ※

Selling Manager can help you keep track of when you ship items and when buyers pay for them. You can mark sold items Paid, Shipped, or Paid & Shipped. From the Selling Manager tab, click the Sold Listings link. Click the option next to an item ( ☐ changes to ☑ ), and select an option, such as Mark Paid & Shipped. Click Confirm Status. Selling Manager tells you your sales record status is updated successfully.

**DIFFICULTY LEVEL**

## Did You Know? ※

Some third-party tools, such as Vendio at www.vendio.com and andale at www.andale.com, also allow you to organize statistics. andale's Manager tool shows you what percentage of your sales is successful, and your top five most successful products by average selling.

○ The File Download dialog box appears.

⑤ Click Save.

○ eBay walks you through the process of saving your data.

⑥ Open your spreadsheet application and open the file containing your data.

○ You can view your sales statistics with an application.

# Get organized with
# SELLING MANAGER

You can save time on many administrative tasks and be more efficient and organized with eBay's Selling Manager, an online tool that enables you to track and manage sales. With Selling Manager, you can easily keep track of items that have sold, been paid for, and shipped; relist items in bulk; archive auction records; and print invoices and shipping labels directly from your sales records. You can also export your sales records to files on your computer, which is useful for keeping your tax records.

Selling Manager is most useful for sellers with medium- to high-volume sales. If you have low-volume sales, then you may not need Selling Manager. You get the most out of Selling Manager if you use it in tandem with eBay's free Turbo Lister tool. To sign up for Selling Manager, go to www.pages.ebay.com/selling_manager/products.html.

You can try Selling Manager for free for 30 days. After the free trial, Selling Manager costs $4.99 each month. For more information about Selling Manager, see task #66.

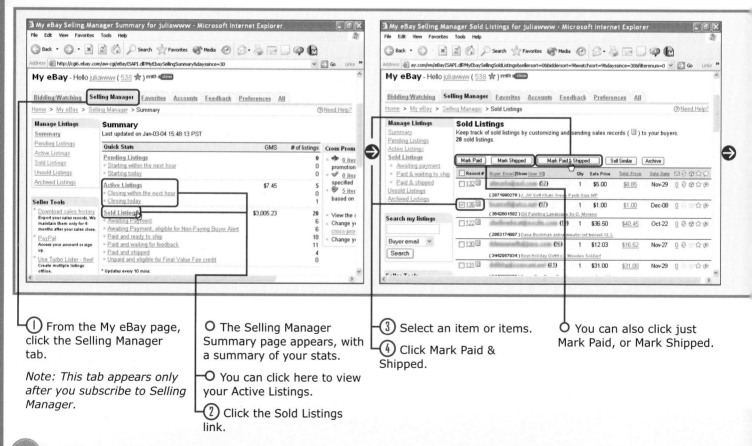

─① From the My eBay page, click the Selling Manager tab.

*Note: This tab appears only after you subscribe to Selling Manager.*

O The Selling Manager Summary page appears, with a summary of your stats.

─O You can click here to view your Active Listings.

─② Click the Sold Listings link.

─③ Select an item or items.
④ Click Mark Paid & Shipped.

O You can also click just Mark Paid, or Mark Shipped.

DIFFICULTY LEVEL

## More Options! ※

If you are a high-volume
eBay seller and list hundreds of
items a month, you can use eBay's
Selling Manager Pro, which offers all
the features of the regular Selling Manager
tool, as well as inventory management. These
tools can help you to determine your products'
success ratio and average selling price; send
and track feedback and invoices; use customizable
seller e-mail templates; and send bulk e-mail to
buyers. For a complete list of Selling Manager Pro
features, go to www.pages.ebay.com/selling_
manager_pro/faq.html. Selling Manager Pro is
free for 30 days and then costs $15.99 monthly.

## Did You Know? ※

If you use Seller's Assistant Basic, you can upgrade
to Selling Manager for free. Get more information
about how to upgrade at www.pages.ebay.com/
selling_manager/upgrade-info.html.

○ The Please Confirm
Status as Paid & shipped
screen appears.

⑤ Click Confirm Status.

○ Selling Manager tells you
your sales record status is
successfully updated.

○ Selling Manager updates
the numbers on the Summary
page, next to Paid and
shipped.

○ You can click Sell Similar
or Archive.

○ Selling Manager helps you
keep track of your payments
and shipments.

# Improve your listings with eBay's
# HTML EDITOR

You can format your listings so they are clear, well organized, and have a nice appearance, using basic HTML attributes. Your prospective bidders take you more seriously when your listings look professional, and this can lead to more sales.

eBay makes it very easy to use HTML, because it provides a small HTML text editor within the auction-listing page.

To use the embedded HTML editor, you simply select from a menu of buttons that represent different HTML attributes, and highlight the text to indicate to which words you want to apply those attributes.

The HTML editor allows you to do things like place your text in bold and italics; select a font, size, and color for your text; center or right- or left-justify it; or create bulleted or numbered lists.

Even if you do not use a lot of HTML tags in your listings, using even a few basic tags can make the difference between one long, monotonous piece of text, and a series of neatly separated and defined paragraphs.

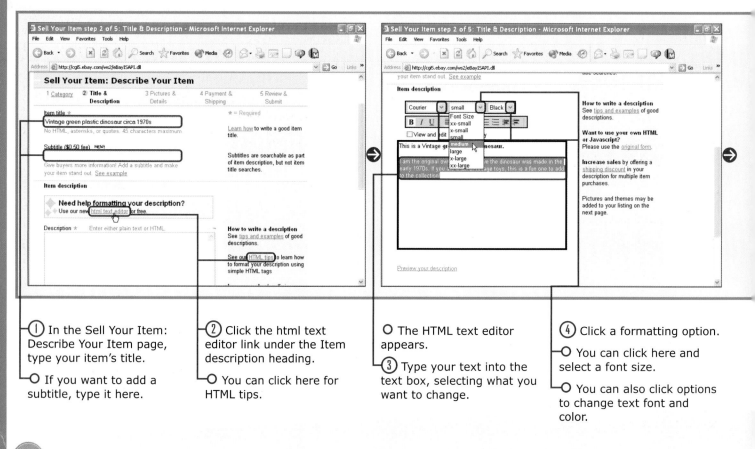

① In the Sell Your Item: Describe Your Item page, type your item's title.

─O If you want to add a subtitle, type it here.

② Click the html text editor link under the Item description heading.

─O You can click here for HTML tips.

O The HTML text editor appears.

③ Type your text into the text box, selecting what you want to change.

④ Click a formatting option.

─O You can click here and select a font size.

─O You can also click options to change text font and color.

# #68

DIFFICULTY LEVEL

## More Options! ⁂

In the Sell Your Item:
Describe Your Item page, you
can click the HTML tips link under
the Item description heading to learn
how to add a <p> tag to separate your
paragraphs, a <br> tag to start a new line
without skipping a space, and the <hr> tag
to add a horizontal rule with your text above
and below it. You can also create different size
headings with the <h1></h1> through
<h6></h6> tags.

## Did You Know? ⁂

The Web offers a number of free HTML
tutorials; for example, www.pagetutor.com,
www.htmlgoodies.com, or Dave's HTML
guide at www.davesite.com/webstation/
html. You can also do a search for HTML
tutorials in your favorite search engine.

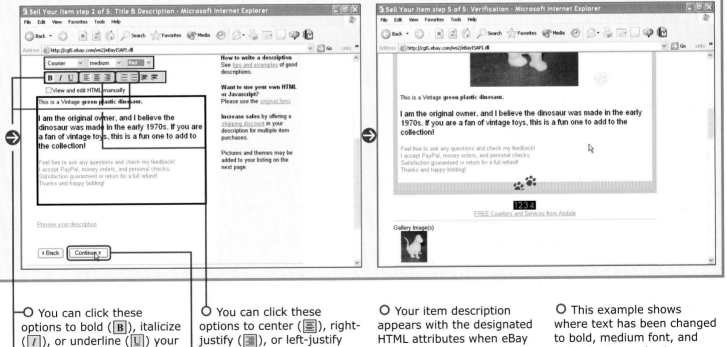

○ You can click these options to bold ( **B** ), italicize ( *I* ), or underline ( U ) your text.

○ You can click here to format bulleted ( ☰ ) or numbered lists ( ☰ ).

○ You can click these options to center ( ☰ ), right-justify ( ☰ ), or left-justify ( ☰ ) your text.

⑤ Click Continue.

○ Your item description appears with the designated HTML attributes when eBay users view it.

○ This example shows where text has been changed to bold, medium font, and red color to emphasize different parts of the listing.

# Market your goods with an
# EBAY STORE

When you open an eBay Store, you can create your own unique presence on eBay, and instill greater confidence in your customers that you are a reputable seller. An eBay Store is an area within eBay that a seller can customize with graphics and their own designated categories. You can also use the eBay Store listing management tools to receive monthly reports on your sales performance.

eBay Stores give you the following advantages: your own directory page and search engine; a chance to feature the store on the main Stores page; promotion

on every one of your item listings and on the related Stores area within eBay's search results pages; and a general eBay Stores link in the eBay home page.

To qualify for opening an eBay Store, you must have a minimum feedback rating of 20, or be ID-verified. A basic eBay Store costs $9.95 each month.

Even if you have an eBay Store, you may also want to list items within the non-store part of eBay. This is because eBay Store items do not currently appear in the eBay main search engine.

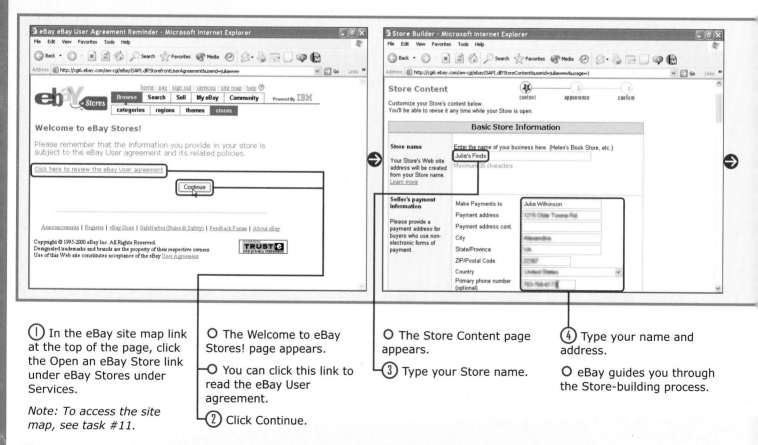

① In the eBay site map link at the top of the page, click the Open an eBay Store link under eBay Stores under Services.

*Note: To access the site map, see task #11.*

○ The Welcome to eBay Stores! page appears.

○ You can click this link to read the eBay User agreement.

② Click Continue.

○ The Store Content page appears.

③ Type your Store name.

④ Type your name and address.

○ eBay guides you through the Store-building process.

## More Options! ※

In addition to the Basic Store,
eBay offers Featured Stores for
$49.95 a month, and Anchor Stores
for $499.95 a month. Featured stores
get priority placement in the eBay Stores
home page, the Shop eBay Stores section
that appears on eBay's search results pages,
and the eBay Stores Directory for the appropriate
categories. With an Anchor Store, eBay gives your
Store one million page visitors monthly, and priority
placement in the Shop eBay Stores section
and the eBay Stores Directory pages.

#69

DIFFICULTY LEVEL

## Did You Know? ※

You can make changes to your Store after you
create it by using the Store Builder tool. To make
changes, go to your Store's home page, click
the Seller, manage store link, and then
select the Edit your store option.

O At the Store Appearance
page, you can select the
store's design.

⑤ Click a pre-selected color
scheme.

O You can click this link to
preview the colors.

⑥ Click here and select a
predesigned graphic.

O You can click this option
to upload a custom graphic,
if you have one.

O eBay continues to step you
through the rest of the listing
process.

O eBay displays your Store
URL and tells you it will be
activated within 24 hours.

# Create your own Store with
# VENDIO

You can sell directly to your customers from a customized Store that works with many automated selling features by using Vendio, a third-party auction service provider. Vendio's interface allows you to sell items directly from a Web site, as well as through eBay or other online selling sites, such as Amazon and Yahoo, or any combination thereof. Vendio also sends daily information about all of the available Store items to Froogle.com, Google's shopping engine.

Vendio Store prices start with the Bronze Plan at $4.95 each month plus 1 percent of the items' final values. However, the maximum final value fee you pay for each item sold is $4.95. For example, if you sell an item for $1,000, you pay a fee of $4.95, rather than $10.00, which is 1 percent of $1,000.

The Vendio Store Gold Plan costs $14.95 each month plus $0.10 for each sold item. For each pricing plan, you can list an unlimited number of items.

To perform this task, you need to first register for a Vendio store from the site at www.vendio.com. For more information about Stores, see tasks #69 and #71.

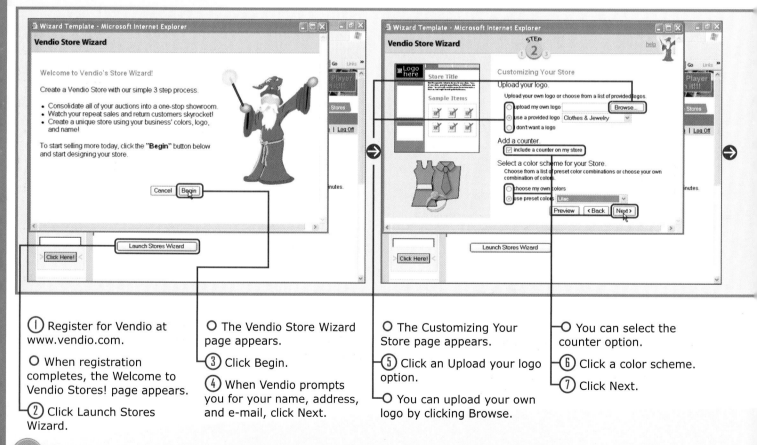

① Register for Vendio at www.vendio.com.

○ When registration completes, the Welcome to Vendio Stores! page appears.

② Click Launch Stores Wizard.

○ The Vendio Store Wizard page appears.

③ Click Begin.

④ When Vendio prompts you for your name, address, and e-mail, click Next.

○ The Customizing Your Store page appears.

⑤ Click an Upload your logo option.

○ You can upload your own logo by clicking Browse.

─○ You can select the counter option.

⑥ Click a color scheme.

⑦ Click Next.

# #70

## More Options! ⁂

To list items on eBay from your Vendio Store, you must sign up for Vendio's Selling Manager. Selling Manager speeds up your listing process by saving your shipping, payment, and marketplace preferences; allows your buyers to calculate their shipping fees; and manages the many post-sale tasks. To sign up, go to www.vendio.com/tours/sm/index.html, and click FREE TRIAL. The cost ranges from $12.95 each month plus a $0.05 listing fee and 1 percent final value fee to $39.95 each month plus a $0.10 listing fee. Vendio also offers a pay-as-you-go plan for $.10 per listing plus 1 percent final value fee and free images.

## More Options! ⁂

Vendio also offers a tool called Customer Manager that helps you manage customer e-mails. For more information see www.vendio.com/my/cm/promo_cm.html.

○ The Company Description and Information screen appears.

⑧ Type a store name.

○ You can type a store tagline.

⑨ Type a store welcome message.

⑩ Type your store's keywords.

⑪ Click Next.

○ The Vendio Store Wizard guides you through the rest of the signup process.

○ Vendio creates your Store.

# Cross-promote your
# EBAY STORE ITEMS

One of the great features of an eBay Store is that shoppers can see thumbnail images at the bottom of a Store listing of items that you designate. They can then go directly to one of those items if they are interested in it and bid on it, which can lead to more sales for you. You can designate what types of items you cross-promote using the Manage your Store area.

You have several options for cross-promoting. You can cross-promote items by Selling format, such as Buy It Now items only or Store inventory items only.

You can promote items with Gallery images first, or only items with Gallery images. You can also select items by when they end, such as those ending soonest or ending last. Or, you can have eBay show your highest-priced items first.

For information on cross-promoting by Store category, see task #72. For more on eBay Stores, see task #69. You can also attract eBay buyers to your auctions using Keywords by eBay and your About Me page as illustrated in tasks #81 and #73.

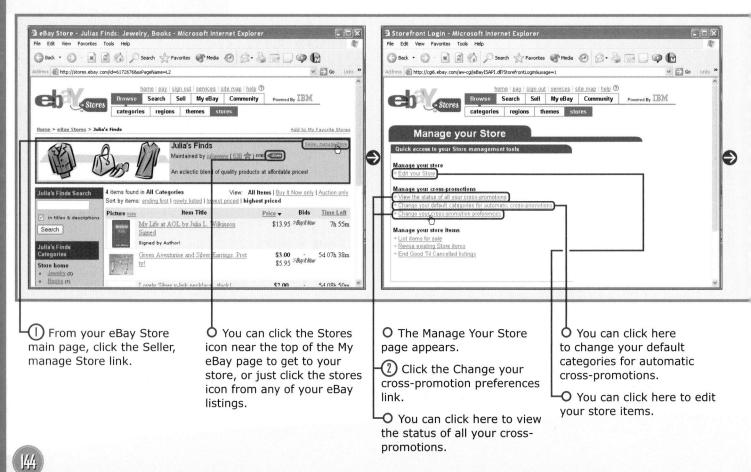

(1) From your eBay Store main page, click the Seller, manage Store link.

○ You can click the Stores icon near the top of the My eBay page to get to your store, or just click the stores icon from any of your eBay listings.

○ The Manage Your Store page appears.

(2) Click the Change your cross-promotion preferences link.

○ You can click here to view the status of all your cross-promotions.

○ You can click here to change your default categories for automatic cross-promotions.

○ You can click here to edit your store items.

## More Options! ☀

To quickly cross-promote
your eBay Store, include item
descriptions that encourage users to
view your other Store items. Prospective
bidders can click the eBay Stores icon to
access your Store. To make this technique
effective, list auctions as well as fixed-price
Store listings, because fixed-price Store listings
do not appear in eBay's regular search, but Store
items in regular auction format do.

# #71

**DIFFICULTY LEVEL**

## More Options! ☀

You can select options for When a user Bids
on or Wins your items, in addition to the
options for when a user Views your items.
From the Cross-promote my items link,
scroll down past When a User Views my
items. You can select to cross-promote
your items by Selling format, by
Gallery images, or by ending times.

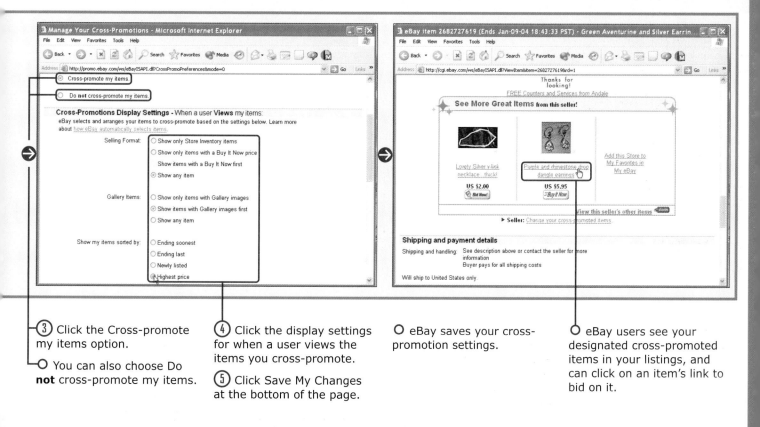

③ Click the Cross-promote
my items option.

○ You can also choose Do
**not** cross-promote my items.

④ Click the display settings
for when a user views the
items you cross-promote.

⑤ Click Save My Changes
at the bottom of the page.

○ eBay saves your cross-
promotion settings.

○ eBay users see your
designated cross-promoted
items in your listings, and
can click on an item's link to
bid on it.

# Manage
# CROSS-PROMOTED
# ITEM CATEGORIES

Using eBay's Store Merchandising Manager, you can boost your Store sales by designating which types of items your eBay Store cross-promotes to eBay users.

eBay shoppers can see thumbnail images at the bottom of a Store listing of items in the same category, or of items in the category that you designate. eBay automatically cross-promotes items that are in the same Store category, but Merchandising Manager lets you change which categories of items you want users to see when they view and bid on your items.

In most cases, you may want to promote items in the same category. For example, from a listing in a Books category, you may want to promote other items in the Books category. But in some cases you may want to promote an item that complements a particular item, but is in a different category. For example, you may want to promote a book light in a book listing.

For more information about cross-promoting your eBay Store items, see task #71.

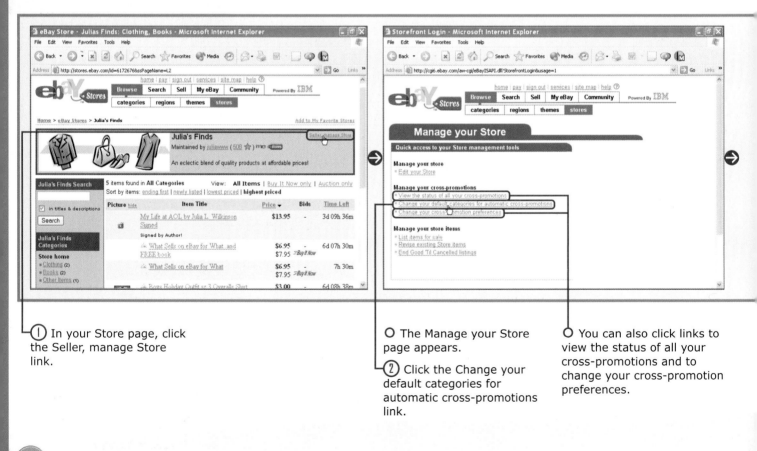

① In your Store page, click the Seller, manage Store link.

○ The Manage your Store page appears.

② Click the Change your default categories for automatic cross-promotions link.

○ You can also click links to view the status of all your cross-promotions and to change your cross-promotion preferences.

## More Options! ⁂

You can see which of
your Store items have manual
and which have automatic cross-
promotions, and which ended items
have had their cross-promotions replaced.
To do this, in the Manage your Store page,
click the View the status of all your cross-
promotions link.

## Did You Know? ⁂

You can turn cross-promotion of your items on or
off, and specify different cross-promotion display
settings. From the Manage your Store page, click
the change your cross-promotion preferences link.
You can select various display options, such as Show
only items with a Buy It Now price, or Show any item.
You can also select how you want to cross-promote
Gallery items and how to sort cross-promoted items;
for example, by Ending soonest or Highest priced.

#72

DIFFICULTY LEVEL

O The Default Categories for
Automatic Cross-Promotions
page appears.

③ Click the change default
categories link under the
category you want.

O The Change Default
Categories for Automatic
Cross-Promotions page
appears.

④ Click here and select a
category that users see
when they view an item.

O You can specify to
promote an item when
someone bids on, or wins
an item.

⑤ Click Save My Changes.

O eBay promotes items
from the category you
designate for items in
that category.

# CHAPTER 8

# Maximize Your Item's Exposure

eBay and some third-party developers offer many ways to attract attention to your items to increase your sales.

One way to promote both your auctions and your business is to create an About Me page. The About Me page is the only place on eBay where you may post links to your Web site, or other Web sites.

You can also use eBay's Gallery feature, which offers a good value at only $0.25. With Gallery, eBay users can preview a photo of your item when searching and browsing, and are therefore more likely to view the auction.

You can buy your way to a better placement within eBay's pages, using a Featured Plus! Listing for an extra $19.95. You can also time your

auctions more strategically using the eBay Merchandising Calendar, and create your own banner ad using Keywords on eBay.

Other tactics, while not as high profile, can also be effective, such as using the bold listing option, and mentioning your other auctions within your auction text.

Sophisticated techniques, such as andale's Gallery tool, showcase thumbnails of your other auctions in your listings. You can also list a strategic item to attract attention to all your auctions and gain buyers' confidence with a SquareTrade Seal of Approval.

Experiment to see which techniques work best for you, and watch your sales increase.

# TOP 100

**#73** Emphasize Listings with Your About Me Page . . . . . . . . . . . . . . . 150

**#74** Give Shoppers a Preview with Gallery . . . 152

**#75** Place Your Item on eBay's Home Page . . . . . 154

**#76** Using Bold and Highlighting to Emphasize Auctions . . . . . . . . . . . . . . . . . . . . . . . . . . . . 156

**#77** Maximize Visibility with Featured Auctions . . . . . 158

**#78** Call Attention to Your Other Auctions . . . . . . . . 160

**#79** Showcase Thumbnails of Related Auction Items . . . 162

**#80** Appeal to Buyers with SquareTrade's Seal of Approval . . . . . . . . . . . . . . . . . . . . . 164

**#81** Attract Traffic to Your Auction . . . . . . . . 166

**#82** Boost All Auctions with a Strategic Item . . . . . . . . . . . . . . . . 168

# Give shoppers a preview with
# GALLERY

When you use the Gallery feature, you can show eBay shoppers a miniature image, or thumbnail, of your auction item when they browse or search in lists of items. According to some reports, you can get from 25 percent to 200 percent more bids by using the Gallery feature. At a cost of only $0.25, the Gallery feature may be your best investment in your auction beyond the basic listing fees.

Because your items are competing against so many other items on eBay, anything that you do to help them stand out increases the chances that people

will bid on them. Some shoppers browse through so many pages of listings so quickly that they may not even take the time to view your item if you do not use the Gallery feature.

You can choose the Gallery feature on the Sell Your Item: Pictures and Details page during the eBay listing process. After you submit your listing, eBay may take a few minutes to recognize your item in its search engine.

---

## LIST YOUR AUCTION

①  In the eBay home page, click Sell.

O  The Sell Your Item page appears.

②  Click the Sell item at online Auction option.

O  You can also select the Sell at a Fixed Price, the Sell in Store Inventory, or the Advertise your Real Estate options.

O  eBay guides you through the listing process.

③  In the Sell Your Item: Pictures and Details page, select the Gallery option.

O  The Gallery option costs $0.25.

O  You can click this link to view an example of a Gallery listing.

O  eBay continues to guide you through the listing process.

**#74**

**DIFFICULTY LEVEL**

## More Options! ※

You can use the Gallery
feature when you shop on eBay.
Try browsing with the Gallery view
feature, instead of viewing the search
results in the default view. To do this, click
the Gallery view link on the left side of an eBay
search or browse results page under the Display
heading. eBay displays auctions on the page in
horizontal rows of gallery images, allowing you to
view many photos of items on one page. For
more information about the Gallery View
feature, see task #19.

## eBay Savvy! ※

Although the Gallery feature is relatively inexpensive,
if your profit margins are slim, the Gallery option
may not be worthwhile for you.

---

**VIEW YOUR AUCTION**

① In the eBay category where you list your item, or eBay's main Search page, type keywords from your item's title in the Search box.

② Click Search.

○ eBay lists items similar to your items.

③ Click the newly listed link.

○ The most recently listed auctions appear.

○ You can view your item with a Gallery preview.

○ eBay shoppers see this photo preview when they browse or search.

# Place your item on eBay's
# HOME PAGE

Every day, eBay features specific categories and subcategories on its home page, the first page people see when they navigate to www.ebay.com on the Web. You can take advantage of the top-level exposure those categories receive, and therefore get more exposure for your own items, by using eBay's Merchandising Calendar. The eBay Merchandising Calendar is a schedule of which categories eBay plans to feature on its home page in the upcoming weeks. You can plan to list items that match those items during that time. You can find this calendar in

the Seller Central section of eBay, located under What's Hot in Seller Services and on the eBay site map.

Because the schedule is subject to change without notice, you may want to check the calendar shortly before you plan to list the items for which you want front-page category exposure. eBay says they make every effort to update the calendar as soon as any changes occur.

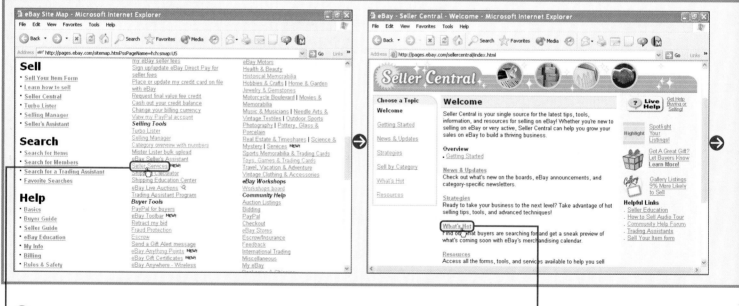

① In the eBay site map, click the Seller Services link.

⊙ The Seller Central page appears.

⊙ The News & Updates link and other resource links appear.

② Click the What's Hot link.

# #75

**DIFFICULTY LEVEL**

## eBay Savvy! ※

To immediately receive
front-page exposure for auctions,
make a note of which categories
eBay promotes on a given day and
quickly list any inventory you have that
fits into those categories. For example, if the
home page promotes Fisher Price toys, you can
quickly list one you have to sell and benefit from
eBay's top-level category exposure.

## eBay Savvy! ※

You can time your auctions to maximize their
effectiveness by using the David's Interactive
Auction Calendar at www.auctionbytes.com/
Email_Newsletter/calendar/calendar.html.

## More Options! ※

For $39.95, you can receive a link to your
item directly on the eBay home page with
the Home Page Featured listing option.
For more information about the Home
Page Featured listing option, see task #77.

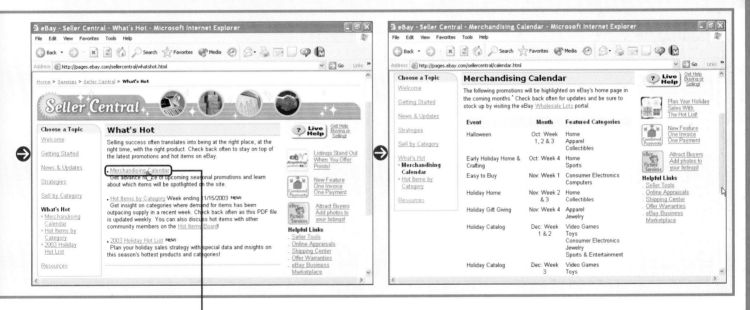

○ The What's Hot page
appears.

○ A link appears to Hot
Items by Category.

③ Click the Merchandising
Calendar link.

○ The Merchandising
Calendar page appears.

○ eBay lists which
categories it will feature in
upcoming weeks.

○ By listing the types of
items specified during the
weeks listed, you ensure
that your items' categories
receive maximum exposure
on the eBay home page.

*Note: For more information
on emphasizing a listing, see
tasks #73 and #76.*

# Using bold and highlighting to
# EMPHASIZE AUCTIONS

You can make your item stand out in the sea of auction items on eBay by using the Bold or Highlight Listing upgrade. These options are especially helpful when eBay has many items similar to yours, and you do not want your item getting lost in the sea of competition. By some estimates, placing the title of your auction in bold text, or in highlighted format, increases your chances of receiving more bids by as much as 25 percent to 35 percent.

The bold listing option costs $1.00, which is a good deal when you sell an item that is of a high enough

estimated final sale value to justify the cost of the feature. The highlight listing option is more expensive at $5.00, which you can justify only for more expensive items.

You may not want to use bold or highlighted text for every listing. For low-priced items or rare items without much competition, the added fees for emphasized text may not be worth it. You can experiment with your auctions to see where these options are most effective.

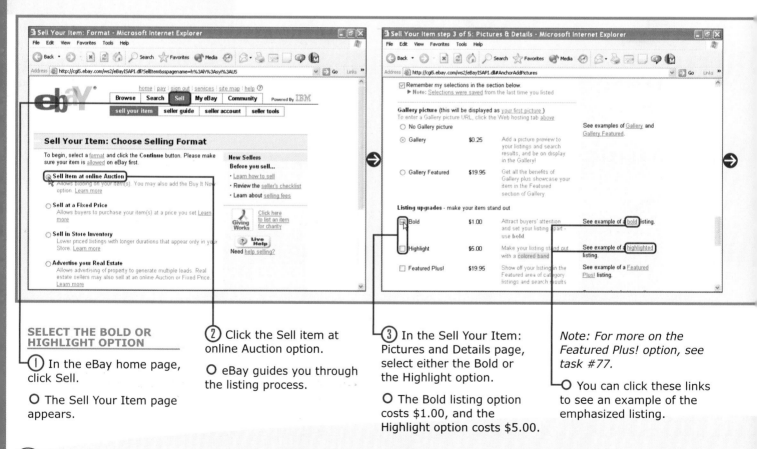

**SELECT THE BOLD OR HIGHLIGHT OPTION**

① In the eBay home page, click Sell.

O The Sell Your Item page appears.

② Click the Sell item at online Auction option.

O eBay guides you through the listing process.

③ In the Sell Your Item: Pictures and Details page, select either the Bold or the Highlight option.

O The Bold listing option costs $1.00, and the Highlight option costs $5.00.

*Note: For more on the Featured Plus! option, see task #77.*

O You can click these links to see an example of the emphasized listing.

## More Options! ※

You can also use HTML to
apply bold formatting to parts of
your item description text to make it
stand out. For more information about
using HTML in auction listings, see task #68.

## Did You Know? ※

eBay sometimes changes fees for additional
features, such as bold and featured listings,
so check the eBay Announcements section at
www2.ebay.com/aw/marketing.shtml periodically,
or pay close attention to the prices on the Sell
Your Item form. eBay reduced the fee for bold
listings in regular U.S. auctions from $2.00 to
$1.00 in March 2003. eBay also reduced the
fees for bold text in eBay Stores, depending
on the duration of the eBay Store listing. For
more information, see pages.ebay.com/
community/news/changes.html.

**#76**

**DIFFICULTY LEVEL**

○ eBay continues to guide
you through the listing
process.

④ At the end of the listing
pages, click Submit Listing.

○ eBay tells you that you
have successfully listed your
item.

**VIEW FORMATTING**

① In the eBay category
where you listed your item,
type search words that
describe your item.

② Click Search.

③ Click the newly listed
link.

○ The search results appear
with your item listing in
emphasized text.

# Maximize visibility with
# FEATURED AUCTIONS

You can use the Featured Auction listing option to increase the visibility of your auctions. When you apply the Featured Auction option to your listings, they appear above the other auctions in their category.

eBay currently offers two kinds of Featured listings. The first kind, Featured Plus!, costs $19.95. Featured Plus! auctions appear at the top of the listings page for that category. eBay also randomly selects Featured Plus! auctions for display in the Featured Items section of related category pages.

The other type of Featured listing is the Home Page Featured Auction listing, which costs $39.95, or $79.95 for multiple quantity listings. When you select the option, your item appears at the top of eBay's all featured items page. Several lucky auctions randomly appear on the eBay home page in the Featured display section, and in the Featured Items section of related category home pages.

For other ways to emphasize your listings, see tasks #68 and #76.

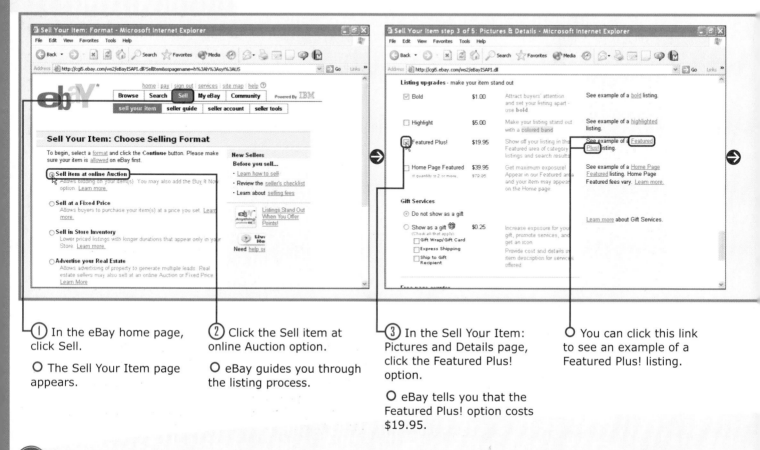

① In the eBay home page, click Sell.

O The Sell Your Item page appears.

② Click the Sell item at online Auction option.

O eBay guides you through the listing process.

③ In the Sell Your Item: Pictures and Details page, click the Featured Plus! option.

O eBay tells you that the Featured Plus! option costs $19.95.

O You can click this link to see an example of a Featured Plus! listing.

## Did You Know? ☀

You need to scroll to the bottom of the eBay home page to see the Home Page Featured Items. Conditions for using the Featured Items options include that the auction item cannot be of an adult nature or in poor taste. For a complete list of prohibited items, see cgi3.ebay.com/aw-cgi/eBayISAPI.dll?Featured, or click Feature my item on the eBay site map, located under Buying and Selling. For more on what items eBay allows, see task #44.

## #77

## DIFFICULTY LEVEL

**Featured Items** — all featured items...
- ✦ Treasure Chest Full Of Old Coins & Gemstones
- ✦ Groovy 70's !! 10 CD Set - 150 Original Songs
- ✦ Playboy First Issue December 1953 Low Grade
- ✦ Nutcracker Suite - Gold Label by Mr. Christma
- ✦ Kids Battery Powered Ride-On Tricycle
- ✦ Lose 95 Lbs By Jan Guaranteed? Best Diet Pill

○ **Alternatively, you can click the Home Page Featured option for $39.95.**

○ **You can click here to see an example of a Home Page Featured listing.**

④ **Click Continue.**

○ **eBay guides you through the rest of the listing process.**

○ **To view your Featured listing, navigate to the category in which your item is listed.**

○ **In this example, the category is Paul Reed Smith Electric Guitars.**

○ **Your item appears in the Featured Auctions section above the non-featured items.**

# Call attention to your
# OTHER AUCTIONS

One of the easiest ways to notify eBay shoppers about all your other auctions is to write a sentence or two in your auction descriptions that invite people to view your other auctions. Calling attention to other auctions is especially effective when you list a popular or otherwise attention-getting item, and when your other auctions are for related items.

You can use bold, italics, or other HTML tags to highlight the sentence that describes your other auctions. eBay shoppers can then go to your other auctions using the View seller's other items link,

located in the blue Seller information box. eBay buyers can also access your eBay Store, if you have one, through its link, which appears beneath the View seller's other items link. For more on using HTML tags, see task #68.

To perform this task, you should know how to create a basic eBay listing. This task builds on this knowledge by showing you how you can use text to point bidders to your other auctions.

For more information about attracting eBay buyers to related auctions, see task #79.

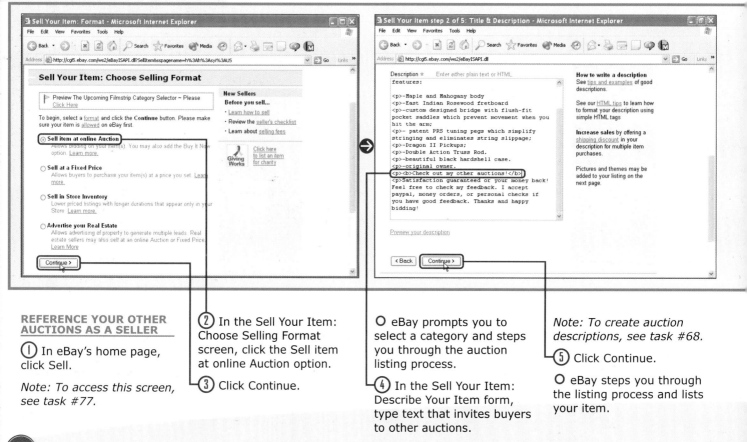

**REFERENCE YOUR OTHER AUCTIONS AS A SELLER**

① In eBay's home page, click Sell.

*Note: To access this screen, see task #77.*

② In the Sell Your Item: Choose Selling Format screen, click the Sell item at online Auction option.

③ Click Continue.

○ eBay prompts you to select a category and steps you through the auction listing process.

④ In the Sell Your Item: Describe Your Item form, type text that invites buyers to other auctions.

*Note: To create auction descriptions, see task #68.*

⑤ Click Continue.

○ eBay steps you through the listing process and lists your item.

## eBay Savvy! ※

You can create a direct link to your other auctions in your item's listing page. Go to any of your auctions, and click the View seller's other items link. Copy the URL that appears in your browser address window, and paste it into your new auction's description. Add the <a href= tag in front of the http tag, the > tag after the 50, and the </a> tag at the end. For example, where xxxx is your seller ID, type the following:

<a href=http://cgi6.ebay.com/ws/eBayISAPI.dll?
ViewSellersOtherItems&userid=xxxx&include=
0&since=-1&sort=3&rows=50>Click HERE to
see my other auctions!</a>

## More Options! ※

Although you cannot post links to your Web site in your auctions, you can post them in your About Me page, which is discussed in task #73.

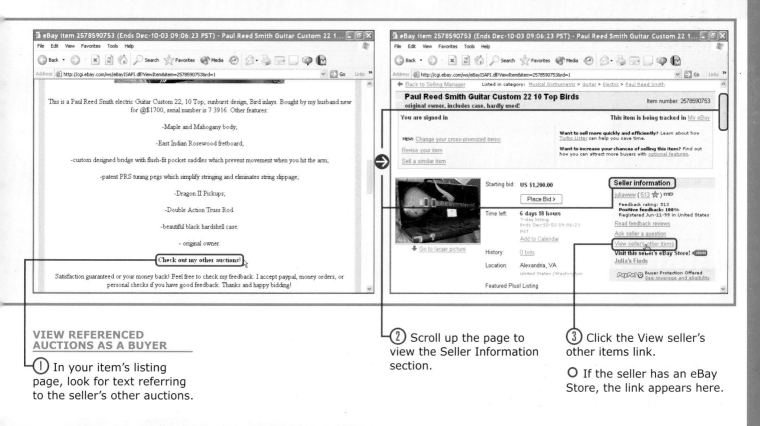

**VIEW REFERENCED AUCTIONS AS A BUYER**

① In your item's listing page, look for text referring to the seller's other auctions.

② Scroll up the page to view the Seller Information section.

③ Click the View seller's other items link.

○ If the seller has an eBay Store, the link appears here.

# Showcase thumbnails of
# RELATED
# AUCTION ITEMS

You can use andale's Gallery tool to show eBay shoppers thumbnail images of your related auction items. This enables eBay users to view small images of your other auction items from your auction descriptions. When eBay shoppers can easily view and access your other auctions, it means increased sales for you.

andale, at www.andale.com, is a third-party auction management service with products that enable you to list and research your auctions, and analyze your sales. You can purchase Gallery as a separate service from andale, or combine it with some of andale's other tools.

andale provides graphics templates so you can customize the look of your Gallery. You can also select whether to have your thumbnail images available from a button in your listing, or directly embedded into your listing.

andale Gallery costs $5.95 a month for up to 200 listings, and an extra $5.95 for each additional set of 200 listings. andale provides a counter service free of charge when you sign up for the Gallery feature.

To perform this task, you must first sign up for the andale Gallery service at www.andale.com.

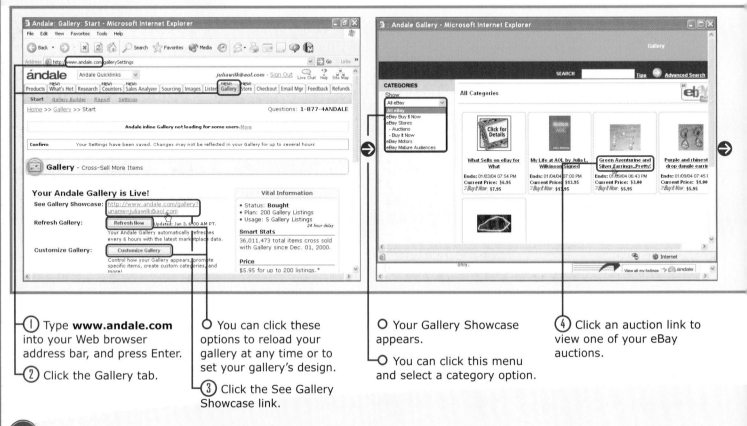

① Type **www.andale.com** into your Web browser address bar, and press Enter.

② Click the Gallery tab.

◉ You can click these options to reload your gallery at any time or to set your gallery's design.

③ Click the See Gallery Showcase link.

◉ Your Gallery Showcase appears.

◉ You can click this menu and select a category option.

④ Click an auction link to view one of your eBay auctions.

## More Options! ※

You can customize your
Gallery so your thumbnail
images show directly beneath
your item's photo in an auction page,
and set other display options. From the
andale Gallery page, click Customize Gallery,
and then select the Gallery in listing option,
which displays up to 50 items in your listing.
Click Continue. You can select an option from
a menu of design themes, color themes, and
fonts. You can also select an option to place
the Gallery in the bottom or the top of the
listing. You can type a business name and
promotion text. Click Continue. You can
select an option to feature up to eight
items, and select custom categories
to display in your Gallery. Click
Done to save your settings.

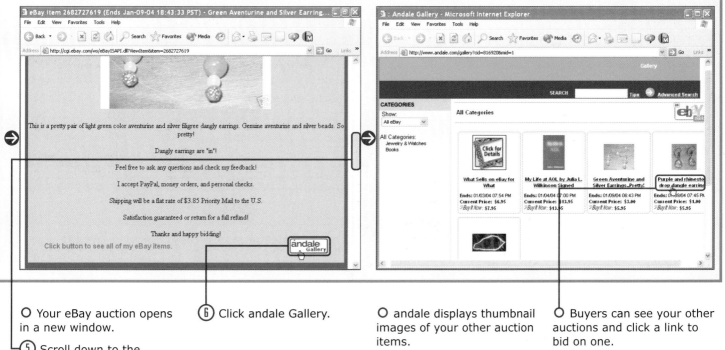

○ Your eBay auction opens
in a new window.

⑥ Click andale Gallery.

○ andale displays thumbnail
images of your other auction
items.

○ Buyers can see your other
auctions and click a link to
bid on one.

⑤ Scroll down to the
Description section.

# Appeal to buyers with
## SquareTrade's
# SEAL OF APPROVAL

You can attract more buyers to your auctions and inspire more confidence in your bidders with a SquareTrade Seal of Approval. SquareTrade Seal benefits include automatic insertion of the seal into your eBay listings, notification when you receive negative feedback, and up to $750 in buyer protection. You also receive activity reports that show you when buyers view your auctions the most as well as buyer alert e-mails that tell bidders you are a SquareTrade Seal Member who cares about giving them a positive buying experience.

To sign up for a SquareTrade Seal of Approval, go to the SquareTrade home page at www.squaretrade. com. The SquareTrade Seal costs $7.50 each month after your 30-day free trial. You can also prepay $67.50 for a year, saving 25 percent off the monthly fees, and get the premium features, which include sales reports, discounts off mediation services, and increased buyer protection.

For more information about using SquareTrade, including mediating a dispute, see task #41.

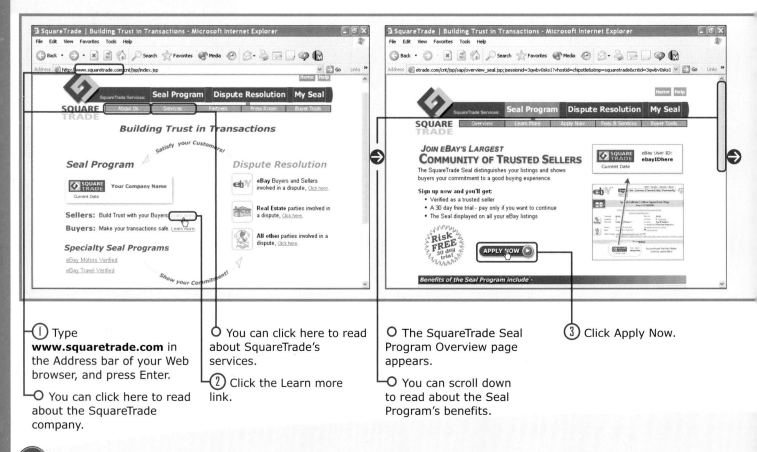

① Type **www.squaretrade.com** in the Address bar of your Web browser, and press Enter.

─○ You can click here to read about the SquareTrade company.

○ You can click here to read about SquareTrade's services.

② Click the Learn more link.

○ The SquareTrade Seal Program Overview page appears.

─○ You can scroll down to read about the Seal Program's benefits.

③ Click Apply Now.

## More Options! ☀

You can get a customized
SquareTrade Seal to use in your
auctions. SquareTrade personalizes
the Seal with your eBay user ID and
that day's date on your eBay listings.
That way, buyers know that the Seal is
really yours. The personalization protects
you from unauthorized use of your Seal.

## More Options! ☀

A Business Reporting Center is coming soon
to SquareTrade. It features over 20 reports
in chart format to help you analyze your sales.
The reports help you to keep track of how your
business performance changes from month to
month, and how your auctions compare to
those of other sellers in the same categories.
The reports are updated daily, and you can
export the data to Microsoft Excel or other
spreadsheet programs.

# 80

## DIFFICULTY LEVEL

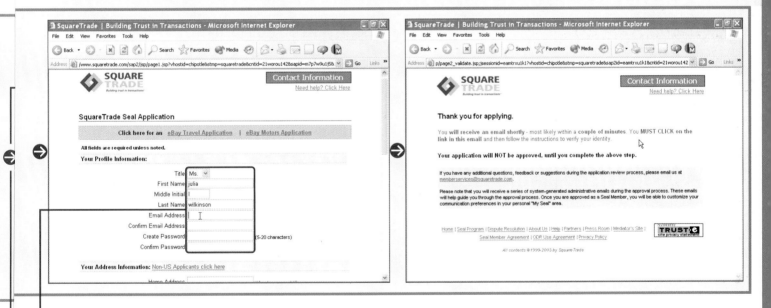

○ The SquareTrade Seal Application page appears.

④ Type your profile information into the form text boxes.

○ SquareTrade guides you through the application process.

○ SquareTrade thanks you for applying and informs you that it will send you an e-mail to confirm your identity.

○ When SquareTrade confirms your identity and activates your account, you receive the SquareTrade Seal of Approval, and eBay inserts the SquareTrade logo into your auction listings.

# Boost all auctions with a
# STRATEGIC ITEM

You can attract more bidders to all your auctions by listing just one special item that attracts a lot of attention. Even if your other items are not as unique or expensive as your strategic item, more bidders are likely to view these auctions. Many eBay sellers agree that this strategy works very well for getting bids for their other items.

If you have a limited inventory of big-ticket items, you can spread out your strategic auctions over time. In this way, your other auctions benefit from being listed with the attention-drawing items for the longest period of time.

You can use various methods to attract bidders to your other auctions: bidders can simply click the View seller's other items link; you can reference the other auctions in your strategic auction description; or you can use the andale Gallery tool to showcase thumbnail photos of your other items. For more on cross-promoting your auctions, see tasks #71 and #72.

This task assumes you know how to list an item. For more information on listing an item, see task #68 and Chapter 5.

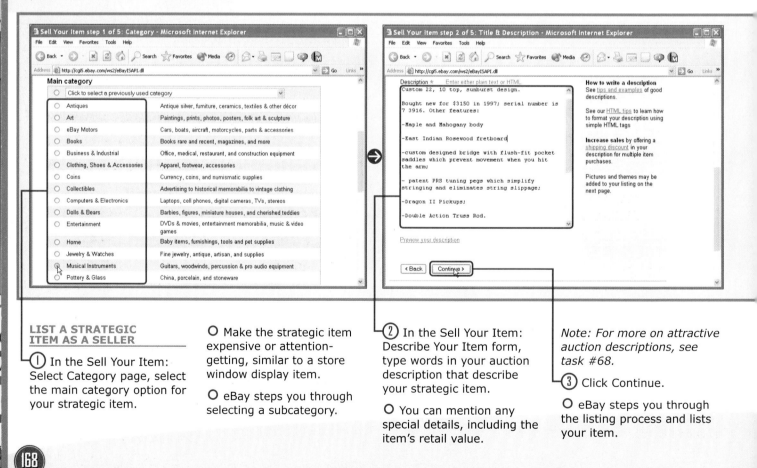

### LIST A STRATEGIC ITEM AS A SELLER

① In the Sell Your Item: Select Category page, select the main category option for your strategic item.

○ Make the strategic item expensive or attention-getting, similar to a store window display item.

○ eBay steps you through selecting a subcategory.

② In the Sell Your Item: Describe Your Item form, type words in your auction description that describe your strategic item.

○ You can mention any special details, including the item's retail value.

*Note: For more on attractive auction descriptions, see task #68.*

③ Click Continue.

○ eBay steps you through the listing process and lists your item.

**# 82**

**DIFFICULTY LEVEL**

### eBay Savvy! ※

To learn the techniques of successful sellers, consider viewing their auctions for up to the past two weeks. You can do so by clicking the Search tab, clicking the By Seller tab, and then typing the seller's eBay user ID in the text box. Select the All option next to Include completed items, and then click Search. You can also learn by participating in the eBay Community Forums. For more information about eBay's Discussion Boards, see tasks #93 to #96.

### eBay Savvy! ※

To improve the click-through rates in your auctions, you can add text to the title and description that reference an item's brand, age, or retail value. You can also use eBay abbreviations to conserve space in an auction title.

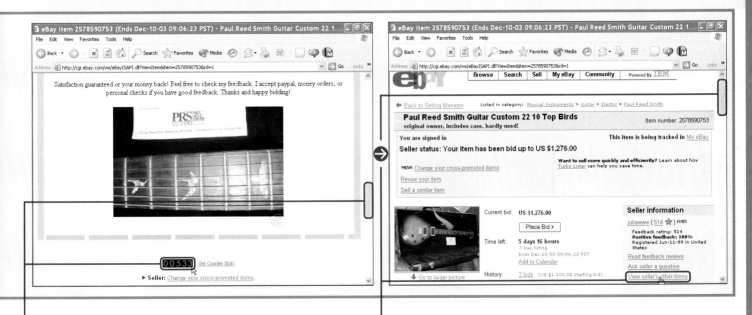

**VIEW A STRATEGIC ITEM AS A BUYER**

① In the item listing page for a strategic item, you can scroll down to the counter stats, which show the number of visits your auction has received.

● In this example, over 500 people viewed this item, which is a high number of people.

② Scroll up to the Seller Information section.

③ Click the View seller's other items link to check the seller's other auctions.

● Buyers who are attracted by your strategic item may bid on your other items.

# CHAPTER 9

# Smart Shipping for Sellers

Packaging and shipping items are among the least favorite tasks that eBay sellers must perform. However, with the tools described in this chapter, you can lighten your workload considerably in this area of your business.

For example, you can easily look up shipping rates online or use flat rates, thus eliminating the need to estimate shipping rates altogether.

You can empower your customers to find out their own shipping information by placing a shipping calculator in your auction listing. eBay customers also appreciate clearly written shipping and packaging terms. You can keep your costs down by using services like U-PIC's discount shipping insurance, ordering low-cost supplies, and even getting free packing supplies. You can pass these savings on to your customers and give yourself an edge over other sellers.

Shipping entails risk for both buyers and sellers. As a seller, you can protect yourself against loss by ordering delivery confirmation, insurance, or both.

Of all the shipping-related tasks, the least enjoyable for most eBay users is waiting in line at the post office. You can eliminate this task by buying and printing your own stamps. You can then either drop off your packages at given locations or have your mail carrier pick them up. Special shippers, such as Craters and Freighters, can handle the shipping of large or awkward items. Once you are familiar with the various shipping services and methods that are available, you can decide what works best for you.

# TOP 100

#83    Create Good Terms of Sale . . . . . . 172

#84    Retrieve Shipping Information . . . . . . . . 174

#85    Place a Shipping Calculator in Your Listing . . . 176

#86    Save Time and Money with Flat Rates . . . . . . 178

#87    Print Your Own Stamps. . . . . . . . . . . . . . . . . . 180

#88    Protect Yourself with Delivery Confirmation and Insurance. . . . . . . . . . . . . . . . . . . . . . . . . . 182

#89    Using U-PIC to Insure Packages . . . . . . . . . . . . 184

#90    Using eBay to Purchase Packing Supplies . . . . 186

#91    Order Free Supplies . . . . . . . . . . . . . . . . 188

#92    Send Large, Valuable, or Fragile Items . . . . . . . . . . . . . . . . 190

Create good
# TERMS OF SALE

You can attract more bidders to your auctions if you clearly state your packaging, shipping, and return policy in your auctions. You can also save time answering e-mails from prospective bidders if you place as much detail in your auctions about your terms of sale as possible. Although eBay prompts you for terms of sale details in the Sell Your Item pages, consider repeating them in the item description area.

Be sure to state what types of payment you accept, how you charge for shipping, and your return policy. Many sellers charge separately for handling or

packaging, so it is a good idea to be clear about those details. You risk getting negative feedback if you surprise buyers with added costs on top of what they pay for shipping. To determine shipping costs, see task #84. To include a shipping calculator in your listing, see task #85.

One successful eBay seller suggests phrasing your sale terms positively — "I accept PayPal and money orders" — rather than negatively — "NO personal checks!" — because negative wording may scare off bidders.

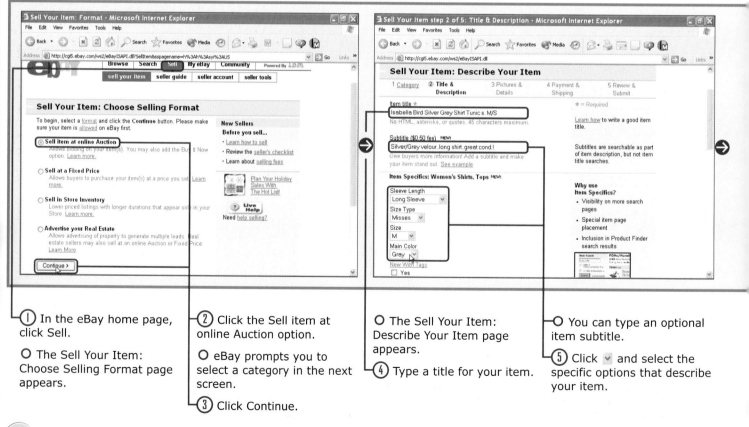

① In the eBay home page, click Sell.

○ The Sell Your Item: Choose Selling Format page appears.

② Click the Sell item at online Auction option.

○ eBay prompts you to select a category in the next screen.

③ Click Continue.

○ The Sell Your Item: Describe Your Item page appears.

④ Type a title for your item.

○ You can type an optional item subtitle.

⑤ Click ▾ and select the specific options that describe your item.

DIFFICULTY LEVEL

## eBay Savvy!

Because buyers may be very sensitive to how much you charge for shipping, consider charging an exact amount — which involves weighing the item and looking up the shipping cost to the destination ZIP code. Exact amounts help you avoid negative feedback from buyers who think you overcharge for shipping. If you charge for handling or packaging costs, clearly state so in the auction description. For more information about calculating shipping costs, see tasks #84, #86, and #92.

## eBay Savvy!

When you buy on eBay, if you do not see the shipping cost specified, you can use the Ask seller a question link on the item's listing page. For more information about the Ask seller a question feature, see task #13.

---

**Sell Your Item step 2 of 5: Title & Description - Microsoft Internet Explorer**

File  Edit  View  Favorites  Tools  Help

Address: http://cgi5.ebay.com/ws2/eBayISAPI.dll

Description *       Enter either plain text or HTML

<p>Isabella Bird Silver Grey long Shirt/Tunic. Shirt is marked XS, but I believe it is more of a Medium. It fits me even with a turtleneck underneath and seems plenty roomy. The label is marked through with marker, so I believe one reason it was so marked is because it was mis-sized.
<p>A soft velvet/velour. Shirt is 82% rayon, 18% silk.  Bought NWOT by me on eBay. I tried it on once but I've never worn it out.
<p>I charge $3.85 flat rate Priority Mail shipping. I do not charge for handling or packaging.
<p>I guarantee satisfaction, or you may return the item for a full refund.
<p>I accept PayPal, money orders, and personal checks.
<p>Feel free to ask any questions and check my feedback!
<p>Thanks and happy bidding!

**How to write a description**
See tips and examples of good descriptions.

See our HTML tips to learn how to format your description using simple HTML tags.

**Increase sales** by offering a shipping discount in your description for multiple item purchases.

Pictures and themes may be added to your listing on the next page.

Preview your description

[ < Back ]  [ Continue > ]

---

**Sell Your Item step 4 of 5: Payment - Microsoft Internet Explorer**

File  Edit  View  Favorites  Tools  Help

Address: http://cgi5.ebay.com/ws2/eBayISAPI.dll

**Shipping costs** *                    Click to minimize

Who will pay for shipping costs?
● Buyer        ○ Seller

Include domestic (United States) shipping rates with my listing:
○ No, skip section below
○ Yes, specify below (faster payment and easier for buyer)

| Flat shipping rates | Calculated shipping rates |
|---|---|
| Same rate for all buyers | Based on buyer address NEW |

To have shipping rates calculated automatically for your buyers based on their address, enter the information below. See how it works.

Package weight      [      ] lbs.     [      ] oz.

Package size        Package/Thick Envelope
                    ☐ The packaging is irregular or unusual.
                    Learn more about weight and package size.

Shipping service    US Postal Service Priority Mail

Seller ZIP Code     22307      (US only)

See the rates that will be offered to the buyer. Try the new shipping calculator.

Shipping rates are calculated on eBay and PayPal.
• No need for you to calculate shipping.
• Buyer can pay as soon as the item ends.

Confirm delivery of your items at the US Postal Service Shipping Center.

Find UPS Drop-off locations at the UPS Shipping Center.

---

⑥ Type your shipping, return, and payment policy in the item description text box.

*Note: For more on adding HTML tags to make your text more interesting, see task #68.*

⑦ Click Continue.

○ In the Provide Pictures and Item Details page, eBay guides you through setting an auction duration, starting price, and picture details.

○ The Enter Payment & Shipping page guides you through selecting the payment methods you want to accept.

⑧ Click to specify who pays for shipping.

⑨ Click whether to include shipping rates.

*Note: For more on shipping rates, see task #84.*

# Retrieve
# SHIPPING
# INFORMATION

You can easily determine the shipping for an item by using the United States Postal Service, or USPS, Web site, which has a shipping calculator for both domestic and international items. Once you know the correct postage, you can place it on your packages and eliminate waiting in line at the post office by either handing the package to your mail carrier or placing it directly in a mailbox or other postal pickup location. You need to know your package's weight and destination ZIP code. You can calculate postage for a postcard, letter, envelope, or package.

The USPS Web site asks you to specify the size of the package. If the length of the longest side of the package plus the distance around its thickest part equals 84 inches or less, the USPS considers the package a regular size. If it is more than 84 inches but less than or equal to 108 inches, the USPS considers it a large package.

You can indicate any special characteristics your package has and choose from different types of mail services, such as Express, Priority, or Parcel Post.

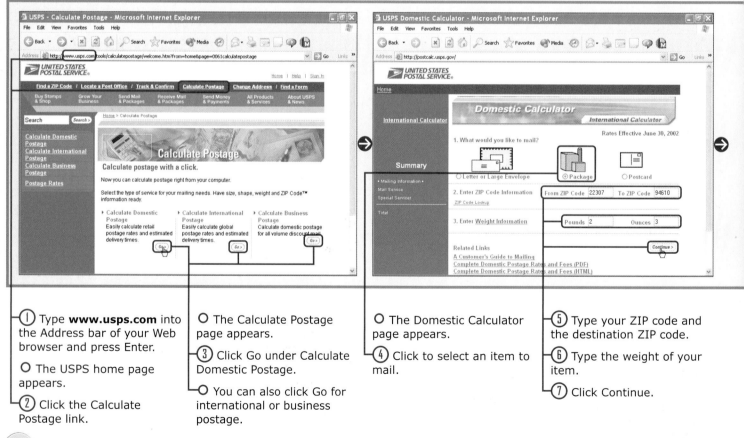

① Type **www.usps.com** into the Address bar of your Web browser and press Enter.

○ The USPS home page appears.

② Click the Calculate Postage link.

○ The Calculate Postage page appears.

③ Click Go under Calculate Domestic Postage.

○ You can also click Go for international or business postage.

○ The Domestic Calculator page appears.

④ Click to select an item to mail.

⑤ Type your ZIP code and the destination ZIP code.

⑥ Type the weight of your item.

⑦ Click Continue.

## More Options!

You can also use the United Parcel Service, or UPS. You can obtain shipping and tracking information at their Web site, www. ups.com. To find shipping rates, go to www.ups.com/content/us/en/shipping/ index.html and click the Estimate Cost link.

**#84**

DIFFICULTY LEVEL

## eBay Savvy!

You can find assembled links about shipping methods and costs on the AuctionBytes Web site at www. auctionbytes.com/Yellow_Pages/Postman/postman.html.

## More Options!

You can add special services to your package on the USPS site, such as certified mail, insurance, registered mail, collect on delivery — or COD — and return receipt for merchandise. To select a special service, click Continue on the Mail Service page that contains shipping rates. The Special Services page appears. You can also select None of These options.

⑧ Click a package size option.

○ You can also type the dimensions of your package.

⑨ Click the package characteristic arrow and select an option, if applicable.

○ Package characteristics range from less than 6 inches long to a film case over 5 pounds or with strap-type closures.

⑩ Click Continue.

○ A table appears with shipping rates for most types of mail service, and estimated delivery times.

○ You can click Continue to add special services to your package.

*Note: For more on the services that USPS has to offer, see task #88.*

# Place a
# SHIPPING CALCULATOR
## in your listing

You can save time and money and increase your customers' satisfaction by placing a shipping calculator in your auctions. This allows customers to determine their own shipping costs, and prevents e-mails from buyers about shipping fees. The calculator can also save you from making errors in estimating shipping on your own.

eBay offers a shipping calculator option in its Sell Your Item forms. eBay's shipping calculator determines United States Postal Service and United Parcel Service shipping charges based on the buyer's ZIP code

within the United States. Buyers can then see the shipping calculator in your listing in the Shipping & payment details section, under the item description.

Although eBay's shipping calculator supports most eBay auctions, it does not calculate shipping for outside the United States or for shipping services that are not shown within the calculator, such as UPS Next Day Air. eBay's shipping calculator also does not calculate the shipping costs of multiple items purchased from one seller. For information about calculating your shipping costs using the USPS Web site, see task #84.

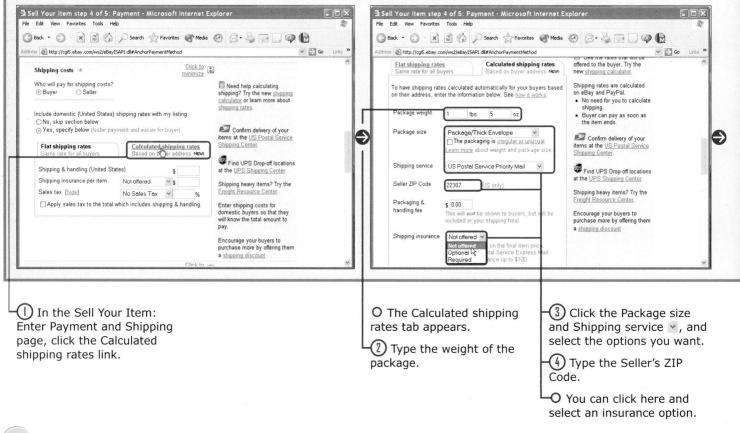

① In the Sell Your Item: Enter Payment and Shipping page, click the Calculated shipping rates link.

O The Calculated shipping rates tab appears.

② Type the weight of the package.

③ Click the Package size and Shipping service ⌄, and select the options you want.

④ Type the Seller's ZIP Code.

O You can click here and select an insurance option.

## More Options! ☀

You can choose from several third-party shipping calculators. AuctionInc's aiShip calculates both UPS and USPS rates, and works with all listing tools. To find out more, go to www.auctioninc.com and click Learn More! under aiShip Shipping Calculator. aiShip costs $0.10 for each auction sale, with a maximum charge of $9.50 each month. aiShip does not charge for unsold auctions or for calculator hits. You can also use the free shipping calculator at www.beesonware.com/shippingcalculator.

## #85

### DIFFICULTY LEVEL

## Did You Know? ☀

eBay's shipping calculator also computes insurance and taxes. Because the item's final price determines the rate, the calculator shows only the shipping insurance rate when the auction ends. For more information about eBay's shipping calculator, go to www.pages.ebay.com/help/buy/ship-calc-buyer-overview.html.

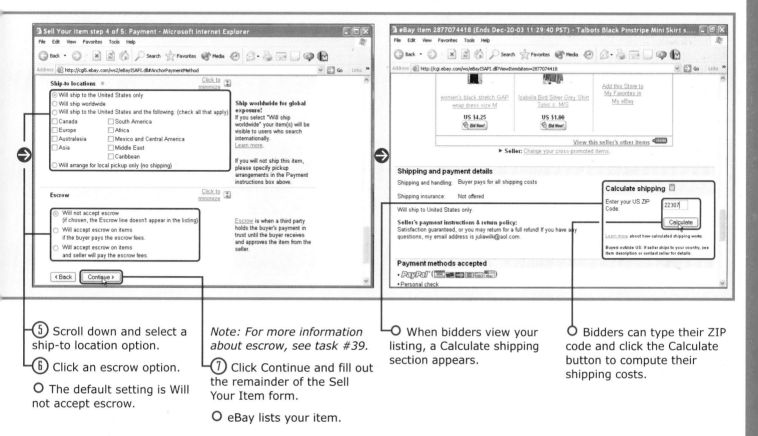

⑤ Scroll down and select a ship-to location option.

⑥ Click an escrow option.

○ The default setting is Will not accept escrow.

*Note: For more information about escrow, see task #39.*

⑦ Click Continue and fill out the remainder of the Sell Your Item form.

○ eBay lists your item.

○ When bidders view your listing, a Calculate shipping section appears.

○ Bidders can type their ZIP code and click the Calculate button to compute their shipping costs.

# FLAT RATES

You can spare yourself the trouble of looking up each item's shipping information by using flat shipping rates in your auctions. A *flat rate* is a consistent rate that is meant to be close to an item's actual shipping cost.

Although some eBay shoppers may expect exact shipping rates, many understand that flat rates can save sellers time and money — savings that a seller can pass on to buyers. If you inform prospective bidders by placing a clear notation in your auction description that you charge a flat shipping rate, buyers can decide if they want to bid on your

auction if they find the shipping amount acceptable. One eBay seller has used flat rates in over 750 auctions, with no buyer complaints.

Flat-rate shipping is especially useful for sellers who list similar types of items that tend to have the same shipping cost.

However, you may not want to use flat-rate shipping for large, heavy items where a margin of error in shipping can add up to a significant amount of money. For more on shipping large, valuable, and fragile items, see task #92.

① In the eBay home page, click Sell.

○ The Sell Your Item: Choose Selling Format page appears.

*Note: For more on creating a listing, see task #68.*

② Scroll down to the Sell Your Item: Describe Your Item page, and type information about your flat rates in the item description text box.

③ Click Continue.

④ Fill out the Sell Your Item: Provide Pictures & Item Details page, and click Continue.

*Note: For more information about this page, see tasks #65 and #68.*

○ The Enter Payment & Shipping page appears.

⑤ Scroll down and at the Include domestic shipping rates with my listing section, click the Yes, specify below option.

⑥ Click the Flat shipping rates tab.

## eBay Savvy!

There are different ways to determine flat rates. One seller uses the average cost of shipping the same product to three parts of the country, and then adds $1.00. This seller sells items with similar weights.

Another seller bases the cost of shipping on the Zone 8 ZIP codes shipping rate, and recovers postage, but not packaging, costs for buyers in Zone 8. If a buyer is in Zones 5 to 7, the seller recovers packaging but not handling costs. If the buyer lives in Zones 1 to 4, the seller recovers postage, all packaging costs, and a small labor charge. To help in calculating flat rates, you can get a postal zone chart at www. postcalc.usps.gov/Zonecharts.

# 86

DIFFICULTY LEVEL

○ The Flat shipping rates tab appears.

⑦ Type the flat rate for your item.

○ You can type a rate for shipping insurance.

─○ You can type a rate for sales tax.

⑧ Click Continue.

○ eBay guides you through the remainder of the listing process.

─○ When a buyer views your listing, your flat shipping rates appear.

# Print your
# OWN STAMPS

You can print stamps and mailing labels from your own printer, thus eliminating long waits at the post office. You can also get free delivery confirmation with Stamps.com.

To use Stamps.com, you must first sign up for the service and download the free software from the Stamps.com Web site. Stamps.com then appears as an icon on your desktop.

Stamps.com offers two different pricing plans: the Simple Plan, which costs 10 percent of your printed postage with a minimum of $4.49 of purchases each

month, or the Power Plan, which costs $15.99 each month in addition to your actual costs for postage. If you buy over $150 worth of postage a month, consider using the Power Plan.

With either plan, you receive a 29-day free trial, with $10 or $20 in free postage during the trial. You also receive a free postal supplies kit, which includes a Getting Started Guide, a sheet of NetStamps labels, a sheet of Internet postage labels, and a sheet of adhesive shipping labels. If you do not cancel this service, Stamps.com charges you on day 30 for using the service.

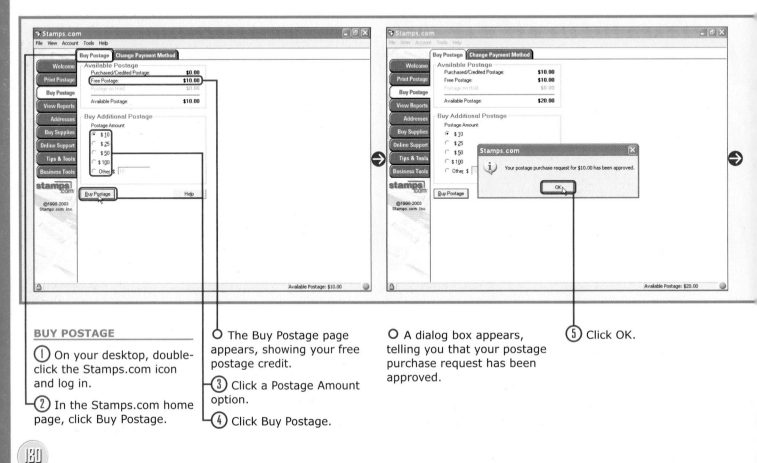

### BUY POSTAGE

① On your desktop, double-click the Stamps.com icon and log in.

② In the Stamps.com home page, click Buy Postage.

○ The Buy Postage page appears, showing your free postage credit.

③ Click a Postage Amount option.

④ Click Buy Postage.

○ A dialog box appears, telling you that your postage purchase request has been approved.

⑤ Click OK.

## Did You Know? ☀

Stamps.com offers several
pickup and drop-off options. If
it is not too large, you can give the
package to your local mail carrier, or
drop packages into any street mailbox.
If you need to add Registered Mail or USPS
insurance, you can take the package to your
local post office. For an additional $12.50, you
can schedule a pickup for an unlimited number
of packages; this option is only available for
Priority Mail, Express Mail, and Parcel Post.
You can schedule a pickup online, or
call 800-222-1811.

**DIFFICULTY LEVEL**

## eBay Savvy! ☀

Stamps.com offers a Hidden Postage feature,
which allows sellers to print shipping labels
without the actual postage value on the label.
Sellers find they get fewer complaints about
shipping charges with this feature.

---

### PRINT POSTAGE

⑥ Click the Print Postage tab.

O A Postage Printing Options dialog box appears.

O Stamps.com explains your different postage printing options.

⑦ Click OK.

⑧ Click a tab for the type of postage that you want.

⑨ Type the return and delivery addresses.

⑩ Click ⌄ and select a mailpiece, weight, and mailing date.

⑪ Click a Mail Class option.

⑫ Click here and select the paper for printing.

O Your total estimated cost appears.

⑬ Click Print.

O Your postage prints.

# PROTECT YOURSELF
## with delivery confirmation and insurance

You can ensure that your packages arrive safely, and help protect yourself from dishonest bidders by purchasing delivery confirmation and insurance. You can also request a return receipt so that the shipping service contacts you when the package arrives.

You can get delivery confirmation at a local post office for between $0.45 for Priority Mail and $0.55 for First-Class and Parcel Post.

The Postal Service does not charge additional fees for online delivery confirmation because the United States Postal Service receives an electronic record of your transaction. However, the online delivery confirmation service is only available to those who use online shipping labels, which are available at sss-web.usps.com/ds/jsps/index.jsp.

The insurance fees for merchandise are $1.30 for up to $50.00 worth of merchandise; and they start at $2.20 for between $50.01 to $100.00 worth of merchandise. The USPS charges $11.20 plus $1.00 for each $100 over $1,000 for between $1,000 and $5,000 worth of merchandise.

This task assumes that you have already performed the steps to retrieve the shipping information for your package per the steps in task #84.

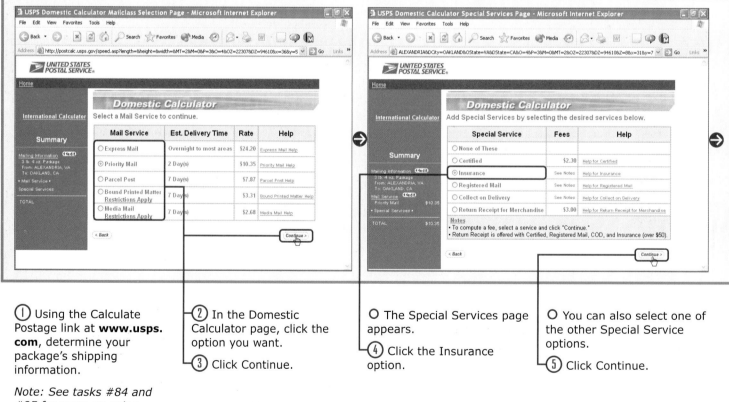

(1) Using the Calculate Postage link at **www.usps. com**, determine your package's shipping information.

*Note: See tasks #84 and #85 for more on using USPS's shipping calculator.*

(2) In the Domestic Calculator page, click the option you want.

(3) Click Continue.

O The Special Services page appears.

(4) Click the Insurance option.

O You can also select one of the other Special Service options.

(5) Click Continue.

# Did You Know?

You can use the Delivery Confirmation option with first-class packages that weigh 13 ounces or less; Priority Mail packages; Parcel Post; media mail — or book rate; bound, printed matter; or library mail. For more information, go to www.usps.com/send/waystosendmail/extraservices/deliveryconfirmationservice.htm.

# Did You Know?

You can also use Delivery Confirmation with extra services, such as Return Receipt for Merchandise; Insured Mail; Registered Mail; Collect on Delivery — or C.O.D.; Special Handling; Merchandise Return Service — where you pay the postage for items sent back to you; Return Receipt; or Restricted Delivery — where only a specified person can receive the piece of mail. For more information, go to www.usps.com/send/waystosendmail/extraservices/deliveryconfirmationservice.htm.

**#88**

DIFFICULTY LEVEL

---

O The insurance amount page appears.

⑥ Type the amount for which you want to insure the item.

─O The maximum insurance amount is $5,000.

─⑦ Click Continue.

O An additional Special Services page appears.

─⑧ Click the Delivery Confirmation option.

─O You can also select None of These or Signature Confirmation.

⑨ Click Continue.

O USPS displays your total cost, including the cost for delivery confirmation and insurance.

# Using U-PIC to
# INSURE PACKAGES

You can save 60 percent to 80 percent on insuring packages by using Universal Parcel Insurance Coverage, or U-PIC. Depending on how many packages you send, you can save hundreds, or even thousands, of dollars each year on your insurance costs.

U-PIC is a discounted insurance service for packages that you ship with major carriers, such as the United Parcel Service, the U.S. Postal Service, and Federal Express. Although the carrier ships the package,

it is insured by U-PIC. U-PIC has no minimum requirements, and offers different programs for different types of shippers.

To use U-PIC, you must first fill out the Request to Provide Coverage form on the U-PIC Web site. U-PIC reviews your form and contacts you to determine what U-PIC program best suits your needs. After U-PIC approves you for coverage, they send you a policy and a supply of claim forms. Then, instead of declaring value with your carrier, you do so with U-PIC.

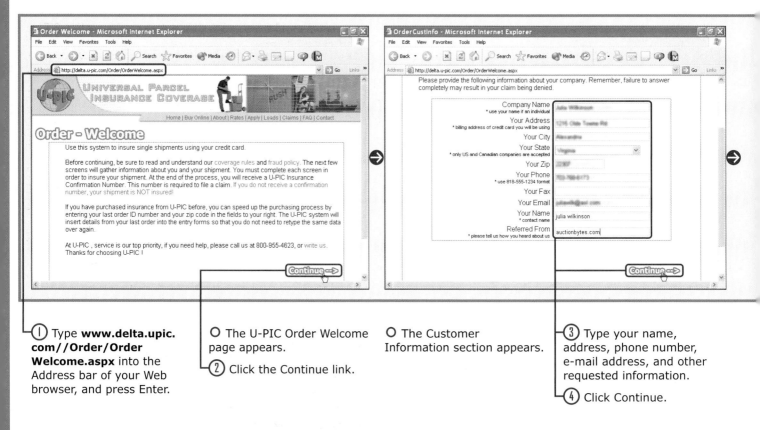

① Type **www.delta.upic.com//Order/OrderWelcome.aspx** into the Address bar of your Web browser, and press Enter.

○ The U-PIC Order Welcome page appears.

② Click the Continue link.

○ The Customer Information section appears.

③ Type your name, address, phone number, e-mail address, and other requested information.

④ Click Continue.

## More Options!

After submitting your personal information with U-PIC in the first order, you do not need to re-type this information for future orders. When you type a previous order ID, along with your ZIP code for security, U-PIC automatically fills in the appropriate fields for you.

# #89

DIFFICULTY LEVEL

## Did You Know?

At any time during the U-PIC order process, you can click the Stop, I'd like to quit link. U-PIC does not process your order until it has your billing information. Until you receive an order ID and confirmation, your package is not yet insured.

## Did You Know?

On the Carrier Service Page, make sure that you select which type of carrier service you want, as the services have different levels of risk, and therefore different costs.

O The Carrier Information page appears.

⑤ Click here and select a Carrier option.

⑥ Click here and select a Carrier service.

⑦ Click Continue.

O U-PIC gives you the price to insure your package and guides you through the rest of the order process.

O When you are finished, an Insurance Confirmation page appears, with the details of your order.

⑧ Click Continue.

O U-PIC finalizes your order.

# PACKING SUPPLIES

Almost every type of packing supply that you need is available on eBay, and you can save a lot of time by purchasing them online. Because many sellers offer good deals, you can also save money. eBay sellers offer everything from bubble wrap and tissue paper to Tyvek mailers and packing boxes.

Because eBay is a ready-made market for shipping supplies, you can get good deals from eBay vendors who sell in bulk. You can also buy multiple packing items from the same seller in order to save money on shipping fees. Several eBay Stores also specialize

in packaging supplies, and you can use the link to a seller's eBay Store, if applicable, to search for more items from a seller. Although you do have to pay shipping fees for packing supplies that you buy on eBay, the dollar value in terms of time saved makes it worthwhile to buy the supplies online.

For more information about obtaining good deals on shipping supplies, see task #91. For more information about buying multiple items from the same seller to save on shipping costs, see task #20.

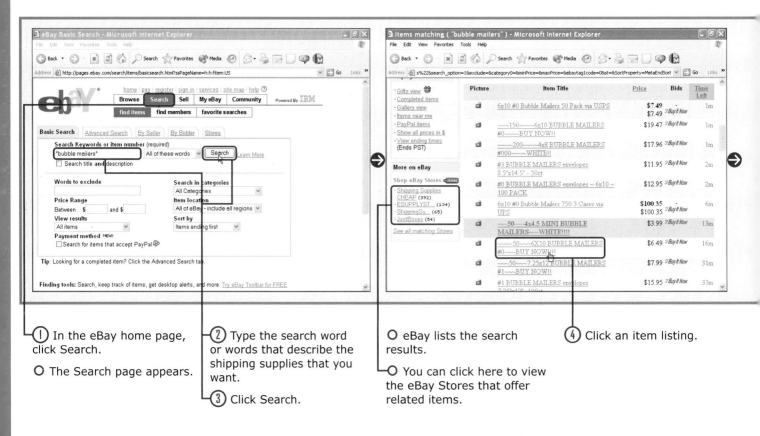

① In the eBay home page, click Search.

O The Search page appears.

② Type the search word or words that describe the shipping supplies that you want.

③ Click Search.

O eBay lists the search results.

O You can click here to view the eBay Stores that offer related items.

④ Click an item listing.

**# 90**

DIFFICULTY LEVEL

## More Options!

Other places to find good deals on shipping supplies include www.papermart.com, www.packagingprice.com, www. uline.com, and www.vikingop.com. You can also check your local Dollar store for attractive and inexpensive boxes. Some retail establishments, such as grocery stores, offer boxes, which they no longer need, for free. Check with the store management about their policy on free boxes.

## More Options!

For more information about packing and shipping supplies and recommendations about good eBay shipping supply sellers, go to the eBay Community Discussion Board on Packaging & Shipping. From the eBay home page, click the Community button, then click Discussion Boards, and then click the Packaging & Shipping link under Community Help Boards. For more on Community Help Boards, see Chapter 10.

○ The details page appears for the listing.

○ A picture of the item appears along with its description.

⑤ Click the seller's eBay Store link to search for related shipping supplies.

○ The seller's eBay Store page appears.

○ You can buy more shipping supplies and ask the seller to combine shipping costs, thus saving you money.

# Order
# FREE SUPPLIES

You can get free packing and shipping supplies from the United States Postal Service when you order Priority Mail or more expensive services, such as Express Mail. You can order them online, and USPS delivers them to you for free.

The USPS.com Web site offers many types of supplies, including cardboard boxes of various sizes, Tyvek mailers, postal tape, mail stickers, and labels. Some of the supplies are for special-sized items, such as long tubes that are ideal for mailing posters and some works of art.

You can also get supplies for different types of mail, such as Priority Mail, Express Mail, and Global Express Mail.

If you use Parcel Post shipping, you cannot receive free USPS supplies, and you still need to buy postage for your packages.

You must only use the free USPS supplies for the type of mail service for which they are intended. Before you check out your free supplies, you must agree that the packaging is solely for sending the type of mail on the supply label, as misuse is a violation of federal law.

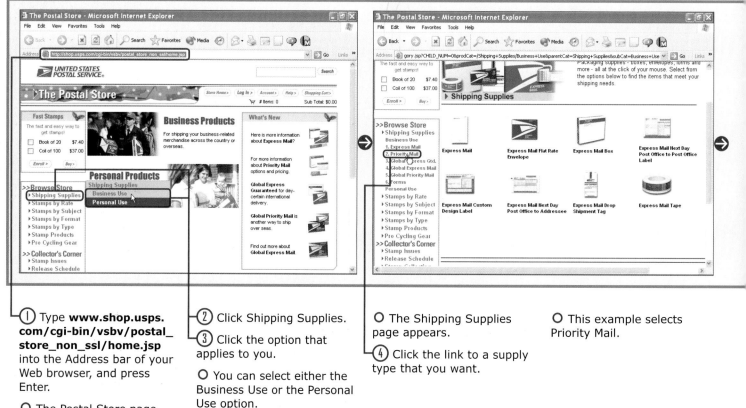

① Type **www.shop.usps.com/cgi-bin/vsbv/postal_store_non_ssl/home.jsp** into the Address bar of your Web browser, and press Enter.

○ The Postal Store page appears.

② Click Shipping Supplies.

③ Click the option that applies to you.

○ You can select either the Business Use or the Personal Use option.

○ The Shipping Supplies page appears.

④ Click the link to a supply type that you want.

○ This example selects Priority Mail.

## More Options!

You can also get free supplies from the United Parcel Service, or UPS, Web site. Type **www.ups.com** into your Web browser Address bar, select the option for your country, and then click the arrow icon. Click the Order Supplies link. You can view the available supplies, and click the Get Now link to order them.

## Did You Know?

The USPS ships supplies through Priority Mail, and may take three to five business days for delivery to domestic addresses, and three weeks to arrive to foreign addresses.

## eBay Savvy!

For another free source of packing supplies, use the plastic bags from your grocery store. They are ideal, lightweight packing materials, and using them saves you from having to throw them away.

**# 91**

DIFFICULTY LEVEL

○ The Priority Mail page appears.

⑤ Click Order Now for the item you want.

○ The Shopping Cart page appears.

○ You can review or change the item quantity.

○ USPS does not charge for these supplies.

⑥ Click Checkout.

○ USPS.com guides you through the rest of the checkout process, and delivers free shipping supplies to you.

# LARGE, VALUABLE, OR FRAGILE ITEMS

In some cases, you may need to ship large, valuable, or fragile items. The packaging and shipping company Craters and Freighters specializes in these items, and offers free pickup at your location, as well as free insurance. You can get an online shipping quote from Craters and Freighters at www.cratersandfreighters.com.

To get a quote for packaging and transporting the item to anywhere in the 48 contiguous states, you need to know the item's destination address, weight and dimensions, value, and when you want the item

to arrive. You can also receive a quote for just the transportation or the packaging.

Although Craters and Freighters can be more expensive than other shipping services, in some cases they offer advantages, such as in-home pickup, and experience in dealing with very large and valuable items. Their rates are best on items that are too big for UPS to ship.

You must register for the Craters and Freighters service before you can receive an e-quote or use their service.

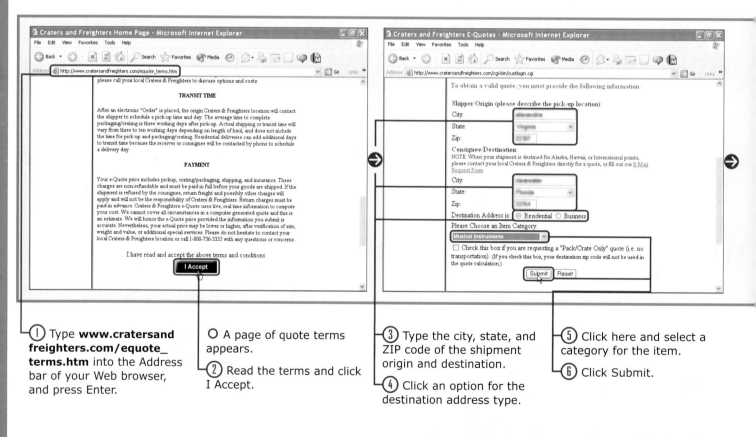

① Type **www.cratersand freighters.com/equote_terms.htm** into the Address bar of your Web browser, and press Enter.

○ A page of quote terms appears.

② Read the terms and click I Accept.

③ Type the city, state, and ZIP code of the shipment origin and destination.

④ Click an option for the destination address type.

⑤ Click here and select a category for the item.

⑥ Click Submit.

# More Options!

You can also send large and heavy items through other shipping services. With UPS, you can send packages that are up to 150 pounds, which measure up to 130 inches in combined length and girth. Oversize and very heavy packages may require special pricing. For more information, go to www.ups.com/content/us/en/resources/prepare/guidelines/index.html.

Other shipping options include Federal Express and www.fedex.com/us. You can get rates by going to and clicking the rates button. For more information on calculating USPS rates, see tasks #84 and #85.

# More Options!

If you register your auction on the Craters and Freighters Web site, then Craters and Freighters lets your bidders determine their packaging and shipping costs directly from your auction listing. Go to www.cratersandfreighters.com/equote_auction_main.htm for more information.

#92

DIFFICULTY LEVEL

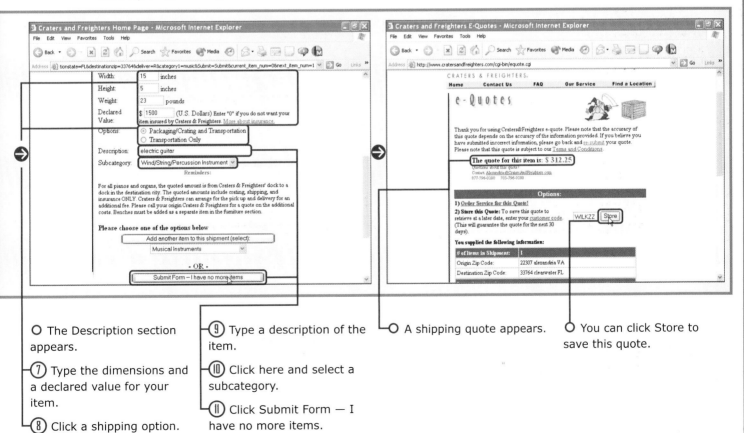

O The Description section appears.

⑦ Type the dimensions and a declared value for your item.

⑧ Click a shipping option.

⑨ Type a description of the item.

⑩ Click here and select a subcategory.

⑪ Click Submit Form — I have no more items.

O A shipping quote appears.

O You can click Store to save this quote.

# CHAPTER 10

# Tap into the eBay Community Gold Mine

You can find a wealth of information and resources in the eBay community. Other auction users are not only a valuable source of information, but also friendship and support. The eBay Discussion Boards cover a wide range of topics, so you can easily find one or more boards that interest you.

For a smaller, more specialized community, you can join an eBay Group and share items like photos and polls with fellow group members.

You can read discussions in the boards as well as start new topics. You can navigate the boards in several ways, such as from the oldest or the most recent post. The Boards Search tool is an excellent way to uncover information that may otherwise be difficult to find.

If you need help immediately, you can use eBay's Live Chat Boards which show the responses of other eBay users right away. You can also explore the topics in eBay's Help boards. eBay community members are extremely helpful, and some member experts even compile comprehensive resources and links in their About Me pages.

You can learn new skills with eBay University's online or offline classes. You can also explore the many resources for online auction users on the Web outside eBay, such as free newsletters.

You can easily navigate all of the Community boards as well as the many layers of the entire eBay site using the eBay site map.

# TOP 100

#93    Find a Home in the Discussion
Boards . . . . . . . . . . . . . . . . . . . . . 194

#94    Browse the Discussion Boards . . . . . . . 196

#95    Get Answers with Live Chat . . . . . . . . . . 198

#96    Get Answers with Message Boards . . . . . . . 200

#97    Using eBay University to Take Classes . . . . . . . 202

#98    Network with eBay Groups . . . . . . . . . . . . . . 204

#99    Find Outside Auction Communities . . . . . . . . . 206

#100    Stay Informed with Industry Newsletters . . . . 208

# FIND A HOME
## in the Discussion Boards

You can learn more about the types of items you like to buy and sell as well as meet friends who share your interests by becoming a part of eBay's Discussion Boards community. The boards are full of knowledgeable eBay users from various fields of interest ready to help new members.

The eBay Category-Specific Discussion Boards contain every type of item you may want to sell or buy, and range from animals to vintage clothing. You can scan the list of categories and decide which interest you the most.

Before you post to a Discussion Board for the first time, read the eBay Board Usage Policies, available in each board's Welcome message. You may also want to *lurk* — read posts for a while without posting — to get accustomed to the topics that the board users discuss. For example, for some questions, the board's regular users may already have a long list of answers, or FAQs. If you are courteous, message board users should receive you warmly.

For more information about the eBay Discussion Boards, see tasks #94 and #96.

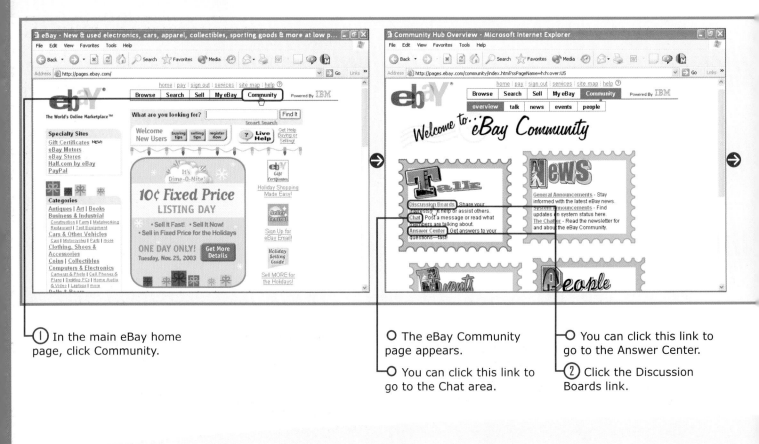

① In the main eBay home page, click Community.

○ The eBay Community page appears.

○ You can click this link to go to the Chat area.

○ You can click this link to go to the Answer Center.

② Click the Discussion Boards link.

## More Options! ※

To post a message on a
Discussion Board, click Login
at the bottom of the Board. A new
screen appears, and eBay prompts
you to log in. Once you log in, an Add
Discussion link appears at the bottom of
the Board. Click the link to make a new
post. You can also reply to an existing
message by clicking the link to the message
to which you want to reply, clicking Post
Message, typing your reply in the Your Reply
box, and then clicking Post Message.

**#93**

**DIFFICULTY LEVEL**

## Did You Know? ※

eBay staff highlight discussions that are particularly
helpful or fun. You can find links to these discussions
on the right side of the Discussion Board screen
under the category's Community heading.

O The Discussion Boards
page appears.

O A list of links to
Community Help Boards
displays here.

O A list of links to Category-
Specific Discussion Boards
displays here.

③ Click the link of a
category that interests you.

O The Discussion Board
page for that category
appears with a Welcome
message.

O You can click this link to
read the Board Usage
Policies.

O You can click a topic
to read it, and join the
Category's community by
reading and posting
messages.

# Browse the
# DISCUSSION
# BOARDS

To find the useful information you need on the eBay message boards, such as tips on where to find inventory and sales techniques from fellow sellers, you must know how to navigate the boards. You can then move easily through discussions to read the posts and get the information you want.

When you click a Discussion Board topic, the first message that appears is the one that started that topic. After that, the messages are numbered sequentially in the order eBay users post them.

You can scroll through the messages using the More button at the bottom of a page of posts. In some cases, you can also scroll forward by a given number of posts using a button with that number on it. For example, if the button has a 25 on it, it scrolls you forward 25 posts. If there are many posts in a given topic, you can use the Recent button to go to the most recently posted messages. This helps you to avoid having to read messages that are weeks or months old.

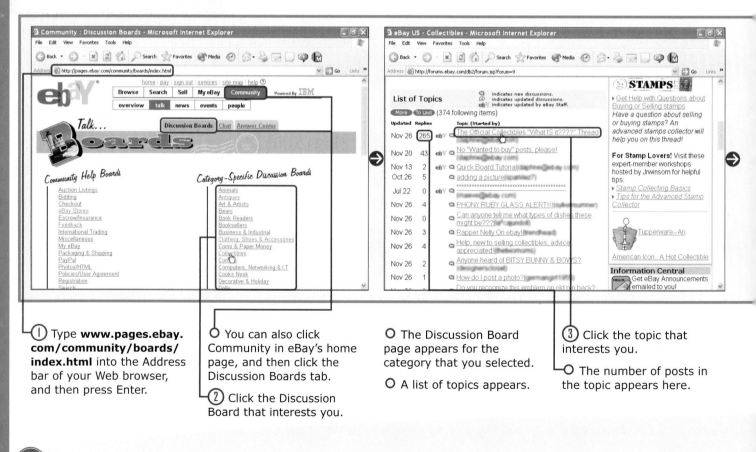

① Type **www.pages.ebay.com/community/boards/index.html** into the Address bar of your Web browser, and then press Enter.

○ You can also click Community in eBay's home page, and then click the Discussion Boards tab.

② Click the Discussion Board that interests you.

○ The Discussion Board page appears for the category that you selected.

○ A list of topics appears.

③ Click the topic that interests you.

○ The number of posts in the topic appears here.

**DIFFICULTY LEVEL**

## More Options! ※

You can also search the
Discussion Boards for keywords.
To do so, click a Discussion Board
link, and then click Search at the bottom
of the topic page. In the search form that
appears, type the word or words you want to
find. Click Search, and eBay displays links to all
the topics that match your keywords.

## eBay Savvy! ※

Some Category Discussion groups have games and
contests, informally run by other board users, designed
to attract users to your auction. You can read the boards
regularly to find out when the contests are run.

## eBay Savvy! ※

You can receive more information about using the
Discussion Boards by accessing the eBay Board
help tutorial at http://forums.ebay.com/db1/
thread.jsp?forum=120&thread=65945.

---

─O The page appears for the
topic you select with the first
messages at the top of the
page, in order from original
message to most recent.

O You can scroll down to the
bottom of the page to use
the navigation buttons to
quickly read the posts.

④ Click Recent.

─O The most recent
messages appear.

─O You can click Previous to
see the page of messages
before this page.

─O You can click To Top to go
back to the first messages in
the topic.

─O You can click a numbered
button to scroll back by that
number of posts.

# Get answers with
# LIVE CHAT

If you have an urgent question, such as about an auction that is about to end, you can receive immediate help using the Chat Boards. Chat Boards allow you to view timely advice from eBay members as soon as you type a question.

Unlike Internet chat rooms, eBay's Chat Boards do not automatically refresh your screen: you must manually do this with the Reload button. Once you refresh, you see the most recent messages, ranging from the last 5 minutes to the last 24 hours. The most recent chat room messages display on the top

of the page, and the chat threads disappear two weeks after the last post. You must be signed in to eBay to make a chat room post.

Once you sign in on eBay, you can choose from several chat rooms, including the original chat room, The eBay Café; The AOL Café, for AOL users; Discuss eBay's Newest Features; and an Images/HTML Board for help with photos and images in your auctions. The eBay Q&A Board is great for general questions.

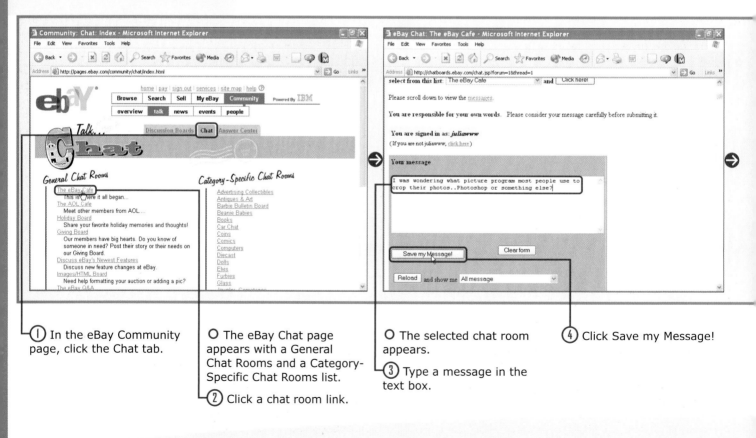

① In the eBay Community page, click the Chat tab.

② The eBay Chat page appears with a General Chat Rooms and a Category-Specific Chat Rooms list.

② Click a chat room link.

② The selected chat room appears.

③ Type a message in the text box.

④ Click Save my Message!

## Did You Know? ※

The time-date stamp next
to a member's eBay ID at the
top of their post shows when they
posted their chat message. The time
is in Pacific Standard Time, or PST. You
can also click the Auctions link to the far
right of the time-date stamp to display
that member's eBay auctions.

## More Options! ※

eBay has many category-specific chat rooms about
everything from advertising collectibles to trading
cards. Category-specific chat rooms are often close
communities that offer help and resources to members.
For example, in the eBay Advertising Collectibles Chat
Room, members post a Welcome Message with this link
to helpful collectibles resources: www.signtech-rta.com
/acboardlinks2.htm. This link includes links to sites
about collectible Absolut Vodka ads, a Pepsi Cola
Collectors Club, and a Cereal Box Archive.

**#95**

**DIFFICULTY LEVEL**

○ The page refreshes, and eBay sends your message to the chat room.

⑤ Click here and select a viewing option.

○ The options range from the last 5 minutes to the last 24 hours.

⑥ Click Reload.

○ eBay refreshes the chat room page.

○ The most recent chat messages appear on the top of the page, which is the opposite of the default order for eBay's Discussion Boards.

○ You can see if anyone has replied to your chat room posting.

# Message Board

## Get answers with
# MESSAGE BOARDS

You can receive answers to your eBay questions using the Community Help Boards, located in the main Boards page to the left of the Category-Specific Discussion Boards. These message boards are a great place to post questions about any subject, from eBay auction listing to shipping, because so many helpful members reply to these boards regularly.

You can also scan these boards to see if similar questions to yours have already been asked and answered. In fact, you may want to first search a specific message board for the word or words about

which you have a question because someone has probably already asked it and the answer is on the board. For information on how to search the boards, see task #94.

The eBay Community Help Boards are in alphabetical order, starting with Auction Listings and ending with Trust & Safety (SafeHarbor).

If you are a beginner, or have a basic question, you may want to post your question on the New to eBay board, located under General Discussion Boards beneath the Community Help Boards.

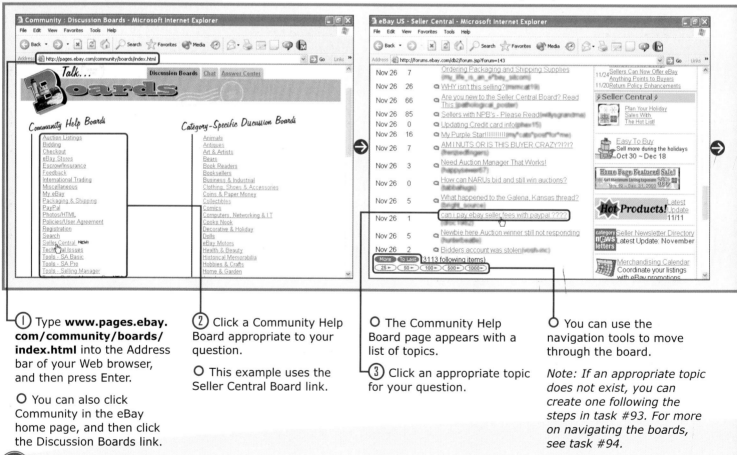

① Type **www.pages.ebay. com/community/boards/ index.html** into the Address bar of your Web browser, and then press Enter.

O You can also click Community in the eBay home page, and then click the Discussion Boards link.

② Click a Community Help Board appropriate to your question.

O This example uses the Seller Central Board link.

O The Community Help Board page appears with a list of topics.

③ Click an appropriate topic for your question.

O You can use the navigation tools to move through the board.

*Note: If an appropriate topic does not exist, you can create one following the steps in task #93. For more on navigating the boards, see task #94.*

# #96

## DIFFICULTY LEVEL

## eBay Savvy! ※

Because eBay changes its
features and policies regularly, it
is crucial for both sellers and buyers
to keep up-to-date on these changes.
You can find valuable information about
changes to eBay features and policies in
the eBay Community area at eBay's General
Announcements Board, located at www2.ebay.
com/aw/marketing.shtml. You can find updates
about any technical problems that the eBay site
may experience as well as system maintenance
and downtimes at the System Announcements Board,
located at http://www2.ebay.com/aw/announce.shtml.

## Did You Know? ※

Several newsletters and Web sites outside eBay report
on the fast-paced auction industry and offer free information
that keeps you informed about the constantly changing
eBay environment. For more about outside auction
communities and newsletters, see tasks #99 and #100.

O The topic appears.

O You can read the question
and any answers that users
have posted.

④ Click Post Message.

O A page appears where
you can reply to the
message.

⑤ Type your question or
reply in the Your Reply text
box.

⑥ Click Post Message.

O eBay posts your message
to the list of existing
messages.

# Using eBay University to
# TAKE CLASSES

You can improve your eBay skills by taking a class at eBay University. eBay University offers both offline classes, which you attend in person, and online classes, which you can access from your home computer. The main eBay University page is located at pages.ebay.com/university/.

Online eBay University classes address topics ranging from Getting Started — the basics of bidding and buying — to Enhanced Listings and Completing the Sale. Online Classes cost $19.95, and you can register for them online at ebayu.vitalstream.com/c1/registration1.html.

You can sign up for offline classes at pages.ebay.com/university/classes.html. In the eBay University Attend Classes page, you can select from a list of cities and dates where the classes are available.

Currently, eBay offers two different offline courses: Selling Basics, which includes opening a seller and PayPal account, creating listings, and setting prices; and Beyond the Basics, which covers more advanced topics, such as starting and marketing an eBay business, using listing tools, and packing and shipping your inventory.

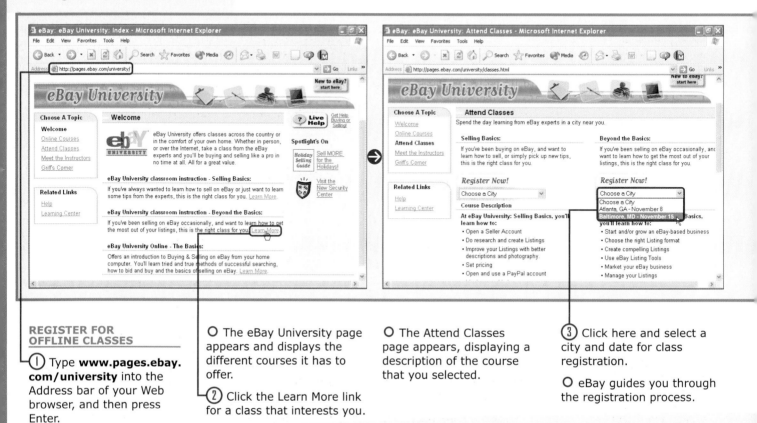

**REGISTER FOR OFFLINE CLASSES**

① Type **www.pages.ebay.com/university** into the Address bar of your Web browser, and then press Enter.

❍ The eBay University page appears and displays the different courses it has to offer.

② Click the Learn More link for a class that interests you.

❍ The Attend Classes page appears, displaying a description of the course that you selected.

③ Click here and select a city and date for class registration.

❍ eBay guides you through the registration process.

## More Options! ⋇

You can take online classes
about a wide range of eBay-
related topics with eBay Workshops.
eBay posts the archives of previous
workshops on eBay at members.ebay.
com/aboutme/workshopevents. Recent
workshop topics include Collectibles, PayPal,
Holiday Selling, and Seller's Assistant Pro
Post-Sales Basics.

## Did You Know? ⋇

If you have specialized knowledge, you can host your own
eBay Workshop. For example, a vintage clothing merchant
hosted a workshop and shared his tips for success. Tips
included very specific and anecdotal examples, such as
that certain plastic aprons from the 1950s sell for over
$100 and that 1950s Christian Dior for Holt Renfrew
dresses can sell for as much as $300 today on eBay.
For more information about eBay Workshop, e-mail
workshopevents@ebay.com or go to members.
ebay.com/aboutme/workshopevents.

# #97

DIFFICULTY LEVEL

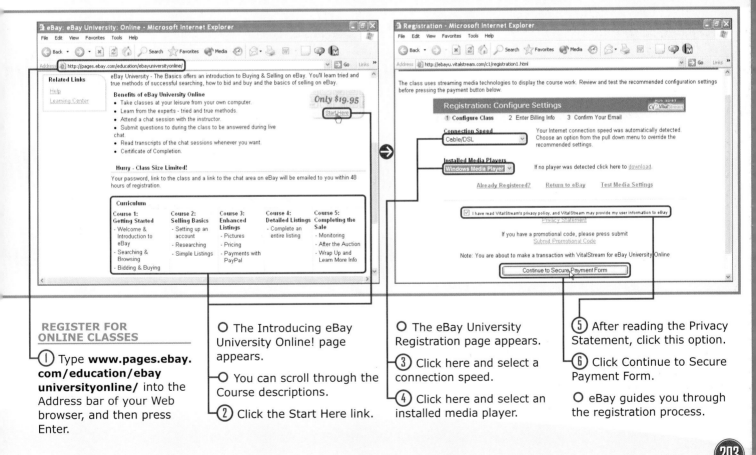

**REGISTER FOR
ONLINE CLASSES**

①  Type **www.pages.ebay.
com/education/ebay
universityonline/** into the
Address bar of your Web
browser, and then press
Enter.

○ The Introducing eBay
University Online! page
appears.

○ You can scroll through the
Course descriptions.

②  Click the Start Here link.

○ The eBay University
Registration page appears.

③  Click here and select a
connection speed.

④  Click here and select an
installed media player.

⑤  After reading the Privacy
Statement, click this option.

⑥  Click Continue to Secure
Payment Form.

○ eBay guides you through
the registration process.

# Network with
# EBAY GROUPS

You can connect with other eBay users who share your interests or geographical location by joining an eBay Group. eBay Groups offer an excellent way to learn more about your field of interest and to get to know your fellow eBay users in a more personal community than that offered by a typical eBay Discussion Board.

People in the same eBay Group can develop their own community by using tools such as polls, photo albums, and calendars.

The eBay Groups home page allows you to view the different categories of groups that are available.

Groups are sorted into categories, such as Collectors Clubs, for those who share a particular collecting or selling passion — for example, for Coins, Pottery/Porcelain, or Stamps; Seller Groups, for different types of sellers, such as PowerSellers and Store Owners; and Regional Groups, with different groups listed by state.

You can browse the list of eBay Groups in the eBay Groups home page, located at groups.ebay.com. You can also search the Groups by keyword or ZIP code to find the type of group you want to join.

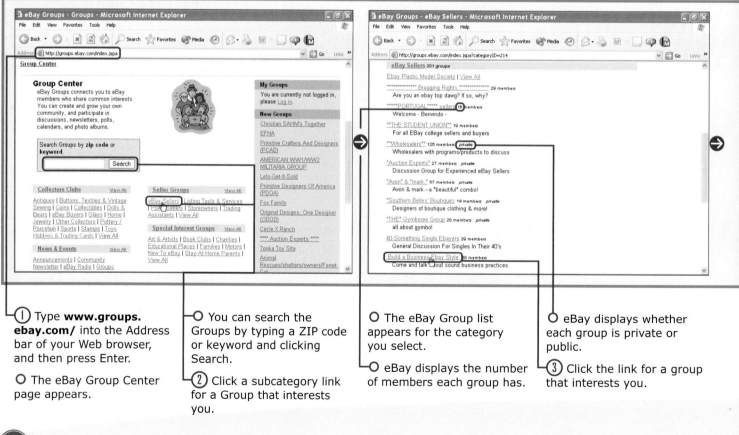

① Type **www.groups. ebay.com/** into the Address bar of your Web browser, and then press Enter.

O The eBay Group Center page appears.

O You can search the Groups by typing a ZIP code or keyword and clicking Search.

② Click a subcategory link for a Group that interests you.

O The eBay Group list appears for the category you select.

O eBay displays the number of members each group has.

O eBay displays whether each group is private or public.

③ Click the link for a group that interests you.

## More Options! ⁂

eBay Groups can be either
public or private, and are marked
accordingly in the list of Groups. If
you want to join a private Group, the
Group Leader can invite you to join, or you
can request to join by clicking the Join Group
link in that Group's page. In the screen provided,
type the reason you want to join, and click Send
Request. eBay tells you that your request has
been sent, and the Group Leader contacts you
if the Group grants you membership.

## More Options! ⁂

For more information on participating or moderating
an eBay Group, go to the eBay Groups Information
Center at groups.ebay.com/forum.jspa?forumID=
1254 and join the group. There you can find
Group Controls, such as Preferences, Invite
Members, and Remove Me.

**# 98**

**DIFFICULTY LEVEL**

○ The eBay Groups page appears for the group you select.

○ eBay displays the Group Leader's ID and a description for the group.

④ Click Join Group.

○ If you have not yet logged in, then eBay prompts you to do so.

○ The eBay Group Discussions list appears.

○ You can click a discussion link to read the discussion or to post a message.

# Find outside AUCTION COMMUNITIES

You can find valuable resources and information about the sometimes-confusing array of auction tools, such as photo-hosting and listing-software services, and other auction-related topics at online communities, such as AuctionBytes and the Online Traders Web Alliance, or OTWA. You can receive information from these sites that you may not find on eBay because they discuss third-party developers as well as alternative auction sites to eBay, such as Amazon, ePier, and Yahoo.

For example, the AuctionBytes site provides a message board community, where you can network and share information with other auction users as well as several resource tables that present information clearly. You can view the Auction Management Services at a Glance chart, which shows the major auction management companies, such as andale and Auctionworks; the auction sites they support; and their prices. You can also view a chart that compares online storefront vendors, and a table that compares the various auction-site seller fees, from Amazon and eBay to Yahoo.

For more information about message boards and networking with other users, see tasks #96 and #98.

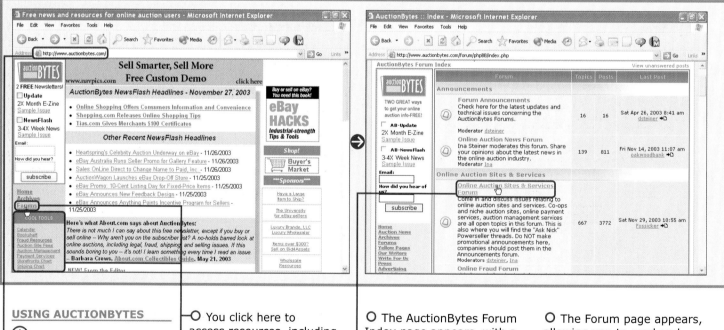

### USING AUCTIONBYTES

① Type **www.auctionbytes.com** into the Address bar of your Web browser, and then press Enter.

O The AuctionBytes Web site appears.

O You click here to access resources, including recommended books, fraud resources, and a chart of fees and services.

② Click the Forums link.

O The AuctionBytes Forum Index page appears, with a list of forums.

③ Click the link of a forum that interests you.

O The Forum page appears, allowing you to read and post messages.

## More Options! ※

To post a message on the
AuctionBytes boards in the
AuctionBytes home page located
at www.auctionbytes.com, click the
Forums link. Select a Forum, and click
the link. Select a topic from the list, and click
the topic link to open it and read the messages.
Click post reply to respond to a message, or click
the new topic button to start a new discussion.

# #99

## DIFFICULTY LEVEL

## Success Story! ※

AuctionBytes has specialty collectors' forums
where people share successes and tips. In one
topic about collectible postcards, a user tells about
selling postcards of roadside attractions from the
1950s to early 1960s for $20 to $50 each.

---

**USING THE OTWA
COMMUNITY**

① Type **www.otwa.com** in
the Address bar of your Web
browser, and then press
Enter.

○ The OTWA page appears.

② Click the Enter the
Community link.

○ The OTWA Forums page
appears.

○ A list of Forums displays,
including the andale
Community Center, Auction
Industry Community Center,
and the Antiques, and
Collectibles Arena.

③ Click a Forum link.

○ The Forum page opens,
allowing you to read and
post messages, and
participate in the OTWA
Community.

# Stay informed with
# INDUSTRY NEWSLETTERS

To keep up with the constantly-changing world of online auctions, you can subscribe to.

You can subscribe to monthly, weekly, or daily auction newsletters. Examples of what you can learn from auction newsletters include advice from collectibles experts, packing and shipping tips, and new features on eBay and other auction sites. Many of the newsletters focus on maximizing your profits and selling tips. One recent newsletter featured articles about selling event tickets on eBay and writing compelling auction copy.

Auction Gold at www.auctionknowhow.com/AG, Cool eBay Tools at www.coolebaytools.com, and Creative eBay Selling at www.silentsalesmachine.com.

Weekly newsletters include AuctionBytes at www.auctionbytes.com and The Auction Guild's TAGnotes at www.auctionguild.com.

You can also search newsletter back issues on some sites, such as AuctionBytes. For more information about online auction communities, see task #99.

Although this example uses AuctionBytes, you can use the steps in this task for other newletters.

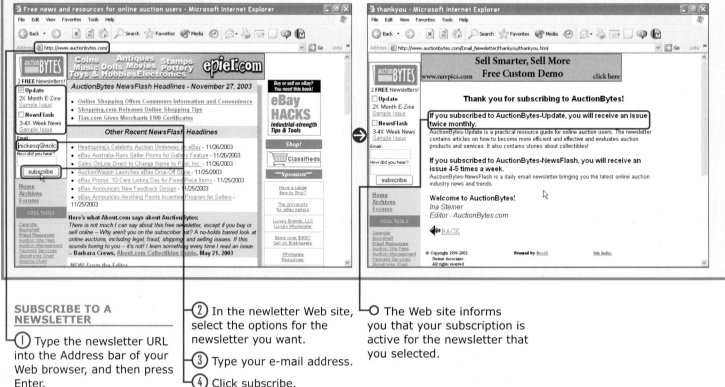

## SUBSCRIBE TO A NEWSLETTER

① Type the newsletter URL into the Address bar of your Web browser, and then press Enter.

② In the newletter Web site, select the options for the newsletter you want.

③ Type your e-mail address.

④ Click subscribe.

○ The Web site informs you that your subscription is active for the newsletter that you selected.

## More Options! ☀

You can search the Internet for more auction-related newsletters. Try conducting a search using the Google search engine at www.google.com, or the Yahoo directory at dir.yahoo.com/Business_and_Economy/ Shopping_and_Services/Auctions/Industry_ Information.

## Did You Know? ☀

eBay also has its own monthly general community newsletter, The Chatter, available at pages.ebay.com/ community/chatter. The Chatter includes hints, articles about eBay members of note, and profiles of eBay staff. The newsletter also offers interviews with representatives of popular collectible manufacturers, such as Precious Moments figurines and Fenton Art Glass. You can read past issues of The Chatter by clicking the Chatter Archive link, available at the lower left side of the main Chatter page. For information about eBay's Category-Specific newsletters available for some eBay categories, see task #62.

# #100

## DIFFICULTY LEVEL

---

### SEARCH A NEWSLETTER FOR INFORMATION

○ In this example, the newsletter is AuctionBytes.

① Type **www.auctionbytes.com** into the Address bar of your Web browser, and then press Enter.

○ The AuctionBytes Web site appears.

② Type your word or words into the Search text box.

③ Click Search!.

○ The search results list appears.

○ You can click an article link to read more about the topic.

# INDEX

## Symbols

" (quotation marks) characters, Basic Search keywords, 4–5

## A

**About Me page**
  seller's personal information, 150–151
  seller's Web site links, 161
**accounts**
  PayPal money transfers, 76–79
  PayPal setup, 74–75
**acronyms, misspelled item bargains, 20–21**
**ad banners, Keywords on eBay, 166–167**
**Ad format**
  bid process, 61
  real estate auctions, 64–65
**Add to My Favorite Searches, add/delete items, 18–19**
**Adobe Acrobat, Hot Categories Report, 17**
**Advanced Search**
  access methods, 6
  Buy It Now Items only, 6–7, 42–43
  Completed Items only, 7, 8–9
  Gallery View, 153
  Gift Items only, 6–7
  Location/International list, 36–37
  Quantity greater than 1, 60–61
  Sort by list, 7
  Sort by menu, 8
  Words to exclude, 6–7
**after-sale problems, 86–87**
**aiShip Shipping Calculator, 177**
**alerts**
  Bid Alert, 38–39
  watch alerts, 39
**Anchor Stores, market service, 141**
**andale**
  Gallery, related auction item thumbnails, 162–163
  hit counters, 116
  image-hosting service, 131
  statistics capability, 135
**Any country, international search, 36–37**
**Anything Points, PayPal, 82–83**
**Asian Arts, Live Auctions category, 68**
**Ask seller a question link, 30–31**
**Auction format, real estate bid process, 65**

**Auction Payments (Western Union), payment service, 73, 80–81**
**Auction Sniper**
  bid groups, 56–57
  browser interface, 57
  snipe service, 54–55
**AuctionBytes**
  auction communities resource, 206–207
  calendars, 124
  NewsFlash newsletter, 208
  weekly newsletters, 208
**AuctionInc's aiShip calculator, 177**
**auctions**
  hit counters, 116
  length issues, 97
  links between, 160–161
  related item thumbnails, 162–163
  schedulers, 117
  strategic item, 168–169
**Audio notification, Bid Alert, 38–39**
**automobiles**
  eBay Motors, 62–63
  vehicle history reports, 63

## B

**background colors, 103**
**backgrounds, image guidelines, 113**
**bank accounts, PayPal money transfers, 76–79**
**banner ads, Keywords on eBay, 166–167**
**bargains**
  hidden cost considerations, 46–47
  last-minute auctions, 40–41
**Basic Search**
  end first items, 41
  Gallery View, 153
  Item location link, 34
  Matching Categories list, 14–15
  misspelled items, 20–21
  My Favorite Searches, 18–19
  Only in this category, 15
  Search title and description, 4–5
  Sort by list, 7
  titles-only limitations, 4–5
  transpositions, 20–21
  versus Browse, 2, 12–13
**Bcc (blind carbon copy), seller questions, 30–31**
**Bid Alert, eBay Toolbar element, 38–39**

**bid groups, snipe method, 56–57**
**bidders, By Bidder market research, 10–11**
**Bidnapper, snipe service, 55**
**BidPay. *See* Western Union Auction Payments, payment service**
**bids**
    Auction Sniper, 54–53
    automobile purchases, 62–63
    Bid Alert, 38–39
    bid groups, 56–57
    charity auctions, 66–67
    Dutch Auctions, 60–61
    increments, 51
    last-minute auction bargains, 40–41
    last-second, 52–53
    non-binding, 65
    odd amount advantages, 58
    price comparisons of common items, 59
    proxy, 50–51
    real estate, 64–65
    real-time auctions, 68–69
    reserve price, 101
    snipe methods, 52–57
**Bids column, item interest information display, 9**
**Bidsage, snipe service, 55**
**BidSlammer, bid groups, 57**
**binding bids, real estate auction, 65**
**blind carbon copy (Bcc), seller questions, 30–31**
**boldface text, item emphasis method, 156–157**
**Books and Manuscripts, Live Auctions category, 68**
**Browse**
    category search method, 12–13
    versus Basic Search, 2, 12–13
**browsers**
    Auction Sniper, 57
    multiple window display, 52–53
**business accounts, PayPal, 73, 74–75**
**Business Reporting Center, SquareTrade, 165**
**Buy It Now Items only**
    Advanced Search, 6–7
    bid process, 61
    fixed-price list, 43, 99
    Gallery View, 42–43
    last-minute auction bargains, 41
    misspelled item bargains, 21
    seller guidelines, 98
**Buyer Protection, PayPal, 87**
**buyers**
    attraction methods, 166–167
    By Bidder market research, 10–11

    Completed Items only market price research use, 8–9
    fraud protection, 86–87
    goodwill promotion, 90–91
    search benefits, 2
    Second-Chance Offers, 108–109
    titles-only Basic Search limitations, 4–5
**By Bidder, market research use, 10–11**

### C

**calculators**
    ship, 176–177
    USPS rate calculations, 174–175
**calendars**
    AuctionBytes, 124
    Merchandising Calendar, 154–155
**cashier's checks, Western Union Auction Payments, 72**
**categories**
    automobile auctions, 62–63
    Browse advantages, 12–13
    combine ship search, 44–45
    cross-promoted, 146–147
    drill down search method, 14–15
    Hot Items list display, 17
    Item Specifics, 107
    Live Auctions, 68–69
    Matching Categories list, 14–15
    newsletters, 125
    Pre-filled Item Information, 106–107
    real estate, 64–65
    top-level exposure, 154–155
    view all, 13
**Category-Specific chat rooms, 199**
**Category-Specific Discussion Boards, 194–195**
**charity auctions, bid process, 66–67**
**Chat Boards, information source, 198–199**
**Chatter, monthly newsletter, 209**
**Checkfree, payment service, 72**
**checks**
    cashiers, Western Union Auction Payments, 72
    personal, payment method, 73
**colors**
    background, 103
    image text, 115
**combine ship cost, multiple item purchase cost reduction method, 44–45**
**comma-delimited file format, Selling Manager support, 134**

# INDEX

commercial real estate, bid process, 64–65
communities
    AuctionBytes, 206–207
    Chat Boards, 198–199
    Discussion Boards, 194–197
    eBay Groups, 204–205
    industry newsletters, 208–209
    message boards, 200–201
    OTWA (Online Traders Web Alliance), 206
Community Help Boards, information resource, 200–201
Community, Hot Items list, 17
Completed Items only
    Advanced Search, 7
    market price search use, 8–9
connection speeds, last-second bid issues, 52–53
contact information, transaction request, 31
copyrights
    photograph addition, 114–115
    VeRO (Verified Rights Owner) Program, 94–95, 114
counters, auction tracks, 116
Craters and Freighters, ship service, 35, 190–191
credit cards
    Anything Points, 82–83
    consumer fraud protection, 87
    PayPal premier/business accounts, 73, 74–75
cross-promotion
    eBay Store sales method, 144–147
    links to other auctions, 160–161
    strategic item auction, 168–169
currency converter, international purchases, 37
Customer Manager, e-mail management, 143

**D**

DAS (Dependable Auto Shippers), automobile purchases, 63
dates
    auction schedulers, 117
    AuctionBytes calendars, 124
DeepAnalysis, market research, 122–123
delimited data files, Turbo Lister support, 119
delivery confirmation, shipper's protection, 182–183
Dependable Auto Shippers (DAS), automobile purchases, 63
desktop, Bid Alert, 38–39
Discussion Boards
    browse, 196–197
    keyword search, 197

    log in process, 195
    lurk before posting messages, 194
    message posts, 195
    message reply, 195
    message scrolling, 196
    usage policies, 194
documents, Hot Items by Category list, 16–17
drill down, category search method, 14–15
Dutch Auctions
    bid process, 60–61
    seller guidelines, 100

**E**

eBay Groups, information resource, 204–205
eBay home page, top-level exposure, 154–155
eBay Motors, automobile purchases, 62–63
eBay Store
    cross-promotion sales methods, 144–147
    market service, 140–141
eBay Toolbar, Bid Alert, 38–39
eBay University, online/offline classes, 202–203
eBay Workshops, information resource, 203
electronic transfers, PayPal, 76–79
e-mail address, user ID search, 11
e-mails
    Auction Sniper, 54–55
    contact information request, 31
    Customer Manager, 143
    Item's I'm Watching notification, 29
    Live Auction reminders, 69
    My Favorite Search results, 18–19
    newsflashes, 125
    PayPal money transfers, 76–79
    PayPal's Winning Buyer Notification, 75
    Second-Chance Offers, 109
    seller questions/answers, 30–31
    VeRO Program notifications, 95
end first items, Basic Search, 41
escrow services
    automobile purchases, 62–63
    payment method, 84–85
eSnipe, snipe service, 55
Everything Else link, all category display method, 13
EZsniper, snipe service, 55

## F

FAQs (Frequently Asked Questions), Discussion Boards, 194
Featured Auction item, 158–159
Featured Plus! item, 158
Featured Stores, market service, 141
feedback
    after-sale problems, 86–87
    goodwill promotion, 90–91
    negative removal, 89, 91
    PowerSellers, 128–129
    Second-Chance Offers, 109
    seller's evaluation, 32–33
Feedback Forum, 90–91
fees
    andale Gallery, 162
    auction schedulers, 117
    bold listing, 156–157
    Buy It Now auction list, 98
    cost reduction methods, 102
    delivery confirmation, 182
    eBay home page item link, 155
    eBay Store, 140–141
    eBay University, 202
    escrow services, 85
    Featured Auction item, 158–159
    Featured Plus! item, 158
    Gallery, 152
    hidden costs, 46–47
    highlight item, 156–157
    image-hosting, 130–131
    insurance, 182
    Keywords on eBay, 166
    reserve price, 101
    Selling Manager, 134
    Selling Manager Pro, 137
    SquareTrade Seal of Approval, 164
    Stamps.com, 180–181
    ten-day auction, 97
    Vendio Store, 142
Fees Overview page, fee tables, 102
Fine Arts, Live Auctions category, 68
Fixed-Price items,
    Buy It Now Items only, 43
    seller guidelines, 99
flat rate ship, time/money saver, 178–179
forums, Feedback, 90–91

Fraud Protection, after-sale problems, 86–87
Frequently Asked Questions (FAQs), Discussion Boards, 194
Froogle, price comparisons of common items, 59
Furniture and Decorative Arts, Live Auctions category, 68

## G

Gallery View
    Buy It Now Items only, 42–43
    gift purchase method, 42–43
    thumbnail images, 152–153
Gift Items only, Advanced Search, 6–7
gifts, Gallery View method, 42–43
GiveSomeBack Bulk Feedback Tool, feedback comments, 33
Giving Works, charity auctions, 66–67
Global Sites, home page element, 37
goodwill, positive feedback, 90–91
Google, newsletter search, 209
graphics, Listing Designer, 104–105
Gutcheck, seller evaluation tool, 32–33

## H

Hammersnip, snipe service, 55
HammerTap, market research, 122
handling fee
    hidden cost, 46–47
    terms of sale element, 172–173
Help Center, site map element, 25
hidden costs, bargain purchase, 46–47
Highest prices first
    Completed Items only market price research, 8–9
    sort method, 7
highlighted text, item emphasis method, 156–157
hit counters, auction tracks, 116
Home Page Featured Auction item, 158–159
Home Page Featured item, top-level exposure, 155
Hot Categories Report, 17
Hot Items by Category list, Seller Central document, 16–17
HTML
    About Me page support, 151
    background colors, 103
    boldface text, 157

# INDEX

**HTML** (continued)
    Listing Designer support, 105
    other auction links, 160–161
    Turbo Lister support, 118–119
**HTML editor, 138–139**

## I

**image-hosting services, 130–131**
**images**
    copyright addition, 114–115
    Gallery thumbnails, 152–153
    image-hosting services, 130–131
    neutral backgrounds, 113
    PhotoShop Elements, 112–113
    related auction item thumbnails, 162–163
    slideshows, 132–133
    text colors, 115
**industry newsletters, information resource, 208–209**
**inkFrog, image-hosting service, 130–131**
**insurance**
    hidden cost, 46–47
    ship protection, 182–185
    U-PIC (Universal Parcel Insurance Coverage), 184–185
**international search, unique items, 36–37**
**Internet, connection speeds, last-second bids, 52–53**
**IrfanView, image editor, 113**
**Item location menu, ship cost reduction method, 34–35**
**Item Specifics, supported types, 107**
**Item Watch Reminder, enable/disable, 29**
**Items end first, sort method, 7**
**Items I'm Watching list, item information display, 28–29**

## J

**Jasc Paint Shop Pro, image editor, 113**
**Jewelry and Timepieces, Live Auctions category, 68**
**Justsnipe, snipe service, 55**

## K

**Kelley Blue Book, vehicle history reports, 63**
**keywords**
    category groups, 15
    Discussion Board search, 197
    eBay Groups search, 204
    titles-only Basic Search limitations, 4–5
    Words to exclude, 6–7
**Keywords on eBay, bidder attraction method, 166–167**

## L

**land, bid process, 64–65**
**last-minute auctions, bargain opportunity, 40–41**
**layouts, About Me page, 150–151**
**lead times, Auction Sniper, 54–55**
**links, other auctions, 160–161**
**Listing Designer**
    item enhancements, 104–105
    versus Turbo Lister, 120
**Live Auctions, bid process, 68–69**
**Location/International list, Advanced Search, 36–37**
**Lowest prices first**
    Completed Items only market price research use, 8–9
    sort method, 7
**lurkers, Discussion Boards, 194**

## M

**mail labels, print, 180–181**
**mail services**
    UPS rate calculations, 175
    USPS rate calculations, 174–175
**market research**
    By Bidder tab use, 10–11
    Completed Items only sort use, 8–9
    DeepAnalysis, 122–123
    HammerTap, 122
    Hot Items by Category list, 16–17
    price comparisons, 59
**Matching Categories list, drill down search method, 14–15**
**mediators, after-sale problem resolution, 88–89**
**Merchandising Calendar, top-level exposure, 154–155**
**message boards, information resource, 200–201**
**Microsoft Excel**
    Gutcheck data export, 33
    Selling Manager tool support, 134
**MissionFish, charity auctions, 67**
**misspelled items, search method, 20–21**
**modems, last-second bid issues, 52–53**
**money orders**
    Payingfast, 73
    Western Union Auction Payments, 73, 80–81
**money transfers, PayPal, 76–79**
**multiple item (Dutch) auctions**
    bid process, 60–61
    seller guidelines, 100
**multiple item purchase, ship cost reduction method, 44–45**

**My eBay**
    Items I'm Watching list, 28–29
    My Favorite Sellers/Stores, 19, 45
**My Favorite Searches, add/delete items, 18–19**
**My Favorite Sellers/Stores, add/delete sellers, 19, 45**
**My Recent Searches list, 29**
**My Recently Viewed Items list, 29**

## N

**neutral backgrounds, images, 113**
**new today link, sort method, 41**
**Newly listed items**
    misspelled item bargains, 21
    sort method, 7
**newsflashes, electronic newsletters, 125**
**newsletters**
    information resource, 208–209
    newsflashes, 125
**non-binding bids, real estate auction, 65**

## O

**offline classes, eBay University, 202–203**
**online classes, eBay University, 202–203**
**Online Traders Web Alliance (OTWA), 206–207**
**Only in this category, Basic Search, 15**

## P

**pack supplies, sources, 186–189**
**packages, terms of sale element, 172–173**
**Payingfast, payment service, 72**
**payment methods**
    Auction Payments (Western Union), 73, 80–81
    Checkfree, 72
    credit cards, 73, 74
    eBay Anything Points, 82–83
    escrow services, 84–85
    Payingfast, 72
    PayPal, 73, 74–79
    personal checks, 73
    services, 72–73
    terms of sale element, 127–173
    Western Union Auction Payments, 72, 80–81
**PayPal**
    account setup, 74–75
    business accounts, 73, 74–75
    Buyer Protection program, 87

    eBay Anything Points, 82–83
    money transfers, 76–77
    money withdrawals, 78–79
    payment service, 73
    premier accounts, 73, 74–75
    shops, 79
    Winning Buyer Notification, 75
**personal checks, payment method, 73**
**personal pages, About Me, 150–151**
**photo albums, timeBLASTER program, 22–23,**
**photographs**
    image editors, 112–113
    image-hosting services, 130–131
**Photoshop Elements**
    copyright tools, 114–115
    image editor, 112–113
**Place a bid page**
    Dutch Auctions, 60–61
    last-second bids, 52–53
    odd amount advantages, 58
    proxy bids, 50–51
    real estate auction, 65
**postage stamps**
    print, 180–181
    USPS rate calculations, 174–175
**postal zone charts, zip codes, 179**
**PowerSeller's tiers, 128–129**
**Powersnipe, snipe service, 55**
**Pre-filled Item Information, supported types, 106–107**
**premier accounts, PayPal, 73–75**
**Price column, market price research, 9**
**print**
    mail labels, 180–181
    postage stamps, 180–181
**Private Auctions, bid process, 61**
**Prohibited and Restricted Items list, 96**
**prohibited items, types, 96**
**Protecting Intellectual Property page, 94–95**
**proxy bids, bid increments, 50–51**

## Q

**Quantity field, Dutch Auction indicator, 60–61**
**questions**
    Chat Boards, 198–199
    Community Help Boards, 200–201
    Discussion Board FAQs, 194
    escrow services, 84
    sellers, 30–31

# INDEX

**questions (continued)**
    seller's payment instructions, 72
    terms of sale, 172–173
**Quick Stats, Selling Manager tool, 134**
**quotation marks (") characters, Basic Search
    keywords, 4–5**

## R

**real estate, bid process, 64–65**
**real-time auctions, bid process, 68–69**
**regional search, ship cost reduction method, 34–35**
**researches, market price, 8–9, 59**
**reserve price auctions**
    bid process, 61
    market price research use, 9
    seller guidelines, 101
**residential property, bid process, 64–65**
**return receipts, delivery confirmation, 182–183**

## S

**sales, measurement tools, 134–137**
**schedulers, auctions, 117**
**Seal of Approval, SquareTrade, 164–165**
**Search title and description, Basic Search limitations,
    4–5**
**Second-Chance Offers, 108–109**
**Seller Central**
    Hot Items by Category list, 16–17
    Merchandising Calendar, 154–155
**sellers**
    About Me information, 150–151
    auction length guidelines, 97
    auction schedulers, 117
    boldface/highlighted text, 156–157
    Buy It Now guidelines, 98
    By Bidder market research, 10–11
    Completed Items only market price research use, 8–9
    copyright/trademark protections, 114–115
    Craters and Freighters ship service, 190–191
    cross-promotion methods, 144–147
    DeepAnalysis market research, 122–123
    delivery confirmation, 182–183
    Dutch Auctions, 100
    eBay Store, 140–141
    Featured Auction item, 158–159
    fee reduction methods, 102
    feedback rate, 32–33
    Fixed-Price item, 99

    flat rate ship, 178–179
    goodwill promotion, 90–91
    hit counters, 116
    Hot Items by Category list market research, 16–17
    HTML editor, 138–139
    image editors, 112–113
    image-hosting services, 130–131
    insurance, 182–185
    intellectual property rights, 94–95, 114–115
    item background colors, 103
    Item Specifics, 107
    Keywords on eBay ads, 166–167
    links to other auctions, 160–161
    Listing Designer, 104–105
    Live Auction terms and conditions, 69
    newsflashes, 125
    package supply sources, 186–189
    payment instructions, 72
    PowerSeller's tiers, 128–129
    Pre-filled Item Information, 106–107
    print mail labels, 180–181
    print postage stamps, 180–181
    prohibited items, 96
    questions for, 30–31
    related auction item thumbnails, 162–163
    reserve price, 101
    search benefits, 2
    second-chance offers, 108–109
    Selling Manager Pro, 137
    Selling Manager tool, 134–137
    ship rate calculators, 174–177
    slideshow uses, 132–133
    SquareTrade Seal of Approval, 164–165
    strategic item auction, 168–169
    terms of sale, 172–173
    titles-only Basic Search limitations, 4–5
    top-level exposure, 154–155
    Turbo Lister enhancements, 118–121
    Vendio Store, 142–143
    View seller's other items link, 44–45
**Seller's Assistant Basic, Selling Manager
    upgrade, 137**
**Selling Manager Pro, 137**
**Selling Manager tool, 134–137**
**ship**
    calculators, 176–177
    Craters and Freighters service, 190–191
    delivery confirmation, 182–183
    flat rate, 178–179
    hidden cost, 46–47

insurance, 182–185
large/valuable/fragile items, 190–191
multiple item purchase cost reduction method, 44–45
package supply sources, 186–189
regional purchase cost reduction method, 34–35
terms of sale element, 172–173
UPS rate calculations, 175
USPS rate calculations, 174–175
**shops, PayPal, 79**
**site map, information display, 24–25**
**slideshows, image presentation method, 132–133**
**Smart Search link, access methods, 5**
**snipes**
Auction Sniper, 54–53
bid groups, 56–57
last-second bids, 52–53
multiple browser window display, 52–53
**Snipeville, snipe service, 55**
**Sort by list**
Basic Search/Advanced Search, 7
Completed Items only market price research use, 8–9
**sorts**
Bids column, 9
Completed Items only, 7, 8–9
end first items, 7, 41
going, going, gone items, 40–41
Lowest prices first, 7
new today link, 41
Newly listed items, 7
Price column, 9
**sounds**
Bid Alert notification, 38–39
watch alerts, 39
**SpareDollar, image-hosting service, 131**
**SquareTrade**
after-sale problem resolution, 88–89
Business Reporting Center, 165
Seal of Approval, 164–165
**statistics**
DeepAnalysis, 122–123
sales measurement tools, 134–135
**Store Merchandising Manager, cross-promoted categories, 146–147**
**strategic items, bidder attraction method, 166–167**
**Submit Your Bid**
Dutch Auctions, 61
last-second bids, 52–53
proxy bids, 51
**symbols, copyright addition, 114–115**

**tax deductions, charity auctions, 67**
**ten-day auction, fee issues, 97**
**terms and conditions, Live Auction, 69**
**terms of sale, information guidelines, 172–173**
**themes**
Listing Designer, 104–105
Turbo Lister, 118–121
**thumbnails**
cross-promotion sales method, 144–147
Gallery images, 152–153
related auction items, 162–163
**tiers, PowerSellers, 129**
**timeBLASTER**
photo albums, 43
search program, 2, 22–23
**timeframes, auction length guidelines, 97**
**times**
auction schedulers, 117
AuctionBytes calendars, 124
**timeshares, bid process, 64–65**
**Title & Description, background colors, 103**
**titles-only, Basic Search limitation, 4–5**
**top-level exposure, eBay home page, 154–155**
**trademarks, VeRO (Verified Rights Owner) Program, 94–95, 114**
**transactions**
after-sale problems, 86–87
contact information request, 31
escrow fees, 85
PayPal money transfers, 76–79
**transpositions, search method, 20–21**
**troubleshoot, after-sale problems, 86–87**
**Turbo Lister**
appearance enhancements, 118–121
Selling Manager support, 136
**typographical errors, search method, 20–21**

**Ulead PhotoImpact, image editor, 113**
**under-bidders, Second-Chance Offers, 108–109**
**unique items, international search, 36–37**
**United Parcel Service (UPS)**
package supplies, 189
package weight/size limitations, 191
ship rate calculations, 175

# INDEX

**United States Postal Service (USPS)**
  package supplies, 188–189
  ship rate calculations, 174–174
**Universal Parcel Insurance Coverage (U-PIC),
  184–185**
**U-PIC (Universal Parcel Insurance Coverage),
  184–185**
**user IDs**
  About Me link, 150–151
  By Bidder market research, 10–11
  contact information request, 31
  e-mail address search, 11

## V

**vehicle history reports, automobile purchases, 63**
**Vendio**
  image-hosting service, 131
  statistics capability, 135
**Vendio Store, market service, 142–143**
**Vendio's Sales Manager, 143**
**Verified Rights Owner (VeRO) Program, 94–95, 114**
**VeRO About Me pages, 95**
**View seller's other items link, 44–45**

## W

**watch alerts, Watch List Items, 39**
**Watch List items, watch alerts, 39**
**Watch this item, add/delete items, 28–29**
**Web pages, eBay's vehicle history report, 63**
**Web sites**
  amazon.com, 107
  andale, 131, 162
  andale's What's Hot, 16
  Anything Points, 82
  Auction Gold, 208
  Auction Guild's TAGnotes, 208
  Auction Payments, 80
  Auction Seller's Resource, 208
  Auction Sniper, 54–55
  AuctionBytes, 55, 124, 175, 206
  AuctionInc's aiShip calculator, 177
  BidSlammer, 57
  Bulk Feedback Tool, 33
  category-specific chat rooms, 199
  Checkfree, 72
  Craters and Freighters, 190
  Creative eBay Selling, 208

currency converter, 37
Customer Manager, 143
DAS (Dependable Auto Shippers), 63
David's Interactive Auction Calendar, 155
Discussion Board tutorial, 197
eBay Groups, 204–205
eBay Motors, 62–63
eBay Toolbar, 38
eBay University, 202
eBay Workshops, 203
eBay's auction format information, 61
eBay's disclaimer, 64
eBay's General Announcements Board, 201
eBay's Giving Works, 66
escrow services, 62, 84–85
Federal Express, 47
Froogle, 59
Google, 209
Gutcheck, 32
HTML tutorials, 139
inkFrog, 130
international eBay, 37
IrfanView, 113
Jasc Paint Shop Pro, 113
Kelley Blue Book, 63
keyword.ebay.com, 15
Keywords on eBay, 166
Live Auctions, 68
MissionFish, 67
OTWA (Online Traders Web Alliance), 207
package supplies, 187
Payingfast, 72
PayPal, 75
postal zone charts, 179
PowerSeller success story, 129
prohibited items list, 159
ship rate calculators, 177
snipe service comparisons, 55
SpareDollar, 131
SquareTrade, 88, 164
Stamps.com, 180–181
System Announcements Board, 201
timeBLASTER, 22
Turbo Lister, 118–119
Ulead PhotoImpact, 113
United States Postal service, 47, 174
U-PIC (Universal Parcel Insurance Coverage), 184
UPS (United Parcel Service), 47, 175
USPS Delivery Confirmation, 182–183
Vendio, 131, 142

Vendio's Sales Manager, 143
WebShots, 133
Yahoo, 209
**WebShots, image-hosting service, 133**
**Western Union Auction Payments, payment service, 72, 80–81**
**What's Hot link**
Seller Central, 16
top-level exposure, 154–155
**windows, display multiple browser, 52–53**
**Winning Buyer Notification, PayPal, 75**

**Words to exclude, Advanced Search, 6–7**
**worldwide sites, home page element, 37**

## Y

**Yahoo!, newsletter search, 209**

## Z

**ZIP code**
postal zone charts, 179
ship cost calculation element, 47

# Introducing Our
## New Consumer Books...

Our new Teach Yourself VISUALLY Consumer books are an excellent resource for people who want to learn more about general interest topics. We have launched this new groundbreaking series with three exciting titles: **Teach Yourself VISUALLY Weight Training, Teach Yourself VISUALLY Yoga and Teach Yourself VISUALLY Guitar**. These books maintain the same design and structure of our computer books—graphical, two-page lessons that are jam-packed with useful, easy-to-understand information.

Each full-color book includes over **500** photographs, accompanied by step-by-step instructions to guide you through the fundamentals of each topic. "Teach Yourself" sidebars also provide practical tips and tricks to further fine tune your skills and introduce more advanced techniques.

By using top experts in their respective fields to consult on our books, we offer our readers an extraordinary opportunity to access first-class, superior knowledge in conjunction with our award winning communication process. Teach Yourself VISUALLY Consumer is simply the best way to learn!

## Teach Yourself VISUALLY **WEIGHT TRAINING**

ISBN: 0-7645-2582-4
Price: $24.99 US;  $36.99 CDN;  £14.99 UK
Page count: 320

# Teach Yourself VISUALLY **YOGA**

ISBN: 0-7645-2580-8
Price: $24.99 US;  $36.99 CDN;  £14.99 UK
Page count: 320

# Teach Yourself VISUALLY **GUITAR**

ISBN: 0-7645-2581-6
Price: $24.99 US;  $36.99 CDN;  £14.99 UK
Page count: 320